Everyday Language

Studies in Ethnomethodology

Everyday Language

Studies in Ethnomethodology

Edited by
George Psathas
Boston University

IRVINGTON PUBLISHERS, INC., New York

HALSTED PRESS Division of
JOHN WILEY & SONS, Inc.
NEW YORK   LONDON   SYDNEY   TORONTO

Distributed by Halsted Press
A division of John Wiley & Sons, Inc., New York

Library of Congress Cataloging in Publication Data

Main entry under title:

Everyday language.

    Includes index.
    1. Communication—Social aspects—Addresses, essays,
lectures. 2. Social linguistics—Addresses, essays,
lectures. 3. Social interaction—Addresses, essays,
lectures. I. Psathas, George. II. Title: Ethnomethodology.
HM258.E83   301.14'08   78-32007
ISBN 0-470-26670-8

10 9 8 7 6 5 4 3 2 1

Printed in the United States of America

Dedicated to the memory of Harvey Sacks,
an original and creative scholar, teacher, and researcher.

Contents

Everyday Language
Studies in Ethnomethodology

Introduction and Dedication

It is not especially easy to assemble a collection of original papers by a number of different researchers whose substantive interests vary widely but whose theoretical and methodological perspectives are very closely shared. Rather, it may be easier to assemble a collection than it is to provide coherence.

A focus on everyday language, spoken and written, unites these studies. All are concerned with discovering and studying the organizational features of natural language whether in the form of telephone conversation openings, the production of a sentence, a newspaper story or a map. Each of the contributors is engaged in the serious quest of discovering the properties of repeatable and recurrent usages and working toward a formal descriptive-analytic account of these discovered properties. There is no hypothesis testing here, no certainty about what will be found before it is found, and no preference for quantitative measurement of the discovered phenomena. The phenomena are first and foremost to be discovered and described. Formal statements can be made about the discovered phenomena and it is in this sense that ethnomethodological studies can achieve rigor and systematization.

Another common bond among these studies is that each contributor is familiar with the work of Harold Garfinkel and Harvey Sacks. Some are

1

more closely attuned to the discovery of methods of practical reasoning, others to the regularities of conversational interaction, while others are involved in developing new combinations of the various themes in ethnomethodology with other theoretical perspectives. Yet it is hard to separate these various strands and perhaps it is less important to do so than it is to recognize their common roots.

The work included represents the result of the collaborative, instructional, or interactive collegial relationships which Garfinkel and Sacks have inspired. Each contributor pursues his own subject and none seeks to deliberately influence anyone else. The nature of the study of natural language, at this stage of development, is such that persons must seek their own discoveries and no worker can simply imitate or parrot his mentor. The nature of the directive provided by Garfinkel and Sacks is that the investigator must seek to study the world of everyday life in order to bring back "news" of discoveries that are to be found there. It is in this sense that each contributor pursues new fields while at the same time remaining indebted to the originary thrust of the two pioneers.

In 1975, shortly after Harvey Sacks sent the paper included in this book, he was killed in an automobile accident. It is difficult to accept his premature loss.

Harvey Sacks was in the prime of life, a prodigious worker, a prolific writer and lecturer, an original mind whose work was only recently beginning to appear in print after having been circulated privately for many years. His influence was, and is, extraordinary—no one can yet assess it. Those contributors who worked most closely with him know what constant stimulation, encouragement, and standards of rigorous work he provided. Others who were inspired by his studies upon reading them can no longer look to him for continuing stimulation. There is no way that the impact of his loss can be assessed—either for the field or for those who were most closely working with him.

The best way to indicate the range and breadth of his mind is to display some of his work, several evidences of which are included in this collection: a transcribed lecture he presented in a course given in 1966; a paper he coauthored and completed prior to his death in 1975; and the work of former students, colleagues and others with whom he collaborated.

In Sacks's earlier work, as shown in the 1966 lecture here entitled "Hotrodder: A Revolutionary Category," he would select from an example or a direct quotation and expand his analysis to reveal the broader implications imbedded in an utterance. Sacks selects a statement made by a young man to a friend about how being "picked up" for drag racing by other drivers depends on the way he is dressed. He focuses on the categories used by members of groups to classify themselves. Other categories, such as "teenager," may be imposed and enforced by outsiders and provide, for members of a culture, ways of understanding who and what such other persons are. Attempts by those so classified to change the categories into which they are placed are of profound significance for the study of social change, for it can be by such efforts to modify the classifications imposed by others, or to advance the classifications developed by themselves, that nonmembers (i.e. those not included in the category by themselves or others) may come to change their perceptions of, beliefs about, and actions oriented toward those ordinarily so classified. Changes in categories, the ways in which they are used, and the rules for their application can be of even revolutionary significance. Sacks demonstrates, in this lecture, the depth of his insights.

In his later work, he gave increased attention to the ways in which interaction proceeds and to discovering the natural organization of such interaction. He was able to benefit from the collection and recording of numerous instances of naturally occurring interactions between ordinary persons in ordinary circumstances and from the work of colleagues and students who joined in the same inquiries. The availability of carefully transcribed materials enabled him to achieve increased rigor and formalization in his work. In the paper on "Two Preferences in the Organization of References to Persons in Conversation and Their Interaction" he works with Schegloff to present a more formal and analytic conceptualization of the rules governing references to persons. Clearly, to be able to focus on such detail in conversations requires a compilation of large amounts of data and a progressive focusing on particular details.

Although his later work moved increasingly toward systematic formalization of the detailed aspects of conversational interaction (i.e. especially "A Simplest Systematics for the Organization of Turn-Taking for Conversation," coauthored with Emanuel Schegloff and Gail Jefferson, (1974) *Language* 50:696-735), he nevertheless retained an interest in and continued to discuss and explore matters which had earlier drawn his attention and which still remain largely neglected by social scientists. Such matters as puns, jokes, and stories, categorization devices, the organization of topics in conversation, the structure of conversational openings, the ways in which conversationalists orient to co-participants in their talk: these and numerous other topics continued to engage his attention.

Sacks was a co-worker par excellence. He shared his data and his observations freely and generously. His lectures, transcribed and mimeographed since the mid-1960's, have been read by large numbers of persons over the years as citations to his unpublished work will attest. This unpublished corpus has achieved national and international circulation and is familiar to researchers and serious scholars of the issues he treated. Characteristic of Sack's style and approach is this body of unpublished but freely available work—he was open, willing to share, genuinely interested in having his ideas discussed, and persistently faithful to the empirical materials on which his research was based. He was original. There is no better way to characterize him. He worked, presented his ideas carefully and systematically, and developed conceptualizations as closely linked to the materials he examined as possible. He enjoyed presenting his work. He shared much and gave much—and expected that each of his students and colleagues would approach such materials with the same interest and respect which he had.

This book is dedicated to him. It is evidence of the influence and importance of his work and of his spirit.

Contributors

Harvey Sacks received his Ph. D. from the University of California, Berkeley in 1966. He taught at the University of California, Los Angeles and was Professor of Social Science at the University of California, Irvine until his untimely death in 1975.

Emanual Schegloff is Associate Professor of Sociology at the University of California, Los Angeles. He taught at Columbia University after receiving his doctorate from the University of California, Berkeley. He has been engaged in research studies of conversational interaction on such topics as sequencing in conversational openings, opening up closings, turn-taking organization, recycling turn beginnings, repair, and the sequential organization of conversation. He has published papers in the *American Anthropologist, Semiotica, Language,* and in numerous volumes of collected research papers.

Gail Jefferson received her Ph.D from the University of California, Irvine and has worked for many years on the close study and analysis of conversation. She has taught at the University of Pennsylvania, The University of Massachusetts (Amherst), the University of California, Santa Barbara, and Manchester University. She has done systematic studies of phenomena heretofore overlooked in studies of interaction, (e.g., laughter, overlap, repair) and has also developed a transcription system for the study of conversation which is now widely used by researchers in this field.

Charles Goodwin is Assistant Professor of Anthropology at the University of South Carolina. He completed his doctoral work at the Annenberg School of Communications at the University of Pennsylvania. He has brought his interests and technical skills in media to bear on the study of conversational interaction sequences by incorporating audio and video recording methods into the collection and analysis of his data.

John C. Heritage was educated at Leeds University and has been a Lecturer in Sociology at Leeds University and the University of Warwick. He has published articles in the fields of social psychology and ethnomethodology and serves on the editorial board of *Sociology*.

D. R. Watson is Senior Lecturer at Manchester University and completed his Ph.D. at the University of Warwick. He has taught at New York State University College at Buffalo and at Lancaster University. In 1975-76 he held a visiting fellowship from The American Council of Learned Societies and was affiliated with New York State University College at Buffalo and the University of California, San Diego. He has published in the fields of ethnomethodology, conversational analysis, interpersonal relations, education, and race relations.

Jeff Coulter, Assistant Professor of Sociology at Boston University, holds the Ph.D. from Manchester University, where he also taught for several years. His work is informed by the ordinary language philosophy of Ryle, Austin, and Wittgenstein, and his current work reflects a convergence of this philosophical tradition with the ethnomethodology of both Garfinkel and Sacks. He is the author of *Approaches to Insanity* (1974) and *The Social Construction of Mind* (1978).

Jim Schenkein is Assistant Professor of Sociology at Queens College and the Graduate School of the City University of New York. His doctoral work was completed at the University of California, Irvine and he has taught at UCLA and the Sociologisch Institut Rijksuniversiteit te Groningen. His research studies have appeared in *Semiotica, Sociology,* and *Language in Society,* and he is currently studying and practicing sociotherapy using audio and video recordings of natural behavior.

George Psathas is Professor of Sociology at Boston University. he completed his Ph.D. at Yale University and has taught at Indiana University and Washington University (St. Louis). His work in phenomenological sociology and enthomethodology has sought to reveal the common bases of these two approaches. His recent studies are of spatial orientation, direction giving, and map making, particularly as these are accomplished by the newly blind.

Melvin Pollner is Associate Professor of Sociology at the University of California, Los Angeles, where he has taught since 1968. He received his Ph. D. from the University of California, Santa Barbara. He has published several papers in ethnomethodology and has done research on—among other topics, mundane reasoning, labeling theory, self-explicating transactions, and reality disjunctures.

J. Maxwell Atkinson is Senior Research Fellow at the centre for Socio-Legal Studies, Wolfson College, Oxford. He received his doctorate in Sociology at Manchester University, where he also taught from 1972-1976.

Hotrodder:
A Revolutionary Category

by Harvey Sacks

Ken: In that Bonneville of mine. I c'd take that thing out, an' if I've gotta tie:, an' a-a sweater on, an' I look clean? (1.0) Ninedy nine percent a' the time a guy c'd pull up to me, in the same car, same color, same year the whole bit, (1.0) roar up his pipes, (1.0) and he's inna dirty grubby tee shirt, an' the guy'll pick the guy up in the dirty grubby tee shirt before uh he'll pick me up.

(2.0)

( ): hheh

Ken: J'st- Just for //. uh-

Al: (Bu') not many people get picked up in a Pontiac station wagon.

I've been focusing on some aspects of teenage kids and cars, but the considerations I've been offering so far don't at all get at what's most important about the phenomenon. And that's what I want to try to do, though the analysis I'll offer has a much stronger sound than I could defend at this point. But I'll do it because something like what I'm saying is, I think, involved, and it's fundamental to see.

A lecture originally presented in 1966. Transcribed and edited by Gail Jefferson.

We could work at it in part by asking such questions as, why do kids go about making up all those typologies of cars—and the typologies they have are really enormously elaborate, and they use those typologies to make assessments of other drivers, and the assessments are not always very nice, as we've seen. Now the question we want to ask is why do they do it? Aren't the terms that are used before they go to work good enough? And what's the matter with them if they aren't? So that's the problem.

One way to get at the problem is to try to see what kind of difference there is between the category "teenager" and the category "hotrodder." I want to argue that they're fundamentally different types of categories; that "hotrodder" is, in a very nontrivial sense, quite a revolutionary kind of category. And I'll be trying to sketch some of the ways that that's so, for that category and others like it.

Because I take it that the issue is really a very deep one, I'll give you some suggestions about a type of category by taking a very ancient and in its way famous example, though probably you don't know the example so it's of some educational value anyway. This is a quotation from Genesis, Chapter 14. It goes like this: "A fugitive brought the news to Abraham the Hebrew who was camping at the terebinths of Namra the Ammorite, kinsman of Eschkel and Amer, these being confederates of Abraham." Now in the history of biblical criticism that's a most important little section and its fundamental importance is at least sketched by the following kinds of considerations. The phrase "Abraham the Hebrew" is apparently unique in the Bible in that it's pretty much the only place where an Israelite who is not talking to some outsider is talked of as a "Hebrew." Its importance lies in the fact that, given the usage "Abraham the Hebrew," biblical critics can feel that that section of the document was not written by the Jews, and thus is some independent information about the historicity of Abraham.

Now categories like "the Hebrew," where the character of the category is that it's used by nonmembers of the category and not by members of the category except when members are identifying themselves to nonmembers, are rather fundamental kinds of categories.

Parenthetically, it's kind of a marvelous quirk about anthropology that an enormous number of tribal names that anthropologists talk of have this character. That is to say, the tribal names the anthropologists write about are very very regularly nonrecognizable to the members of those tribes and often mean things like "outsider" "stranger" in some language other than the language of the named tribe. And that's because by and large if somebody is told of a tribe by a member of another tribe, they get the name of the tribe in the other tribe's language.

Elizabeth Colson, in an absolutely marvelous ethnography called *The Makka Indians,* traces such a naming. She says "they received the name Makka in 1855 when they made their treaty with the United States government. The government interpreter was a Klallum who gave the treaty makers the Klallum name for the Cape Flaherty people. This has been the official name for them ever since. Today most people speak of themselves as Makka though some of the older people say they dislike the name because it doesn't belong to them and they don't understand its meaning." That's from page 76. If you look at page 12 in Radcliffe-Browne's *The Andaman Islanders* you'll find the same kind of reference, and it's a very very frequent thing.

Now we can say introductorily that there are certain categories which are owned by a group other than those to whom they apply. A term like "the Hebrew" in the ancient Near East was that sort of term. Right now the term "Negro" is being treated as that sort of term; i.e., the Muslims are attempting to treat the term "Negro" as one which, if it is used, would be recognized to be used by a nonmember. Roughly, we could say that what the dominant categories basically own is how it is that persons perceive reality. And there's an order of revolution which is an attempt to change how it is that persons see reality. I don't mean that in a casual way, and I'll try to deal with it with respect to the difference between "teenagers" and "hotrodders."

A week or so ago I mentioned the claim that psychoanalysis is a bourgeois discipline, and mentioned some of the ways one can see the sense of such a claim. Another of the ways one can formulate the sense of that claim turns on the way that psychoanalysis is concerned to defend the fact that adults own reality. That defense is made against, in the first place, what they call "neurotics." And Menninger has a magnificent phrase—he speaks of neurotics as "disloyal to reality." What neurotics are, from the psychoanalyst's point of view, are children who can pass as adults. (And I think from the psychoanalysts' point of view, a psychotic is a retired child.) Now what that involves is an attempt to refuse to recognize the claims to be dealing with reality on the part of such categories as "neurotics," "psychotics," and, say, "children."

We can note in passing that there have been tremendous revisions of history involved in psychoanalysis, and one of the most striking is the business of an Oedipus complex. People regularly talk about an Oedipus complex as though what Freud says about the Oepdipus plays are perfectly obvious, whereas if you read them without first starting with Freud's way of looking at them, it seems to me at least it's perfectly obvious that they're just about the exact opposite of what's proposed. They're perfectly clearly about infanticide, not parricide. And the parricide theme, if anything, is a rationalization for an institution of infanticide, in a play written for adults by adults. After all, Oedipus is to be done away with by an oracle that precedes his birth (and one would presume that, if anything, there might be some guilt about that). Furthermore, while the ones who set out to kill the infant Oedipus know what they're doing—i. e., they're adults killing a child—Oedipus, when he kills his father, doesn't know what he's doing—i.e., he knows he's an adult killing an adult, he doesn't know he's a son killing his father.

There are, of course, real problems that adults have to come to terms with about children. Most of these problems are completely unknown and fantastic in their character. For example, there is, in a perfectly good sense, a children's culture: a culture with its artifacts, songs, games, etc., a culture that is unbelievably stable. So, for example, if you look at a book called *The Lore and Language of School Children* by Peter and Iona Opie, there's good evidence that the songs sung by London school children four hundred years ago are still sung, purely orally transmitted, without any officials taking care of the transmission, where the words have even passed out of the English language—transmitted only by children. The same goes for a series of other phenomena associated with children's culture.

And there's enormous interest to how that gets done and what it might mean and what things like it might mean, for example, for reformulating the relationship of children and adults, where, instead of saying that adults are bigger and better versions of children, one might treat them as alumni.

Of course it's very important that children have a notion of dependence, in contrast to a notion of their own culture as stable and independent, because for one, presumably, if children realize that they're not dependent in important senses, and realize, for example, that the norms regulating the treatment of children are enforced by adults on adults and whatever children did adults would have to take care of them because they could be embarassed, sanctioned, thrown in jail, etc. (to be sure, all adults could renounce all children, but pretty much no given adult could renounce any given child), they might come to see that there is an enormous dependence of adults on children; for example, adults are dependent on the response that children give to them, like show them a little affection now and then.

Now none of that stuff is officially recognized. It's not recognized in just the way that Marxists would say that the dependence of our culture on the laborer is not recognized; i.e., it's not only not recognized by those on top, it's not recognized by those on the bottom, either. And the kinds of revolutions that then try to take place are attempts to reconstruct how it is that things are seen. where the attempt in part is for some category to get to enforce a view of themselves, a view which will be held by others; a view which the category administers and not the others. And a big difference between the categories "teenager" and "hotrodder" is that "teenagers" is a category that adults administer. What's known about "teenagers" is enforced by adults. And of course there is a parallel situation for Negroes vis-a-vis whites.

I'm suggesting that a notion of independence is trying to be asserted against the notion of independence now enforced. The notion of independence that's held for, say, Negroes and children is, in a radical way, asociological. They should become independent one at a time. And by following the ways that are defined by the dominant culture. Be a good boy and grow up, keep clean, get a good job. You can do it, it's your problem. That formulation of independence is enforced by the adults. Can some way be found whereby independence can be internally administered? There are simple and trival solutions which people sometimes come up with, but they're in that genre. The attempt, say, to buy a state by the Negroes is that kind of an attempt; they'll define what makes for success.

What is crucially needed is to bring about a change in what it is anybody sees when they see one of these things (teenager, Negro, etc.). And then to be able to control what they know about one when they see one. And the question of how you could control this is of course an extremely complicated one. Kids know that if they're in cars they're going to be seen as teenage drivers. I've talked about this phenomenon before—there are ranges of other categories other than "teenager" that somebody could be seen as. What are the occasions under which that category would be chosen uniquely? If somebody's driving a car and that somebody could be seen as a teenager, then they're seen as a teenager. Now what can kids do to shift that around or begin to modify it? And remember, what we want to have is a set of modifications that are administered by members. And that means, for example that *they* will recognize whether somebody is a member of one or another category, and what that membership takes, and *they* can do the sanctioning.

Now the character of the sanctioning does not need to involve at all that anybody gets together and beats somebody up. But how it is otherwise enforced is most extraordinary in a way. It used to be the case, maybe it still is, that sports-car drivers flicked their lights when they passed each other. Now a Volkswagen driver might flick his lights at a sportscar driver and be absolutely ignored. It isn't in the first place the fact that if a sports-car driver flicked his lights at a Volkswagen somebody would put a bomb in his car, but it was his business to defend all other sportscar drivers on each occasion in which somebody who wasn't properly a member flicked his lights. And members of the category "sport-car drivers" made that their business.

That's much related to drag racing in the streets, because although in this little story we've been looking at, this fellow proposes that he pulls up in a Bonneville (alternatively formulatable as a Pontiac station wagon), and another fellow pulls up in a Bonneville, and now they have a drag. While that's conceivable, if the hotrod culture is properly self-enforced, then if he does it to anybody else they just won't drag with him. They will not accept him as a proper person to drag with, no matter how fast his car is, or whatever else. It's not a car for doing drag racing. Since everybody by and large, including "teenagers," simply takes his Detroit car and drives it, when you in one or another ways radically modify the car and get the title "hotrod" applied to it (with of course the possibility of subversion present—i.e., you get a hotrod built by some company specializing in fixing up cars), then anybody who sees such a car needn't wait to see who's driving it, they can know it's a hotrod and there's a hotrodder in it. And what is known about hotrodders—what they do with their cars, how they look, how they behave—these are things that hotrodders can enforce on each other and defend against nonmembers.

Crucially, for the issue of self-enforcement, since hotrods are used only by kids or by adults "disloyal to reality," then once you have one, one important thing you're going to do with it is play with it. And that makes you tremendously dependent on others' willingness to recognize that you have one, and e.g., to recognize what its status is: good, the best, rotten. The point is, once you make yourself a candidate hotrodder, then you subject yourself to the controls that the set of members have and enforce. And the notion that it's merely the fun of driving fast that's involved, and the sorts of consequences of that notion (e.g., such a notion may be part of the basis for setting up places where kids can drag safely), is doomed simply by virtue of the fact that that sets up an administration of the phenomenon which is not theirs.

Further, one can begin to see the interest of kids in sanctioning kids driving ordinary cars, since kids driving ordinary cars permit the retention of the "teenage driver" category with all that's known about it, and its crucial feature that it's a category loyal to and administered by adults. Moreover, kids driving ordinary cars can be doing something for which there ought to be a psychiatric category, but we don't have one; i.e., we don't have a psychiatric category for something like a "fink"—a fink being a disloyal member of a lower category. (I don't know why there's not been a psychiatric category for "scab and "fink" and things like that. It's kind of an interesting problem, I suppose.) If you look at that long utterance I've been dealing with, in which the kid proposes he could go out looking nice and clean and drive his car fast and a cop wouldn't pick him up, what's being proposed of course is that he could put on the appearance of a nice-kid teenager driver who doesn't drag race, and get into a drag, and the cops wouldn't get him. That is, he could look like he's loyal to adults while he's really being loyal to hotrodders. Where of course his co-participants take it that that's just talk, that what he's doing is being disloyal to hotrodders.[1]

Now one of the things you have to see, which sets these sorts of tasks into a framework of their real possibility, is this. We're dealing in the first instance with a category. They're not groups. Most of the categories (women, old people, Negroes, Jews, teenagers, etc., etc.) are not groups in any sense that you normally talk about groups, and yet what we have is a mass of knowledge known about every category; any member is seen as a representative of each of those categories; any person who is a case of a category is seen as a member of the category, and what's known about the category is known about them, and the fate of each is bound up in the fate of the other, so that one regularly has systems of social control built up around these categories which are internally enforced by the members because if a member does something like rape a white woman, commit economic fraud, race on the street, etc., then that thing will be seen as what a member of some applicable category does, not what some named person did. And the rest of them will have to pay for it. And somehow those categories live with that problem by and large, and members go around trying to live up to the best image of that thing as provided by the enforcing culture.

Those systems of control are not enforced by any government, there are no officials, most members never know each other, but they live and die awaiting what will be in the next day's newspaper about what one of them did. I would bet that in the period between the assassination of the president and the discovery of who did it (not only "who" by name, but what category he was a member of), that every depressed group in the country sat in mortal fear of the fact that they did it. And had they done it, it would then be a fact of their lives. At best they can argue, well, there are good ones and bad ones among us.

It's been, I think, teenagers who have made a raft of attempts to break that kind of situation. From hotrodders to surfers to beatniks to whatever else, they've been engaged in setting up independent corporations which everybody is eventually forced to recognize on their own terms And in that regard, then, one can specifically see the tie to drug users, who are in effect saying, let them all retain their perceptual structure of reality, we'll make our own. Of course in the case of kids, the problem of their attempted revolution is really fantastic, since they lose members at an incredible rate. Other sorts of revolutions might have more chance of success insofar as they can retain members.

In any event, we want to see that it's not simply the case that, for example, the fact that Eskimos have seventeen different categories of snow whereas we have only one means that Eskimos are much more interested in snow than we are, or the fact that kids have fifty-seven categories of cars means that they're much more interested in cars. Rather, the fact that kids have such categories, and focus on those categories, can be ways that more or less fundamental attacks are being launched against a culture which is stable by reference to everybody seeing the world for what it is, without regard to whether it's pleasant or not, whether they come out on top or not, and not seeing that they can do anything about it.

It's in that regard, then, that the important problems of social change, I would take it anyway, would involve laying out such things as the sets of categories, how they're used, what's known about any member, and beginning to play with shifts in the rules for application of a category and with shifts in the properties of any category.

NOTES

1. Here is another story with similar features, told by the same kid in the absence of the other two boys. The activity here, and perhaps in the other fragment as well, might be described as "passing," an activity which might be akin to finking or scabbing. In this case the proposal is he's putting on the appearance of just a normal everyday car and its normal everyday driver while he's really being loyal to another category similar to hotrodders — i.e., surfers. ((GJ))

    Ken: Oh-Oh wait. In Mammoth my Jeep I've got surf stickers all over the back windows you know?
    Louise: Mm//hm
    Ken: An' up there they <u>hate</u> surf. Surf is the lowe//st thing,
    Louise: Oh I <u>know</u> that. heh
    Ken: in the world. An' all the adults frown upon it, the kids hate'em, they see me, an' they used to throw rocks. =
    Louise: ehheh heh!
    Ken: you know?
    Ken: An' I was avoiding <u>rocks</u>. So I finally decided this isn't for me y'know, I took razor blades, took all my surf stickers off? So it looked like just a normal everyday Jeep, you know, an' I was driving around town, an' nobody throwin rocks, or anything, it felt so good, y'know?

Two Preferences in the Organization of Reference to Persons in Conversation and Their Interaction

Harvey Sacks and
Emanuel A. Schegloff

*In conversation, persons have occasion to refer to other persons.
Sacks and Schegloff examine here two preferences in such references.
The first, minimization, involves use of a single reference form and the
second, recipient design, involves the preference for "recognitionals,"
e.g. name. Names may be used not only because the person is known
but also in preparation for subsequent use in the conversation even
when the person is not already known by the recipient/hearer.*

*When recognition is in doubt, a recognitional with an accompanying
(questioning) upward intonational contour, followed by a brief pause
(or "try-marker") may be used. The argument advanced by the authors
is that members' uses of these, and succeeding try-markers in sequences,
provide evidence for the preferential structure of efforts to achieve
recognition in reference to other persons in the course of a conversation.
Thus, the close examination of members' conversational interaction can*

This paper was written in the summer of 1973 while the authors were teaching at the
Linguistic Institute, University of Michigan. Its publication has been delayed by the ill-
fated nature of several publications for which it had been scheduled.

reveal not only the organized, methodical practices they use but also the structure of preferred solutions to particular problems that arise in conversation.

1. Research into the social organization of conversation has, as one type of product, the isolation of a "preference" operating for some domain(s) of conversation and the depiction of the organizational machinery through which that preference is effected. A variety of such preferences and their organizational instruments have been studied. It regularly turns out that various of them are concurrently relevant, concurrently applicable, and concurrently satisfied.

However, on some occasions in which some such two preferences appear to figure, the actually produced talk does not concurrently satisfy them.[1] Examination of such materials is particularly useful. They can, for example, give support to the proposal that *separate* preferences are involved, a possibility that the regularity of their concurrent satisfaction obscures. Furthermore, examination of such materials permits the extraction of a "second order" organization directed to an *integration* of preferences on occasions when their potential concurrent satisfiability is not realized.

The study of various such second order devices suggests that they do provide resources which organize adjustment of the concurrently applicable preferences when both are not satisfiable. What is more interesting is that the second order devices themselves represent *types* of solutions, a common one being to prefer satisfaction of one of the applicable preferences, the other being relaxed to such a point as will allow the preferred to be achieved: *The nonpreferred of the two is not suspended but "relaxed step by step."*

We have found this type of solution in a variety of domains in conversation,[2] operating on occasions when two concurrently relevant and applicable preferences that are usually concurrently satisfiable, do not happen to be. Here we shall address this problem and describe its solution on one of those domains—that of reference to persons by the use of reference forms.

2. Two preferences which we have found widely operative in conversation are those for "minimization" and for "recipient design." Each of these is relevant and applicable in the domain of "reference to persons." Each has an expression specific to that domain.

The specification of the general preference for minimization in the domain of reference to persons is of the following sort: *On occasions when reference is to be done, it should preferredly be done with a single reference form.* The point is this: For reference to any person, there is a large set of reference forms that can do the work of referring to that one (e.g., he, Joe, a guy, my uncle, someone, Harry's cousin, the dentist, the man who came to dinner, et cetera). Reference forms are combinable, and on some occasions are used in combination. But massively in conversation, references in reference occasions are accomplished by the use of a single reference form. [As in: (1) Did *Varda* tell you what happened this weekend? (2) Hey do you have a class with *Billy* this term? (3) *Someone* said at the end of the class "Could you pl-please bring in a microphone next time?" (4) If *Percy* goes with *Nixon* I'd sure like that.][3] Thereby a preference for minimization is evidenced.

The specification of the general preference for recipient design in the domain of reference to persons is: *If they are possible, prefer recognitionals*. By "recognitionals" we intend, such reference forms as invite and allow a recipient to find, from some "this-referrer's-use-of-a-reference-form" on some "this-occasion-of-use," who, that recipient knows, is being referred to. By "if they are possible" we mean: If recipient may be supposed by speaker to know the one being referred to, and if recipient may suppose speaker to have so supposed. The speaker's supposition will be evidenced by, for example, use of a first name, first names being a basic sort for recognitionals. Several easily observable phenomena attest the operation of this preference. Having noted that first names are a basic sort for recognitionals, suffice it to remark that they are heavily used. The point is this: In view of the aforementioned availability of a large set of reference forms for any possible referent, nonrecognitional forms (and indeed minimized recognitional forms—e.g., "someone") are available to any speaker for any recipient about any referent. Against the background of those resources, the heavy use of first names evidences a preference for recognitionals. Furthermore, names are not only heavily used when known: they may be introduced for subsequent use when not already known to recipient, thereby arming him with the resources he may thereafter be supposed to have. The strength of the preference should therefore be appreciated to involve not only maximum exploitation of the use of recognitionals consistent with some current state of "if possible," but to involve as well an interest in expanding the scope of possibility. From recipients' point of view also, the preference is extendable. For instance: a nonrecognitional having been done, recipient may find from other resources provided in the talk that he might know the referred-to, while seeing that the speaker need not have supposed that he would. He may then seek to confirm his suspicion by offering the name or by asking for it, characteristically offering some basis for independently knowing the referred-to, as in the following:

	B:	Wh-what is yer friend's name.
	B:	Cuz my <u>son</u> lives in Sherman Oaks.
(5)	A:	Uh <u>We</u>nzel
	B:	(Mh-mh) no.
	B:	And uh,
	B:	If she uh
	A:	She lives on Hartzuk.
		(1.6)
	B:	No I don' even know that street.

These and other such phenomena evidence the recipient design preference which, to repeat, is: If recognition is possible, try to achieve it.

From this last discussion it should be apparent that there are extensive resources which provide for the compatibility of the preferences with each other, i.e., which allow the two preferences to be concurrently satisfied. The compatibility can be appreciated from either preference's point of view: names are prototypical and ideal recognitionals in part because they are minimized reference forms as well; and the stock of minimized forms includes a set (of which names are only one sort) which are for use as recognitionals. (It should be noted that names do not have their uniqueness of reference serve to account for their recognitional usage—for they are, of course, not characteristically unique.)

Massive resources are provided by the organization of reference to persons through reference forms for references that satisfy both preferences concurrently, and those resources are overwhelmingly used.

3. Turning to incompatibility, that possibility is structurally recognized, sometimes engendered, and potentially restricted in size via a form available to intending referrers, which involves use of such a recognitional as a first name, with an upward intonational contour, followed by a brief pause. We shall call this form a *"try-marker."* Use of such a form is understood to be appropriate if a speaker anticipates that the recognitional form being used will on this occasion, for this recipient, possibly be inadequate for securing recognition. If recipient does recognize the referred-to, such success is to be asserted in the brief pause which the referrer will have left for such assertions. (An "uh huh" or a nod can be used to do this.) A recipient's failure to insert such an assertion in the pause evidences the failure that the try-marker evidenced suspicion of; recognition is supposed as absent, and in that case a second try is in order. A second try will be treated as in aid of recognition, and also obliges that its success be acknowledged or a third try is in order etcetera, until either they agree to give up or success is achieved.

(6)

A: Ya still in the real estate business, Lawrence
B: Wah e' uh no my dear heartuh ya know Max Rickler
    h (.5) hhh uh with whom I've been 'ssociated since
    I've been out here in Brentwood// has had a series
    of um--bad experiences uhh hhh I guess he calls it
    a nervous breakdown. hhh
A: Yeah ((at double slashes))
A: Yeah

(7)

A: . . . well I was the only one other than than the uhm
    tch <u>Fords</u>?, Uh Mrs. Holmes Ford? You know uh//
    the the cellist?
B: Oh yes. She's she's the cellist. ((at double slashes))
A: Yes
B: ye//s
A: Well she and her husband were there. . . .

The existence and common use of such a form obviously bears on a consideration of the concurrence of the preferences for minimization and recipient design, and it bears as well on a consideration of their relative strengths. Since the try-marker engenders a sequence, involving at least recipient's assertion of recognition (an occurence which is in marked contrast to the usual use of recognitionals which do not have success asserted by recipient), and perhaps involving a multiplicity of reference forms as well, and since it generates a sequence whose desired outcome is "recognition," the try-marker is evidence for the preference for recognitionals being stronger than the preference for minimization. (Were minimization stronger, then, when recognition via a minimal recognitional were doubtful, a minimal nonrecognitional would be preferred.)

Note, however: the try-marker engendered sequence has a minimal form used first, even when its success is doubted, and when others are available for combination with it; and in each subsequent try also uses a single form; and between each try it provides a place for the assertion of recognition, the occurence of which stops the sequence. Thereby, the try-marker evidences the nonsuspension of the preference for minimization, and that it is relaxed step by step in aid of recognition and only so far as the achievement of recognition of this referent by this recipient obliges.

Note, finally, that since the try-marker involves the use of an intonation contour applied to a reference form, and followed by a brief pause, its use is not constructionally restricted to some particular recognitionals or to subsets of them; whatever recognitional is otherwise available can be try-marked, and thereby used by referrer to initiate a recognition search sequence.

An initial second-order device for coordinating an adjustment between locally incompatible preferences having been found, it is common to find others. Consider then the use of "who."

```
          A:   Hello?
          B:   'Lo,
          B:   Is Shorty there,
          A:   Ooo jest- Who?
(8)       B:   Eddy?
          B:   Wood₊ward?
          A:          ⌊Oo jesta minnit.
               (1.5)
          A:   Its fer you dear.
```

Note about it first, that it is done as a full turn by a reference recipient after an unmarked (without upward intonation or a pause) recognitional. More precisely, it occurs as a next turn on the completion of one in which a recognitional reference figures, which its use locates as unrecognized. Note further that its use engenders a sequence very similar to the one initiated by a try-marker, in which recognitionals are tried by referrer, one at a time, a pause between each for an assertion of recognition, and a stopping of the sequence by an evidencing of recognition by recipient. Then, the principle of a preference for recognition, with a relaxation but not suspension of minimization, is preserved when an incompatibility between the two, consequent on the use of a minimal recognitional that does not yield recognition, is noticed by recipient. A reconciling device is then available for initiation by referrer or by recipient.

Certainly there are differences between the referrer-initiated and the recipient-initiated recognition search sequences. The second try in the "who" engendered sequence is very commonly a repeat of the problematic reference form. The try-marker engendered sequence does not have that feature, is in that regard potentially shorter, as it is also by virtue of its first try potentially working. On the other hand, "who" engendered sequences very commonly occur as inserts into other sequences, and when they do, the assertion of recognition can be dispensed with in favor of recipient, on recognition, proceeding with his next move in the sequence his "who" interrupted. In that move he will characteristically display, but not assert, his recognition in a way alike to how he proceeds if no failures had been involved.

B: I'll get some advance birthday cards. heh
heh ((pause)) and uh Ehhh Oh Sibbi's sister
had a baby boy.

(9)   A: Who?

B: Sibbi's sister

A: Oh really?

While there are differences, then, between the referrer-initiated and recipient-initiated recognition search sequences, both evidence the type of solution to a preference incompatibility which it was our aim here to notice and characterize.

NOTES

1. For simplicity of exposition we consider such a case as involves just two preferences here.

2. See e.g., Harvey Sacks, Emanuel A. Schegloff, and Gail Jefferson, "A Simplest Systematics for the Organization of Turn-Taking in Conversation," *Language* (1974): 696–735.

3. These fragments and those cited subsequently are drawn from a large and varied collection of recorded ordinary conversations. For transcription conventions see Appendix I.

Identification and Recognition in Telephone Conversation Openings

Emanuel A. Schegloff

In this paper Schegloff considers how parties in a telephone conversation display and achieve identification and recognition of each other, i.e., manage to show and tell who they each are and whether each knows who the other is and whether or not he is recognized by the other. The caller and the answerer are shown to produce and use, in their first utterances and turns at talk, considerable resources for accomplishing the task.

Telephone conversations are particularly valuable for dealing with these issues since the speakers do not have sensory access to each other except through their voices and speaking. Identification and recognition can be studied as these occur in the talk—audiotape recordings providing adequate access to the phenomena.

This paper was prepared at the invitation of the Bell Telephone Company and the Massachusetts Institute of Technology for the centennial anniversary of the invention of the telephone, and was written with that occasion in mind. Parts of it have been previously published in Ithiel DeSola Pool (editor), *The Social Impact of the Telephone* (Cambridge: M.I.T. Press, 1976). It is here printed in full for the first time, with no revision, and with acknowledgement to the M.I.T. Press for permission. An earlier version of some portions of the paper was presented at the Conference on the Pragmatics of Conversation, Institute for Advanced Study, Princeton, New Jersey, April, 1974.

The scope and range of Schegloff's paper is extraordinary, for he not only addresses an interesting and important topic of study but also displays, in systematic and rigorous fashion, how conversational analysts work. The transcripts of actual telephone conversations are presented. These are arranged in subgroups which present the variety of methods used by speakers to display and achieve identification and recognition; a number of issues displayed in the data are explored, particularly those structural matters which can be studied by examining the turn-by-turn sequential organizations of utterances; and then an effort is made to develop a description and analysis of the systematics of the organizational structure of identification/recognition. The power of this approach is demonstrated in two ways: first, exploration and illumination of a heretofore unexamined topic, —how speakers display and achieve identification and recognition; and, second, presentation of the methodical procedures by which such work can be accomplished.

I

The work in which my colleagues and I have been engaged is concerned with the organization of social interaction. We bring to the materials with which we work—audio and videotapes of naturally occurring interaction, and transcripts of those tapes—an interest in detecting and describing the orderly phenomena of which conversation and interaction are composed, and an interest in depicting the systematic organizations by reference to which those phenomena are produced.

What people do on the telephone is talk. Conversations on the telephone are, accordingly, natural materials for investigators working in this area, not because of any special interest in the telephone, but because they are instances of conversational interaction.

Materials drawn from telephone conversation *can*, however, have special interest. One feature of materials in which the parties lack visual access to one another was specially useful early in our work, when it helped obviate arguments about the possibility of successfully studying conversation and its sequential organization without examining gesture, facial expression, and the like. Telephone conversation is naturally studied in this manner, and shows few differences from conversation in other settings and media. The materials we have examined include a substantial number of telephone conversations and there are few areas of investigation in which we have had occasion to segregate them by virtue of important (or even unimportant) differences in how phenomena were organized. Indeed, the gross similarity of telephone and other talk has contributed to our confidence that a great deal can be found out about the organization of conversational interaction without necessarily examining video materials (however important and interesting it is to do so in any case). The talk people do on the telephone is not fundamentally different from the other talk they do.

Our work over the last several years has yielded the description of a variety of the orderly phenomena of which conversation is composed, and initial efforts at depicting the systematic sequential organizations by reference to which those phenomena are produced, such as the organization of turn-taking in conversation,[1] the organization of repair in conversation,[2] and, less systematically as yet, the organization of sequences.[3] A number of reports have dealt with elements of another type of sequential organization, the overall structural organization of the unit "a single conversation," which operates on openings, closings, and some aspects of what transpires in between, describing several sorts of sequences which are regularly involved.[4] It is in the overall structural organization of a conversation—in its opening and closing—that the distinctive characteristics of various "types" of conversation may most prominently appear. The opening is a place where the type of conversation being opened can be preferred, displayed, accepted, rejected, modified—in short, incipiently constituted by the parties to it.[5] With all the similarity between talk on the telephone and other talk settings—in the systematic ways turns are allocated, sequences built, trouble repaired, words selected, and the like—openings are a likely place in which to find differences. And, indeed, the openings of telephone conversations generally do have a distinctive shape. One element of it is this: we regularly find in the telephone openings a type of sequence not much found in "face-to-face" conversation—a sequence in which the parties identify and/or recognize one another. Even when no sequence devoted to this job occurs, the issue (identification/recognition) is worked through. This paper is about those sequences and that issue.

I do not report about this topic, however, because of its specialized appearance in telephone conversation, but because identification appears to be generically relevant in interaction and its recognitional variant especially important among humans.

When social behavior is differentiated by reference to its recipient or target, investigators can hardly escape the importance that attaches to the processes by which identification of recipients is made. Biologists, for example, concern themselves with the differential capacities of the various species to identify conspecifics, nestmates and intruders, males and females, conspecifics at various stages of life, members of various "castes," and even particular individuals and the methods by which such identifications are made.[6]

Humans, of course, make these sorts of identifications, both categorial and "recognitional," (i.e., of particular, "known" others), and differentiate their behavior toward them accordingly. We are just beginning to appreciate the degree of detail to which such differentiation—by "recipient design"—is applicable, but a sense of its range may be gleaned from considering that on the one hand the very occurrence or not of interaction may be contingent on it, and on the other hand, should conversation be entered into, the selection of words in the talk will be sensitive to it (e.g., the reference terms employed).[7] Identification is important, then, to all the domains in interaction in which a formally constituted system, built for anonymous usability (not for use by particular classes of speakers for particular classes of recipients), is used to produce particularized talk (turn-taking organization, sequence construction, and word selection are such domains). In regard to openings, it is especially worth noting its centrality to the "gatekeeping" issue for interaction concerned with which of those who are potential cointeractants actually enter into an occasion of interaction.

No elaborate consideration of gatekeeping for interaction can be entertained here. One of its basic rules may be noted, however. Grossly put, such persons may (or may be required to) enter into interaction who have done so before. Necessary qualification, refinement, and supplementation aside, I am noting in a slightly different way what others have noted before:[8] that "acquaintanceship" is one major basis for the undertaking of an interaction. Indeed, the vast majority of conversational interactions must certainly be between "recurrent parties," i.e., parties who talk to one another recurrently. If access to interaction is organized, and therefore at least partially restricted, and acquaintanceship is one basis for its occurrence, then recognition by one person of another will be important because recognition is central to the possibility of "social relationships." It can, therefore, be expected to be subject to some potentially elaborate organization.

In human social interaction, identification and/or recognition of others is largely accomplished through sighting by one of the visual appearance of the other, as the few descriptions we have of these phenomena make amply clear.[9] When personal recognition of "other" occurs, and especially when it is prospectively reciprocal, a display of its accomplishment, subtle or elaborate, is made, and constitutes a "social,"—as distinct from "cognitive"—event, an event in interaction therefore.[10] The celebrations of recognition and its importance in the classic texts of Western culture, in the problem of recognition under conditions of partial masking of identity, address themselves to these central features. In the return of Odysseus, markedly changed physical appearance frustrates recognition by intimates, and the action is stopped precisely between the achievement of recognition cognitively and its display as an interactional event;[11] the drama involved in the story of the allocation of Isaac's inheritance between Jacob and Esau turns on a recognitional problem grounded in Isaac's failing eyesight.[12]

When recognition is made problematic (as in literary texts), its processes can come to have texture as events, to have an obvious interest, drama, and centrality. In the normal course of daily routine, however, and especially by virtue of their accomplishment by visual inspection in the "pre-beginning" of interaction, they are somewhat resistant to study and appreciation. What one biologist reports about the social insects is to a large degree true of humans (if we read "eyes" for "antennae"): "recognition. . .seems outwardly a casual matter, usually no more than a pause and sweep of the antennae over the other's body."[13] A body of materials in which the identification and recognition of potential interaction co-participants is routinely problematic and has its solution carried through in such a manner as to make it more readily accessible to empirical inspection is, therefore, of considerable potential value to students of the organization of social interaction.

Telephone conversations supply such a body of materials. In them, recognition is regularly enough relevant, cannot be accomplished visually, and cannot be accomplished before and as a condition for the beginning of the interaction. The work of recognition has a sequential locus in the talk, occupying or informing a sequence of conversational turns, and is thereby accessible to research approaches developed to deal with turns and sequences. Attention to these sequences may contribute to our knowledge of one type of conversational opening; and by exploiting the special "visibility" of interactional work on recognition on the telephone, it may contribute to our understanding of it in other settings of conversation and interaction as well.

This, then, is another of a series of studies on parts of conversational openings. Its data base is made up of about 450 openings, the parties to which vary on the standardly relevant parameters—age, sex, region, social class, etc.—which here, as elsewhere in our studies of the sequential organization of conversation, are not relevant to the matters I shall be concerned with. This series of studies (including the present contribution) may be thought of as preliminary studies for an eventual examination of the systematic organization of opening sections as parts of overall structural organization; or they may be thought of as "brush-clearing" studies for the interactional analysis of particular openings of particular conversations, serving to help "partial out" those aspects of an opening that are products of an underlying systematic organization so as to allow more pointed analysis of what is particularly being done in some particular conversational opening.[14]

I shall proceed in the following manner: In Section II, I display in a number of segments something of the range of data with which we need to come to terms. In Sections III and IV, I discuss somewhat discursively several segments which allow bringing to notice some of the major themes underlying the organization with which we are dealing. In Section V, I begin again from the beginning, somewhat more analytically and systematically, introducing several new themes and points, and hopefully showing how the observations of Sections III and IV are systematically produced. I shall conclude with a discussion of the relationship of the two tacks I have taken.

II

For reasons that will become apparent, the sequential focus of identification/recognition work in the conversations with which we are concerned is in the second turn, i.e., the caller's first turn. Those turns are, overwhelmingly, constructed from a very small set of types of turn components. Nine types may be listed, with exemplary displays, some of which occur infrequently, and/or largely in combination with others. (See Appendix I for a glossary of symbols used in the transcripts. The arrows locate the phenomenon for which the segment is cited.)

    1) greeting terms:

A:	H'llo:?	
→ B:	hHi:,	(1)
	(TG, #1)	
M:	Hello	
→ J:	Hello	(2)
	(MDE, #91)	
C:	Hello::,	
→ A:	Good morning.	(3)
	(NB, #112)	
B:	Hello:,	
→ R:	Howdy.	(4)
	(ID, #277)	

    2) answerer's, presumed answerer's, or intended answerer's name or address term (in varying combinations, of first name, title + last name,[15] nickname, etc.) in one of a range of interrogative or quasi-interrogative intonation contours.

C:	Hello:.	
→ M:	Miz Parsons?	(5)
	(JG, #73a)	

```
     I:   Hello,
 ──►N:   Irene?                                              (6)
              (ID, #244)


     L:   Hello here.
 ──►S:   Colonel Lehroff?                                    (7)
              (CDHQ, #353a)

     C:   Hello:
 ──►R:   'hh Mother?                                         (8)
              (JG, #41c)

     M:   Hello:
 ──►E:   Gina?                                               (9)
              (MDE, Supp.)

     M:   Hello?
 ──►J:   Marcia?                                            (10)
              (MDE, #99)

     C:   Hello?
 ──►G: · Charlie?                                           (11)
              (CF, #157)

     H:   Hello?
 ──►R:   Harriet?                                           (12)
              (RB, #186)
```

3) answerer's, presumed answerer's, or intended answerer's name or address term (in varying combinations of name components) in one of a range of
   assertive, exclamatory, or terminal intonation
   contours.

```
     C:   Hello?
 ──►M:   Charlie.                                           (13)
              (CF, #155)

     T:   Hello::,
 ──►E:   Uh Tiny.                                           (14)
              (CDHQ, #306)

     P:   Hello?
 ──►L:   Phil!                                              (15)
              (CDHQ, #299)

     M:   Hello
 ──►G:   Mommy,                                             (16)
              (MDE, #98)
```

4) question or noticing concerning answerer's state

P:	Hello::,	
→ A:	Are you awa:ke?	(17)
	(NB, #105)	

I:	Hello:,	
→ A:	Did I waken you dear,	(18)
	(ID, #235)	

AL	Hello,	
→ B:	Hi. // C'n you talk?	(19)
	(DS, #184)	

F:	Hello:,	
→ S:	Hello. You're home.	(20)
	(RK, #190)	

F:	Hello:,	
→ R:	Franklin are you watching?	(21)
	(RK, #189)	

5) "First topic" or "reason for the call"

F:	Hello:	
→ R:	Whewillyoubedone.	(22)
	(JG, #55)	

F:	(. . .)-o.	
→ C:	Yeah I'm jus leaving.	(23)
	(JG, #55)	

M1:	((Hello))	
→ M2:	What's goin' on out there, I understand y'got a robbery,	(24)
	(WGN, #2)[16]	

L:	H'llo:,	
→ C:	Hi, 'r my kids there?	(25)
	(LL, #8)	

6) request to speak to another ("switchboard" request)

A:	Hello	
→ B:	Is Jessie there?	(26)
	(NB, #118)	

S:	((Hello))	
→ B:	Iz yur (eh) gramother there	(27)
	(JG, #62)	

```
M:   Hello:,
C:   May I speak to Bonnie,                    (28)
        (ID, #289)

A:   Hello:?
I:   ú Can I speak to Dr. S _____          (29)
     please,
        (ID, #254)
```

7) self-identification[17]

```
B:   H'llo?
D:   Hi Bonnie. This is Dave.                 (30)
        (ID, #234a)

R:   Hello,
M:   Hey:: R:i:ck, thisiz Mark iz            (31)
     Bill in?
        (#198)

M:   Hello?
D:   Hi. = Thisiz David Williamson           (32)
        (JG, #34a)

M:   Hello? =
C:   = Hello it's me.                         (33)
        (MDE, Supp.)
```

8) Question re identity of answerer

```
L:   Hello:,
M:   H'llo, is this Kitty?                    (34)
        (LL, #27)

M:   Yhello,
L:   H'llo who's this,                        (35)
        (LL, #23)
```

9) a joke, or joke version of one of the above (e.g., mimicked intonation, intendedly incorrect identification, intendedly funny accent, etc.)

```
Ba:  Hello?
B:   Hello?
Ba:  Hello?
B:   Hello?                                   (36)
Ba:  Hi Bonnie.
B:     Hi he heheheheh 'hh
Ba:         heheheh
        (ID, #287a)
```

```
        L:   H'llo::,
 ───►M:   H'llo::    ((intended intonation echo))
        (1.0)
        L:   H'llo? =                                      (37)
 ───►M:   = H'llo?   ((intended intonation echo))
        L:   Oh hi.
             (LL, #9)

        C:   Hello?
 ───►G:   Grrreetins.   ((gutteral "r"))                  (38)
             (CF, #160)

        C:   Hello?
 ───►G:   Helloooooo,                                     (39)
             (CF, #160)

        C:   Hello?
 ───►G:   Is this the Communist Party Head-               (40)
             quarters?
             (CF, #147)

        M:   Hello?
 ───►G:   Hi = This is your daughter chewing              (41)
             on beets.
             (MDE, #93)
```

Very nearly all second turns are composed of these component types, singly (as presented above, for the most.part) or, frequently, in combinations of various sorts. In fact, if one omits requests to speak to another (collection 6 above) as a single component or one of several (usually the other is a greeting which precedes), the overwhelming majority of second turns after "hello" are composed of collection 1 (greetings), collection 2 (other's name interrogative), collection 3 (other's name declarative), or a combination of collections 1 + 2 or 1 + 3. The various turn types that are constructed with these nine components and the various combinations of them initiate a range of different types of sequences: greeting sequences, request sequences, request for confirmation sequences, question/answer sequences, apology sequences (post "Did I wake you," for example), and others. In each of them, however, the identification/recognition issue is addressed.

It is worth noting that all the data segments displayed above have "hello" (however variously inflected) as their initial turn. Elsewhere,[18] I have examined the major other type of initial turn: self-identification. I tried to show that who answered a ringing phone, and with what type of intial turn, was "recipient designed," even though the particular recipient was at that moment unknown. The determination of who should answer, and with what, is sensitive to putative orientations of an at-that-moment unknown caller to a set of potential answerers of the phone he has called. At a phone whose callers are not expectably recognizables and are not expectably oriented to answerers as recognizables, answerers' first turns routinely are designed to afford categorial confirmation that the caller reached what he intended, typically by self-identification (e.g., "American Airlines"), a self-identification which projects a type of identification for caller (e.g., "customer") and aspects of the type of conversation getting under way (e.g., "business"). For a phone whose callers may be oriented to a set of potential answerers who are recognizables, answerers' first turns regularly supply a voice sample—"hello" is its conventional vehicle—as materials from which confirmation of reaching the intended locus may be achieved, but no overt self-identification. The confirmation may be achieved by recognition, and the caller's first turn is the place in which such recognition, or trouble with it, can be displayed.

It is by reference to this placement that the turn-types constructed from the components listed above address the identification/recognition issue. Even the request to speak to another (the "switchboard request"), which seems to claim the nonrelevance of identification or recognition of current recipient,[19] displays a recognition of recipient as "not the intended recipient" or an inability to recognize answerer as intended recipient. The vast majority of second turns address the identification/recognition issue for caller. I will initially focus on the latter issue. For this focus it is useful to group together those second turn components which specifically initiate an indentification/recognition *sequence* (collections 2, 7, and 8) when constituting the sole or final component of the turn, and those which are informed by that issue while not addressing a sequence to it overtly (all the other components).[20] For simplicity of presentation, I will consider from the first group mainly the turn-type composed of interrogative name (collection 2 above), sometimes preceded by a greeting, and from the second group the turn-type composed of a greeting alone or greeting plus name in "assertive" intonation (collection 3).

III

Greetings are generally, and not incorrectly, treated as the first exchange of a conversation. It is important to note, however, that they are, as well, the end of a phase of incipient interaction—what I referred to earlier as "pre-beginnings." Routinely, the actual exchange of greeting terms follows a set of other activities, such as lookings, eye aversions, pace changes, body, head, and arm maneuvers.[21] One important component of the pre-beginning is identification of other(s) in the scene. Among the possible outcomes of the pre-beginning are that no interaction is entered into; that a passing exchange of greetings only is undertaken;[22] that greetings are followed by further talk of variously projected length; or that some talk is begun but without greetings. If some talk is undertaken, the first turns regularly display (by each party for the other) understandings of the outcome of the pre-beginning phase. The types of turn employed begin to constitute a conversation of some type, and are selected, at least partially, by reference to determinations made in the pre-beginning, among them the identification made there. For example, a greeting, e.g., "Hi," in first turn can display a claim of recognition by its speaker of its recipient, and can make reciprocal recognition relevant, if it has not already occurred nearly simultaneously.[23] An "excuse me" in first turn can display an identification of its recipient by its speaker as a "stranger" (as well as displaying, for example, that something other than a full or casual conversation is being initially projected, but rather a single sequence, very likely of a "service" type). The proferring of a greeting can, then, be one way of displaying to another that he has been recognized, and can be a way of soliciting reciprocal recognition. The completion of a greeting exhange can involve, therefore, claims by the parties to the exchange that they have recognized each other.

On the telephone, visual access is denied, and typically there is no pre-beginning. But by the time of the caller's first turn, the answerer's first turn has occurred (with occasional exceptions), and with it, its voice and manner. A caller's use, in his first turn, of a greeting term alone, or a greeting term plus an address term "terminally intoned" or other of the earlier-listed components in this class, constitutes a claim by caller that he has recognized the answerer from the answerer's first turn. And it invites reciprocal recognition from the single, typically small turn it constitutes. In being selected from the set of possible turn-components at just the point that recognition of the answerer is claimed, it shows itself as well to be recipient-designed, i.e., selected by virtue of who the recipient is. It carries, then, the promise that the caller is, for this answerer, one who can be recognized from this resource. In doing so, it initiates an effort to have the identifications (in such cases, the recognitions) accomplished *en passant*, while doing an otherwise relevant part of the opening (a greeting exchange), and without building a special sequence to accomplish that work.

The doing of an initial greeting in second turn[24] has two aspects at least. First, it is the first part of a basic sequential unit we call an "adjacency pair," whose simplest form is a sequence of two turns, by different speakers, adjacently placed, typologically related such that the occurrence of some particular type of first part strongly constrains what occurs in the next turn to be one of a restricted set of second parts.[25] In the case of the adjacency pair initiated by a first greeting, of course, its recipient properly responds with a second greeting, or greeting return. Second, it is a claim to have recognized the answerer and a claim to have the answerer recognize the caller. These two aspects of the caller's initial "Hi" are intertwined. A first greeting having been done, a second greeting is what should relevantly occupy the next turn. But as the first greeting displays recognition, so will a second greeting; it will thus do more than complete the greeting exchange, it will stand as a claim that the answerer has reciprocally recognized the caller.

Regularly answerers do follow callers' initial greetings with return greetings, accomplishing thereby both an exchange of greetings and an exchange of recognitions.

```
      A:    H'llo:?
  →   B:    hHi:,                               (42)
  →   A:    Hi:?
              (TG, #1)

      M:    Hello
  →   J:    Hello                               (43)
  →   M:    Hi
              (MDE, #91)


      A:    Hello::,
  →   B:    Hi:::,                              (44)
  →   A:    Oh: hi::: 'ow are you Agne::s,
              (NB, #114)
```

That is, the callers' "recipient-designed" use of such a turn type in T2 (as I shall hereafter refer to the second turn of the conversation, the caller's first turn) is regularly successful. It is employed with such recipients as callers suppose, and, on the whole, suppose correctly, will recognize them from a small voice sample. Recipients of such turns are aided in accomplishing the recognition by the information, supplied by the form of the turn, that the caller has rights, and grounds for supposing, that he can be so recognized. Such information can considerably restrict the set of candidate recognizables they search to discover who the caller is. Recipients display their reciprocal recognition by doing a sequentially appropriate second part for the type of sequence initiated by the caller, a sequence which is (in the cases here under consideration) not overtly directed to identification, and can be occupied with some other opening-revelant job, such as greeting.

If answerers/recipients do not recognize callers from the initial "Hi" (or other sequence start, not overtly identificatory), several courses are available to them.

Sequentially, the initial greeting has made a second greeting relevant, but a second greeting will claim the answerer's recognition of the caller. Answerers who do not recognize the caller may withhold the return greeting in order not to claim a recognition they have not achieved. Thus:

C:	Hello?		
➤G:	Hello.		(45)
➤	(1.5)		
		(CF, #130)	
C:	Hello?		
➤Y:	Hello Charles.		(46)
➤	(0.2)		
		(CF, #145)	
L:	Hello,		
➤B:	Hi Linda,		(47)
➤	(0.1)		
		(ID, #212a)	

The caller's first turn is followed by a gap of silence.

Such a sequence of events is familiar to us from other instances of this sequential structure.[26] The first part of an adjacency pair not only makes one of a set of type-fitted second parts relevant in next turn, but typically displays a preference for one of them. Questions may be built to display preferences for yes or no answers; requests prefer grants rather than rejections; offers and invitations prefer acceptances, etc. The occurrence of a gap following the first part displays the incipient possible occurence of a dis- or less preferred second part. It affords the speaker of the first part an opportunity to back down from the turn-type he has done, revise it so that it displays a different preference (so that the second part that is apparently "in the cards" will be the preferred one for the reconstructed first part), etc. If the speaker of the first part does not do so, then its recipient may do the dispreferred second, or may continue to withhold it and do another pre-dispreferred, affording the speaker of the first part yet another opportunity to modify it before the dispreferred second is done. He may do this by "questioning" all or part of the first part of the adjacency pair with what we have elsewhere termed a "next turn repair initiator (NTRI)."[27]

In the sequential environment under discussion here, the first part greeting, as we have noted, involves more than the initiation of a greeting exchange; it invites recognition. The preferred next, then, is a display of recognition, a display which is accomplished by completing the adjacency pair which is the vehicle for the recognition exchange with a second greeting. The withholding of the second greeting may then be understood as pre-the dispreferred—no recognition.

The alternative courses which follow are familiar as well. The speaker of the first part, we noted, may modify his stance, may modify his turn, and back down from the constraint placed on the next turn. In the present sequence type, that would involve backing down from the claim that the recipient recognize him from a voice sample alone. One way of doing this is to supply additional resources for the recognition, which weakens the claim of degree of recognizability. The two sequences presented below follow this course:

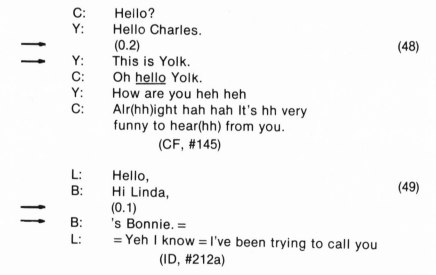

```
        C:    Hello?
        Y:    Hello Charles.
──▶           (0.2)                                          (48)
──▶     Y:    This is Yolk.
        C:    Oh hello Yolk.
        Y:    How are you heh heh
        C:    Alr(hh)ight hah hah It's hh very
              funny to hear(hh) from you.
                  (CF, #145)


        L:    Hello,
        B:    Hi Linda,                                      (49)
──▶           (0.1)
──▶     B:    's Bonnie. =
        L:    = Yeh I know = I've been trying to call you
                  (ID, #212a)
```

In both segments, the upgrading of resources by the caller as a way of backing down from the strength of the initial claim to recognizability (i.e., from voice sample alone) is sufficient to allow the achievement of recognition, which is displayed in the next turn. In both cases as well, the snag in the sequence is further dealt with, in #49 by a claim that the full self-identification was unnecessary, the recognition having been already achieved (and indeed, only the slightest of gaps had developed before B's upgrade). In #48, C recognizes caller, display by the "oh" (which marks both success and success "just now") that he had not recognized before, and produces the return greeting, but uses for it what I will call "the big hello," which is used with "long time no see" recipients or "unexpected" callers. Then, one turn later, he explicitly comments on the unexpectedness of this caller, finding therein a bit of warrant, and a diagnosis, for having failed to recognize from the voice sample alone.

The third of the segments we are examining, #45, in which a gap follows the T2 greeting, is resolved in a different manner. Here, the opportunity—indeed, given the length of the gap, the opportunities—for the caller to upgrade the recognitional resources are not taken. (Very likely we have here an instance of the sort of "option cycle" discussed in formal turn terms elsewhere,[28] the gap being occupied by alternating options for the prior speaker to continue—here to upgrade the resources—and for the recipient to start up—here, eventually with a repair initiator—the options being several times passed by the relevant party.) Finally, the recipient breaks the gap, with "who's this."

"Who's this" makes explicit, and embodies in a sequentially consequential turn, C's failure to recognize. Following, as it does, a turn in which is implicated an invitation to recognize, it disappoints that invitation. It thus appears to be the dispreferred next turn which the 1.5 second gap foreshadowed. Its form, however, is notable. It does not simply declare the failure of recognition, as is done, for example, in another segment in the corpus, "I can't place you." Rather it is a form of question we call a "next turn repair initiator" (NTRI).[29] NTRIs are directed to trouble of some sort in a prior turn, which the speaker of the prior turn has not repaired elsewhere in the prior turn, or in the "transition space" immediately following it. Generally, NTRIs afford the prior speaker, the speaker of the trouble source, another opportunity in the turn that follows to repair that trouble. If that is done, the speaker of the NTRI may, in the turn after *that,* do whatever turn-type was made sequentially appropriate by the turn that contained the trouble. Thus, if the trouble-source turn was a first part of an adjacency pair, its second part may follow the NTRI and the repair it solicits.

In the segment under examination here, the T2 "Hello"has been offered as the resource from which recognition should be achieved. The gap of 1.5 seconds has displayed the incipient failure of the recognition, and provided an opportunity for the caller to repair the turn, for example, by upgrading the resources from which the recognition might be made. She does not do so. "Who's this" located the source of trouble—the insufficiency of the resources for achieving recognition—and provides another opportunity, in the turn that follows, for G to repair the trouble, for example, by giving her name. Had the sequence developed that way, and the name been a sufficient repair to allow recognition, then the still relevant second part of the greeting pair might have been produced. The sequence would then have gone:

> C: Hello?
> G: Hello.
> (1.5)
> C: Who's this.
> G: ((Gloria))
> C: ((Oh hi, Gloria.))

In such a sequence, the caller would have been marked as the speaker of the trouble source, the difficulty having been with the resources supplied for recognition, as in #48 and #49.

The sequence, however, does not develop this way.

> C: Hello?
> G: Hello.
> (1.5)
> C: Who's this.   (49a)
> C: Who is this. = This is your (0.2)
> friendly goddess,
> G: OHhh, hhh, can I ask for a wish
> (CF, #130)

G somewhat turns the tables on C by affording *him* yet another opportunity to accomplish the recognition from less than a full self-identification, making his failure to recognize, rather than her failure to give her name, the trouble source. She does this by availing herself of a device available to recipients of questions, the "joke first answer."[30] Her "joke first answer" preserves the sequentially appropriate type of turn for the question it follows, a self-identification. But instead of self-identifying by name, she does a joke self-identification, and one which supplies potential clues for recognition (e.g., that she is a friend, that she is female, etc.) as well as a further voice sample. C does thereupon recognize her, displaying his recognition with the "success marker" described earlier, and continues not with a greeting return, but with a turn-type fitted to the joking self-identification that precedes it.

In the data segments I have examined, there are differences in who ends up moving to fix the snag that the gap after the second turn displays, with derived interactional consequences for who is "at fault," the caller for not supplying sufficient materials from which to be recognized, or the recipient for failing to recognize. In all cases, however, the gap in which a return greeting is momentarily withheld is understood by the parties to display trouble with recognition. Whichever of the parties breaks the silence, it is with identification-revelant talk. And in cases in which an intitial gap after T2 is followed by the caller with additional talk which is not identification-relevant and fails to secure recognition, the same sequel may ensue, and ensue recurrently until some next gap is followed by identification-relevant talk. For example:

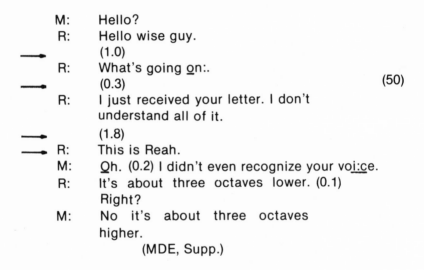

```
        M:    Hello?
        R:    Hello wise guy.
  ──▶          (1.0)
        R:    What's going on:.
  ──▶          (0.3)                                    (50)
        R:    I just received your letter. I don't
              understand all of it.
  ──▶          (1.8)
  ──▶  R:    This is Reah.
        M:    Oh. (0.2) I didn't even recognize your voi:ce.
        R:    It's about three octaves lower. (0.1)
              Right?
        M:    No it's about three octaves
              higher.
                        (MDE, Supp.)
```

When the self-identification is done, recognition is achieved, and a next turn displays it. (Of course, it happens that even self-identification does not achieve recognition right away, and sometimes not at all, as in wrong number calls.)

The segments I have examined all began with a greeting or greeting + address term in second turn. But as was noted at the beginning of this discussion, this T2 turn-type was selected for convenience from the set of T2 turn-types which do not overtly address the identification issue. We have found that the identification theme underlies these sequences, their success being at the same time a success of reciprocal recognition, and their failure being not a failure of greetings but a failure of recognition. This holds equally true for the other not overtly identificational turn-types which get used in the caller's first turn. If recognition, or at least some identification, is not achievable from that turn, then the identification issue is raised in the ensuing turn. Regularly, of course, no such trouble arises, because the use of a nonidentificational turn-type at T2 is recipient-designed. When it is not, or when it fails despite its recipient design, then identification trouble becomes overt. To cite but one instance: even the call to a bank during a robbery answered by the robber cited earlier (#24) shows this sequence:

M1:	((Hello))	
M2:	What's going' on out there, I understand y'got a robbery,	
→	(0.8)	
→ M1:	Uh yes, who's this speaking, please?	
M2:	WGN	(51)
M1:	WGN?	
M2:	Yessir,	
	(0.7)	
M1:	Well this is the robber, (0.2) or the so- so called robber, I guess,	
	(WGN, #2)	

It is because nearly every turn-type in the second turn which appears to evade the identification/recognition issue is vulnerable to its immediate appearance—by a "who's this" or by a gap which is understood as displaying the need for self-identification—that it seems that the identification/recognition issue is generically relevant at second turn, whatever the overt composition of the utterance placed there.

Two turn-types for T2 are a partial exception here, for they may delay the relevance of identification by a turn or two. Both the switchboard request at T2 ("May I speak to. . .?" "Is X there?") and some questions regarding the answerer's state (in particular "Did I wake you?") may get their answers with no gap, without that displaying claimed recognition by answerer of caller. It seems likely that this is so because each of these turn-types is a possible pretermination of conversation with this answerer at this time (the "Did I wake you?" question being a possible "pre-first-topic closing offering,"[31] to be followed, if answered positively, with an offer to call back). However, should the caller try to press beyond this sequence without self-identification and without having been recognized, except for proceeding to a closing sequence, the identification issue regularly gets raised. For example:

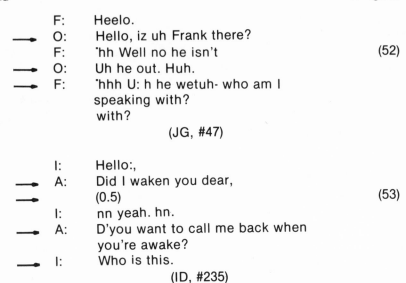

```
    F:      Heelo.
→   O:      Hello, iz uh Frank there?
    F:      'hh Well no he isn't                        (52)
→   O:      Uh he out. Huh.
→   F:      'hhh U: h he wetuh- who am I
            speaking with?
            with?
                    (JG, #47)


    I:      Hello:,
→   A:      Did I waken you dear,
→           (0.5)                                        (53)
    I:      nn yeah. hn.
→   A:      D'you want to call me back when
            you're awake?
→   I:      Who is this.
                    (ID, #235)
```

It appears then that identification/recognition is generically relevant at the very beginning, at best deferable for a turn or two if it appears the conversation between the current parties may terminate thereafter. This is so whether the turns overtly address the matter or not. We have been examining the set of cases in which they do not. We will shortly turn to the other major class of turn-types, those which are overtly addressed to the identification/recognition issue at T2. Before doing so, two additional matters concerning the class we have been discussing require brief treatment: deception and mistakes.

We have noted that the not-overtly identificational second turn is recipient-designed, selected for use to such a recipient as caller supposes will recognize him from it. The caller thereby displays a claim on the answerer and on their relationship. Failure of the recipient to recognize may reflect on the state of the relationship, and we have seen that there can be some manuevering sequentially which can place the blame on one or another party. Another possibility is open to the nonrecognizing answerer than withholding a next turn, and that is deception, in which the answerer returns the greeting (if that is what is required by the turn-type done at T2) although no recognition has been accomplished. It is not unlikely that many answerers' return greetings are deceptions when produced, but are never "caught" because a next turn by the caller suffices to allow the answerer to achieve the recognition he had not achieved at the moment of the claim, a resource on which answerers may rely in choosing this tack. Such deceptive uses may thus routinely escape notice both by callers and by analysts. They do, however, sometimes become visible, and sometimes are "caught." A few instances will suffice:

            A: Hello
            B: Hi: (54)
    ⟶   A: Hi: (0.3) Oh H̲i Robin
                    (EN, #183)

Earlier we noted the use of some "oh"s to mark success and to mark success "just now." In #54 above, the "oh" displays the point at which recognition is achieved, and the re-greeting is proved to be "honest" by affixing the caller's name to it. But thereby we (and caller) are allowed to see that A's first "Hi" in T3 was deceptive; it claimed recognition, although, it turns out, it had not been achieved.

Another, more dramatic, instance:

            S: Hello
            R: Yeah. Hi::::. How are you boyfriend
    ⟶   S: I'm good. How are you.
    ⟶   R: Ha ha ha. You don't know which
                    of these girls you eh that talking
                    to you.
            S: Huh?
    ⟶   R: You do not know which one of
                    your girlfriends is talking to you.
            S: Yes I do.
    ⟶   R: You do.
            S: Yeah.   (55)
    ⟶   R: And so who.
            S: Is this Mary?
    ⟶   R: Ahh haa! I knew it, see::, I knew
                    I wasn't the only girl you had on
                    your string.
                    (1.0)
            R: This is Lena.
            S: L̲ena! // How are ya honey.
            R: Ha ha
            R: Oh I'm fine. How are you. Listen,
                    how did. . .
                    (JG, #49)

In this segment, some fairly overt joking is going on, the elderly lady caller clearly enough not being S's girlfriend. Still, the sequence displays a direct orientation to the possibility of deceptive claims of recognition, as does the following segment, in which a young teenage boy calls his mother at work and disguises his voice:

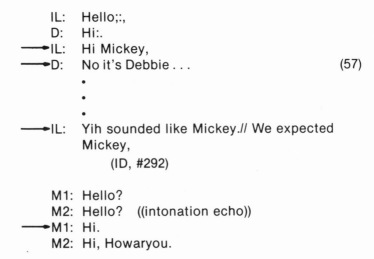

	C:	Dresses?	
		(0.8)	
	R:	Oh. Hi Cathy, ((disguised voice))	
→	C:	Hello:	
→	R:	(Hewo) d'ya know who <u>this</u> is?	
	C:	Yeah.	
→	R:	˙hh Who.	
	C:	This is my boyfriend?	(56)
	R:	˙hh Huh?	
	C:	Are you my.boyfriend?	
	R:	Uh <u>huh</u>,	
	C:	Oh. Okay.	
		(0.5)	
	R:	Okay whaddiyuh wanna eat for dinner.	
		(JG, Supp.)	

The deception of answerers' recognition claims can, then, be matched by deception on the caller's part. And such deception seems aimed at luring the answerer into making a mistaken recognition. Such mistaken recognitions, of course, occur without a deception as bait. Thus:

	IL:	Hello;:,	
	D:	Hi:.	
→	IL:	Hi Mickey,	
→	D:	No it's Debbie . . .	(57)
		•	
		•	
		•	
→	IL:	Yih sounded like Mickey.// We expected Mickey,	
		(ID, #292)	

	M1:	Hello?
	M2:	Hello? ((intonation echo))
→	M1:	Hi.
	M2:	Hi, Howaryou.

```
        M1:  Okay, Howaryou.
        M2:  I'm just fine thank you.                    (58)
        M1:  Did you get the note?
        M2:  What note.
───▶M1:  Oh it's Gary,
        M2:  Yeah,
───▶M1:  Oh I'm sorry.
        M2:  (      ) that's okay.
                    (LL, #18)
```

The second of these cases especially can remind us that even when the shoals of recognition appear to have been skirted in the opening sequences, identification/recognition issues may yet need to be overtly addressed; to the risks of nonrecognition are added those of misrecognition.

IV

The caller's first turns which initiate a sequence specially directed to the identification issue fall into two classes: those directed to self-identification, and those that appear occupied with identification of the answerer.

On the whole, self-identification is not much done in the caller's first turn.[32] Examination of those openings in which it does occur reveals:

a. Many of the instances have a caller's first turn in the *form* of a self-identification which nonetheless operates in the manner of the turn-types discussed in the previous section. For example:

```
        M:  Hello? =
───▶G:    = Hello it's me.                              (59)
        M:  Hi.
                    (MDE, Supp.)
```

```
        P:  Hallo? =
───▶C:    = Hi it's only me.                            (60)
        P:  Hallo there, you,
                    (CG, #182a)
```

In such openings, though the form of caller's first turn is self-identificatory, it is largely by voice recognition (supplemented by the clue supplied by use of the "It's me" form, which may be used specially by nuclear family members) that it works.

b. Another subset of the instances have a self-identification in the caller's first turn followed in that turn by another turn component, regularly the first part of an adjacency pair. It is the latter turn component which is then sequentially implicative, constraining the next turn, and the self-identification does not in that case occupy its own sequence. Two main types of component follow the self-identification: switchboard requests and "How are you" type questions. Thus:

> S: Hello:.
> —▶P: Pt. 'hh H:i. This is Penny Rankin
>   from Lincoln I'm a friend of Pat's.
>   can I speak t'her at all?   (61)
> S: She:re.
>   (RF, #180)

> C: Hello.
> —▶M: Good evening. My name is Murray
>   Murray and (I've called to talk to   (62)
>   Alice Andrews).
> C: (Yes, just a minute).
>   (JG, #53)

"Switchboard requests" are regularly followed by an identification question (e.g., "who's this," "who is calling," etc.) from the answerer, and the cases above appear to be anticipations of this question. Such anticipation is especially in point when the one being asked for is not usually associated with that number, in which case the unprefaced switchboard request is vulnerable to being heard as a wrong number. This is the case in #61 above, and is clearly shown in #63.

> I: Hello:,
> —▶JM: Hello. i- This is Jan's mother.   (63)
> I: Oh yes.
> JM: Is Jan there by any chance?
>   (ID, #233)

Here the switchboard request is started in turn 2 ("i-" being the start of "is Jan there . . ."), but is cut off to do a self-identification first. It is also characteristic, though not invariable, about T2 preswitchboard self-identifications that they are not by first name (hence for recognition), but are by first name + last name, sometimes by, or supplemented by, recognitional descriptions, and that they sometimes use the frame that shows that the self-identification is not intended to solicit recognition: "My name is."

Another component type that follows a T2 self-identification in our corpus is the "How are you" type question.

> R: Hello.
> ─►L: Hi Rob. This is Laurie. How's
> everything. (64)
> R: ((sniff)) Pretty good. How 'bout you.
> L: Jus' fine. The reason I called was
> ta ask . . .
> (LM, #199)

Such cases share with others, in which T2 self-identification is not followed by another turn component, the feature of projecting an abbreviated opening and a quick move to first topic or reason for the call. An instance of such abbreviation in which the T2 self-identification is not followed by another component:

> C: Hello.
> ─►G: Charlie? = Gene.
> C: Oh, Hi. = (65)
> ─►G: = The whole weekend I forgot to tell
> you, I have this book, . . .
> (CF, #164)

These cases, then, appear to be related to #22–25, in which first topic is initiated in the caller's first turn. Here, the risks of nonrecognition entailed by that procedure are avoided by self-identification in the caller's first turn, at the cost of one turn (the first topic being initiated in the caller's second turn) but avoiding a fully expanded opening section.[33]

The caller's first turn is not the main position for self-identification. Such self-identifications as appear there seem to be, for the most part, derivative from other sequential interests. When self-identification by name is done, it mainly occurs in the caller's second turn. When the opening develops in that way, the caller's first turn is occupied with the major turn-types yet to be discussed here: an address term for the answerer (or intended or presumed answerer), in interrogative or quasi-interrogative intonation, alone or preceded by a greeting term. Because the use of title + last name in that position frequently displays that recognition is not a relevant outcome of the sequence,[34] I will not deal with cases of that sort in what follows.

Sometimes, of course, the use of interrogative name in the caller's first turn displays a real uncertainty in the caller's recognition of the answerer from the initial "hello." Sometimes, indeed, the caller's recognition of the answerer is incorrect, as in several calls in our corpus in which mother and daughter are mistaken for each other. For example:

```
        M:   Hello?
 ──► E:      Tina?
        M:   This is Martha.
 ──► E:      Well if I had said "Martha" you
             would've said "This is Tina".              (66)
        M:   Oh, Esther! // hih hih
        E:                    (yah) hih hih heh heh hah
        E:   ⌈Hi:*
        M:   ⌊hih heh* hah
 ──► M:      ˙hhh Hi:: I didn' recognize your
             voi:ce. Either.
                  (MDE, Supp.)
```

In some cases, then, when the caller's "guess" at T2 is correct, it is marked as uncertain. The form thus raises the issue of the possible inadequacy of voice sample for recognition, a theme to which we shall return. It should be noted, however, that in many cases of this form of T2, caller's recognition of the answerer nonetheless seems certain enough (consider again #65 above, in which interrogative name is used, though it appears that the caller does not doubt identity of answerer); and even when it does reflect a serious uncertainty, the form has other sequential uses and consequences as well.

One sequential consequence of the "confirmation-request" form of this turn-type may be appreciated by contrast with a form of turn identical to it in all respects but intonation, and that is "assertive" name with or without a preceding greeting. We have seen that the latter form constrains its recipient to do a greeting in return, which displays reciprocal recognition (whether achieved or not). The alternative, we saw, was to ask the caller for a self-identification, which displays a potential failure, and disappoints an expectation the caller claimed a right to have.[35] The "interrogative name" form of second turn adds to these possibilities "confirmation" and "disconfirmation + correction" (and overwhelmingly it is the former of these which occurs) as turn-types for next turn, both possibilities allowing avoidance of identification/recognition of caller at that turn position. It is, then, a more flexible instrument than the same components in "assertative" or "declarative" intonation, in allowing, but not requiring, deferral of recognition of a caller.

Most importantly, interrogative name in caller's first turn operates as a "presequence." That term is used to collect a variety of turn-types which initiate a sequence understood to be specifically preliminary to a later turn or sequence, one which will be placed in the presequence speaker's next turn or not, depending on what is placed in the turn following the presequence. The most accessible instance is the preinvitation; questions of the form "Are you doing anything?" or "What are you doing?"—especially just after, or even in, the opening—are understood to preface an invitation; if the answer to the preinvitation is "no" or "nothing," the next turn will have the invitation; other answer types may result in no invitation, or in a report of what the invitation would have been, e.g., "I was gonna say let's go to the movies." A range of sequence types can take "pre-"'s; there are prerequests, preannouncements,[36] etc., as well as the "generalized pre-"—the summons—described elsewhere.[37] The T2 interrogative name takes a form identical to some summonses, but is more properly understood as a pre–self-identification.

One use of some presequences, for example of preinvitations, is the avoidance of dispreferred second parts. A prospective inviter can guard against the possibility of an invitation being rejected by using a preinvitation first; some answers to the preinvitation can project acceptance of the invitation, others its prospective rejection, and in the latter case the invitation may be withheld.

Another use of some presequences, for example of prerequests, is the avoidance of relatively less preferred first parts of adjacency pairs. For some projected outcomes, alternative sequential routes are possible, of which one may be structurally preferred to another. Thus, for example, my late colleague Harvey Sacks argued that offers were structurally preferred to requests as a way of getting transfers accomplished. Where such preferences between alternative sequence types, and therefore between alternative first parts of adjacency pairs, operate, a presequence can elicit from its recipient the preferred first part. Thus, a prerequest can get an offer next, obviating the need for actually doing the request (sometimes; the offer may be of something other than the projected request).

The use of an address term in interrogative or quasi-interrogative intonation in caller's first turn operates in the second of these ways. Although recognitional identification is the preferred form of identification[38] (most importantly for reference to third persons, but for self-identification as well), and name is the preferred form of recognitional identification, all the evidence we have so far reviewed points to the fact that *for achieving recognition from co-participant,* self-identification by name is less preferred than recognition by "inspection." The heavy use of non-identification-relevant turn-types discussed in the preceding section, and the substantial absence of self-identification from the second turn even when identification is directly addressed in a sequential locus in which identification/recognition is focused and where the answerer's initial, strong interest is in "who is calling," all point to the relative dispreference for self-identification as a route for achieving recognition. How does interrogative name in the caller's first turn serve as a pre-self-identification which can potentially avoid self-identification? And why is it needed?

It will have been noted that I have frequently referred to the intonation of the turn-type under discussion as "quasi-interrogative." Sometimes, and especially when displaying a serious doubt about the identity of the answerer, callers employ a fully inflected interrogative intonation (in many of these cases following a slight gap of silence after the first "hello"). But for many of the occurrences of the turn-type being examined, a less inflected intonation is used (hence "quasi-interrogative"), rather like what has elsewhere been termed a "try-marker."[39] In the organization of reference to persons in conversation, recognitional reference (of which name is the basic type) is the preferred reference form "if possible." The latter constraint concerns a supposition of the speaker that his current recipient knows the one being referred to, and that the recipient can be expected to suppose that the speaker so supposed. This is a specification, in the domain of reference to persons, of the general recipient design preference: don't tell the recipient what you ought to suppose he already knows; use it. This principle builds in a preference to "oversuppose and undertell." But even with "oversupposition," or because of it, a speaker may suppose a recipient knows the one to be referred to (and knows that one by name), but have doubts about it. In such cases, a speaker regularly employs the name with a slight upward (or "quasi-interrogative") intonation, marking the reference as a "try." It is this intonation which characterizes the caller's T2 pre-self-identification use of answerer's name.

When recognition of self by other is at issue, as it is at T2, the speaker's supposition concerns whether recipient knows him, and by what resource that recognition can be secured; the relevant recognitional resource may be voice sample. But here the preference to oversuppose and undertell may be especially guarded against oversupposition, if not countered by an inclination to undersuppose and overtell,[40] avoiding the interactional consequence of presumptuous and embarrassingly disappointed claims, and the technical organizational consequence of dispreferred sequence expansion. When the supposition that the recipient can recognize by voice sample is doubted, then the try-marker may be employed, qualifying not the recipient's knowing who he (recipient) is, and not (in these cases) the speaker's knowing who the recipient is, but qualifying the supposition that the recipient will know, from the voice sample which that turn supplies, who the speaker (i.e., caller) is.[41] The reciprocity of recognition is nicely caught in the use of form which also can display the possible inadequacy of voice sample for the caller's recognition of the answerer.

The try-marked address term in the caller's first turn can then work as a pre-self-identification by (1) providing a voice sample, (2) displaying a doubt that the recipient will be able to recognize the caller from it, (3) providing a next turn in which the recipient can display recognition if it is achieved, (4) providing an option in the next turn which will not exhibit failure of recognition if recognition does not occur, and thereby (5) allowing caller to supply, and to project the possibility of supplying, in his second turn, self-identification by name from which the recipient can achieve recognition, if recognition is not achieved from the T2 turn and displayed in the turn following. The pre-self-identification thus provides the possibility of success without recourse to the less preferred route of self-identification, while retaining the possibility of the less preferred route should the presequence not avoid it.

The pre-self-identification can have a number of outcomes. Its greatest success, achieved in a substantial proportion of the cases in which it is used, is "evidenced recognition" in next turn. From the voice sample it supplies, and sometimes from other "clues" that are put into the turn (for example, such wholly or partially self-identifying address terms as "Mommy"), the answerer achieves a recognition, and displays it in the next turn in a way that obviates the possibility of deception. The basic form of evidence is inclusion in the recognition-exhibiting turn of the caller's name, usually as an address term, occasionally as a "try."

```
        A:   Hello.
——▶B:   Connie?                              (67)
——▶A:   Yeah Joanie
             (JG, #65a)
```

I: Hello:,
→B: H'llo Ilse?   (68)
→I: Yes. Be:tty.
       (ID, #231)

F: ₍Hello?*
M: ˡHello,*   (69)
→M: H'llo, Donna?
→F: Oh. yeah, Hi Jim,
       (JH, #86)

I: Hello:,
→D: Hello mo:m?   (70)
→I: Debbie?
       (ID, #296)

No self-identification by name is then in point, and the opening continues.

A closely related but somewhat weaker class of outcomes, which adds another substantial proportion of cases, is that of "unevidenced recognition claims." Again, the device to display a claim of recognition is a greeting term. It may occupy the turn (after the pre-self-identification) alone, or it may be preceded by the "oh" previously described as a marker of "success" and "success just now," which upgrades its strength as a claim of recognition.

A: Hello:?
→B: Shar'n?   (71)
→A: Hi!
       (RB, #185)

C: Hello.
→M: Hello, Charlie?   (72)
→C: Oh, hi.
       (CF, #153)

It may also be upgraded by the addition after it of other turn components, especially first parts of adjacency pairs (the characteristic one in this sequential environment being "How are you") which set constraints on the next turn to be a fitted second part, and thereby immediately advance the opening past identification.

```
        C:   Hello?
  ──►M:   Hello, Charlie?
  ──►C:   Oh hi. // How are you.              (73)
        M:            How are you.
        M:   Hey listen . . .
              (CF, #146)
```

Or the greeting as recognition claim may be upgraded productionally, by raised amplitude, pitch, or duration.

```
        S:   Hello::?
  ──►J:   H'llo, Sima?                       (74)
  ──►S:   hhhHI!
              (TAC, #122)
```

The import of these unevidenced recognition claims can be equivocal. Regularly, they are taken by callers to display recognition. An exchange of recognitions is thereby completed, no self-identification by caller is necessary, and the opening proceeds to other components. Sometimes, however, especially when the recognition-marking greeting is not upgraded, the caller proceeds to a self-identification in his second turn anyway, perhaps sensitive to the deception potential of an unevidenced recognition claim, and the inclination to undersuppose, or at least not press oversupposition too far.[42]

```
        B:   'hhh Hello,
  ──►Ba:  Hi Bonnie,
  ──►B:   Hi. =                              (75)
  ──►Ba:  = It's Barbie. =
        B:   = Hi.
              (ID, #275a)
```

```
        L:   H'llo:,
             (0.3)
  ──►M:   Hello, hi Laura,                   (76)
  ──►L:   Hi:
  ──►M:   Howyadoin it's Michael.
        L:   Hi Michael, how are you.
              (LL, #30)
```

```
        J:   Hello,
  ──►B:   Hello Jim?
```

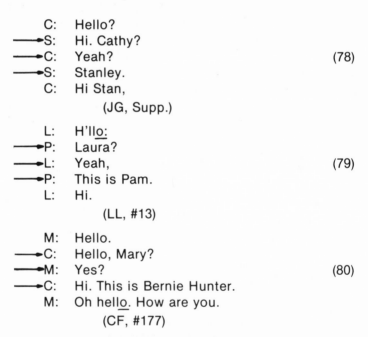

—→•J: Hi-,   (77)
——→B: Hi, it's Bonnie.
    J: Yeah I know
         (ID, #246)

The "upgraded" recognition claims, thus, appear to operate like the evidenced recognitions in allowing deletion of self-identification by caller, and thus shade into that class of next turns to the presequence.

The major class of next turns after the pre-self-identification is even more equivocal. The prototype turn component here is "yes" or "yeah," but the range of its intonational shadings is vast, and its sequential import seems at least partially tied to them. In a very large proportion of the cases, "yeah" or "yes" in next turn is treated by caller as evidencing the failure of the presequence to achieve recognition by the answerer, and the projected self-identification is then produced in the caller's second turn. For example:

        C: Hello?
——→S: Hi. Cathy?
——→C: Yeah?   (78)
——→S: Stanley.
        C: Hi Stan,
             (JG, Supp.)

        L: H'llo:
——→P: Laura?
——→L: Yeah,   (79)
——→P: This is Pam.
        L: Hi.
             (LL, #13)

        M: Hello.
——→C: Hello, Mary?
——→M: Yes?   (80)
——→C: Hi. This is Bernie Hunter.
        M: Oh hello. How are you.
             (CF, #177)

But even the apparently polar intonational values—a clearly interrogative "Yes?" or an emphatically assertive "yeah!"—which might appear to display confirmation-of-answerer's-identity-but-no-recognition-of-caller on the one hand, and confirmation + recognition on the other, do not unequivocally elicit regular sequels. There are T4 self-identifications after enthusiastic "yeah"'s which might be taken to exhibit recognition:

```
        H:   Hello?
  ──►G:   Henry?                                           (81)
  ──►H:   Yeah!
  ──►G:   Yeah. It's Gary. Is Neil there?
             (LL, #33)
```

```
        E:   Hello,
  ──►G:   Eddy,
  ──►E:   Ye̲:h.                                             (82)
  ──►G:   Guy Huston.
             (NB, #109a)
```

And caller may not self-identify by name in fourth turn after a pre-self-identification, even when the prior turn has been a fully interrogative "Yes?". For example:[43]

```
        L:   H'llo,
  ──►E:   Laura?
  ──►       (0.5)                                           (83)
  ──►L:   Yeah?
  ──►E:   Hi,
             (0.5)
        L:   Hi. // Erin?
        E:          Didju-
        E:   Yeah.
             (LL, #17)
```

```
        H:   H'llo:?
  ──►R:   Harriet?
  ──►H:   Yeah?                                             (84)
  ──►R:   Hi!
        H:   Hi̲:.
             (RB, #186)
```

```
        C:   Hello.
  ──►J:   Hello, Charlie?
  ──►C:   Yeah?                                             (85)
  ──►J:   Did I wake you up?
        C:   No. It's alright.
             (CF, #171)
```

But it is not only after interrogative "yeah?" that the callers may fail to deliver in their second turn what they apparently had prefigured in their first. In 25 of approximately 60 calls in which callers did an interrogative or quasi-interrogative address term in T2 or its equivalent, no self-identification by name appears in T4 or its equivalent. Instead, these second turns by callers contain all the various turn components earlier listed as components of T2, except the one actually used in the preceding T2 in that call. Thus, roughly half of the 25 are composed of greetings and/or some version of the "how are you" question, 3 are "Did I wake you"'s, 3 are switchboard requests, 5 start first topic, and one is a mock self-identification:

$$
\begin{array}{lll}
\text{A:} & \text{Hello:,} & \\
\text{\textbf{B:}} & \text{Hello M::\underline{A}?} & \\
\text{\textbf{A:}} & \text{Ye:\underline{AH}! =} & (86) \\
\text{\textbf{B:}} & \text{= It's \underline{m:e}.} & \\
& \text{(RF, \#179)} &
\end{array}
$$

Those components behave sequentially in T4 as they did in T2: they invite recognition from less than name self-identification, but (1) they do not require it at T3, which lowers the degree of their claim, (2) they supply a second voice sample, which upgrades the resources for recognition that have been provided, and (3) in a higher proportion of the cases, the composition of the turn provides additional clues for recognition (for example, in the five first topic starts).

The withholding of self-identification by name from T4 as well as T2, when T2 has prefigured it, supplies additional evidence of the relative dispreference for that recognition resource, and the persistence of the effort to secure recognition from inspection. It shows a second way in which the pre-self-identification contributes to the potential avoidance of self-identification. Not only does it get a "safer" (i.e., from "who's this") position for possible recognition at T3, but if recognition does not occur there, the other less-than-self-identification turn-types may be tried at T4 and get recognition at T5. Furthermore, the persistence of the effort to get recognized without self-identification at T4 can inform answerer that the caller has reason to suppose such recognition is possible, even if not at T2. Indeed, in only two cases of the 25 in which T4 employs a non-self-identificatory turn-type, does the "who's this" (to which it is, of course vulnerable) occur. And in one of them, the "who's this" follows a switchboard request in T4, a turn-type regularly followed by "who's this."[44] In the other 23 cases, recognition is secured without self-identification. Sometimes, it is evidenced recognition in T5:

    B: Hello?
    J: H'llo, Barb?
    B: Mmhm?   (87)
    J: Is uh: Larry there?
——▶B: No he's not home yet Jim, . . .
            (JH, #81)

Sometimes the recognition is achieved and evidenced only late in T5:

    M: Hello,
    C: H'llo Marcia?
    M: Yea:h.   (88)
    C: Oh it's good to heah yur voice-
            sound like yur in a hurry though.
——▶M: 'hh <u>Yea</u>:h kind of- hi C- is- you're
            home! Carolyn.
            (MDE, #102)

Sometimes, the evidence of recognition does not come until a later time, but caller appears to "mark time" until it appears:

    J: Research Design,
    P: Jim?
    J: Yeah.
    P: Wha' d'ya say.   (89)
    J: Oh:: not much.
    P: What's doin.
——▶J: Not a damn thing Jeff.
            (JG, #66)

Sometimes, no evidence from address terms ever appears. It is completion of one sequence after another through which recognition is evidenced. The pre-self-identification thus has considerable success in allowing avoidance of self-identification.

Still, most openings in which a pre-self-identification is employed at T2 have a self-identification done at T4. And, in most cases, a display of recognition occurs in the next turn, and reciprocal recognition has been achieved (see #78–80). But it must be recalled that self-identification by name is only a resource, although the basic one. Recognition still must be achieved by its recipient, and this is not guaranteed. This is so especially since those doing a self-identification will include those who could not suppose they could be recognized by inspection at T2, and who could not suppose that they could be recognized by inspection at T4: in short, those whose supposition of recognizability by this recipient is tinged with doubt. And, we noted earlier, T4 self-identification by name could be try-marked.

Indeed, the same evidences of trouble in accomplishing the recognition after a non-self-identificatory turn-type at T2 can be found after self-identification at T4. Recognition may not come directly upon provision of the name, and the delay can reflect trouble in recognizing even from that resource.[45]

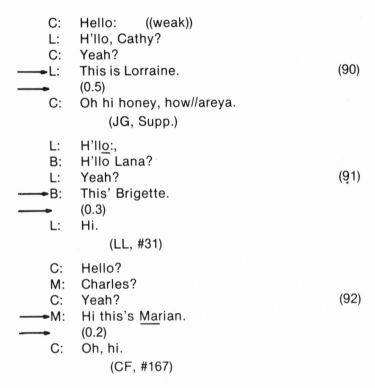

C:	Hello: ((weak))	
L:	H'llo, Cathy?	
C:	Yeah?	
→L:	This is Lorraine.	(90)
→	(0.5)	
C:	Oh hi honey, how//areya.	

                    (JG, Supp.)

L:	H'llo:,	
B:	H'llo Lana?	
L:	Yeah?	(91)
→B:	This' Brigette.	
→	(0.3)	
L:	Hi.	

                    (LL, #31)

C:	Hello?	
M:	Charles?	
C:	Yeah?	(92)
→M:	Hi this's Marian.	
→	(0.2)	
C:	Oh, hi.	

                    (CF, #167)

In these cases, a display of recognition eventually comes, after a gap. It is notable that the caller does not break into the gap to add further resources, as was the case with gaps after the not overtly identificatory T2 turn-types. Of course, it must be recalled that, here, callers have already supplied the basic resource for securing recognition. With what shall they upgrade the resources?

Still, there is a version of that phenomenon (in which the caller upgrades when trouble is exhibited) at T4 as well. It is, however, a bit subtler than at T2. Here, the self-identification offered is first name. It is delivered in turn-terminal intonation. If there is not an immediate start of a recognition display, even if no appreciable gap develops, the caller upgrades the resources—by the addition of last name.

L:	H'llo̲:,	
M:	Laura,	
L:	Ye̲:s, ((intonation echo))	(93)
➤M:	It's Peter. (0.7) Williams.	
L:	HI: just a minute, let me close the uh thing.	

(LL, #25)

B:	Hello,	
A:	Hi. Susan?	
B:	Ye:s,	(94)
➤A:	This's Judith. Rossman.	
B:	Judith!	

(TAC, #121)

We do not find the gap after self-identification broken by the caller at T4 as we did at T2 because the caller may not let it develop in the first place. In these cases, it appears that callers are hyperalert to the possible insufficiency of first names as self-identifications, and at the first evidence that recognition is not occurring—no immediate recognition at completion of their turn—they are ready to supplement. It is of interest then to note that in both cases, when recognition *does* occur, it is displayed with a much upgraded recognition display—the "big hello." It is the "big hello" that callers can look for at the very beginning of their self-identification, and, not finding its beginning there, know that they may need to supplement their self-identification. The basis for expecting a "big hello" and the need to supplement the basic "first name" to get recognition cannot be elaborated here.[46]

Finally, we find after the T4 self-identification the other development noted earlier in the T2 environment: a gap develops, the caller does not break it with supplementary resources, and the recipient initiates repair.

K:	Hello,
B:	Kim, // it's Bonnie.
K:	Yeah.

⟶   (0.4)
⟶K: Who?   (95)
  B: Bonnie. =
  K: = Hi, where we//re you.
  B: Remember ME:?
  K: Where were you. = I though you said
        Connie. (   )
                (ID, #223a)

  I: Hello:,
  K: Hello. (0.2) uh May I speak to Missiz
        Mallett uh Dallett.
  I: Yes. Speaking.   (96)
  K: uh This is uh Ken speaking.
⟶   (0.4)
⟶I: Who is speaking?
  K: Kay.
⟶I: Ken?
  K: uh: who attend uh last quarter English
        two C,
  I: Oh yes
                (ID, #232)

  M: (Hello.)
  L: Hi. Is Mrs. (Sturbridge) home?
        (0.5)
  M: What?
  L: Is Mrs.-Marcia?
  M: Yeah
  L: Oh HI. I didn't recognize your voice. =
⟶   This is Linda.
⟶   (1.0)
  M: Linda,
  L: Rubin.   (97)
        (2.0)
⟶M: I-uh can't place you.
        (1.0)
  L: Have I got the- is this three eight
        four five oh six five,
  M: No. = you really have the wrong number.
        //But-
  L: And is your name Marcia? =

M: = Yes! //heh
L: Isn't that swee:t
         (MDE, #88)

Although this last case is a "wrong number," that only turns out to be its outcome. From inside its developmental course, it is not a wrong number until L's fifth turn. Until then, she is first not recognized by voice inspection, then not recognized by her friend from first name self-identification, and after a 2.0 second gap, is not recognized even from a last name supplement. The possibility that she has reached a wrong number does not follow immediately after the last of these three failures; a gap of one second passes before she begins her inquiry. Those who prefer not to call and not to answer the telephone have, perhaps, such interactional perils in mind.

V

The preceding two sections have somewhat discursively depicted the main, structurally engendered, sequential developments through which recognitional identification is worked throughout, and they have offered interactional accounts of particular sequences representing some of these possibilities, tracing their workings on a turn by turn, moment by moment basis. Much of what has been discussed draws on other organizations much more general in their domains than the recognition problem. The import of the gap is provided for first by the turn-taking organization, which provides for its status as an event; and secondly by the organization of sequences, adjacency pairs, and agreement/disagreement which provides a sequential consequence, and an interactionally interpreted import, for the gap. But is there an independent structure which engenders these possibilities and underlies the particular sequences with their interactional drama?

One apparent finding that emerges from the preceding discussion is that much of what occurs by reference to the recognition issue happens in sequences of quite distinctly other types. It is tied not to a form of sequence, but is overlaid onto sequences of various types by virtue of the positioning of their first part, that positioning being first and, more particularly in our treatment, second turn of the conversation. These positions are defined by reference to the overall structural organization of the conversation. They are the first turns of its respective participants, and much of the material we have been exploring pertains to an organization built around first turns of participants. That organization appears to run parallel to whatever other organization operates there, e.g., the particular sequence type used there, running underground as long as they run compatibly; but if they don't, the one we have been examining takes priority.[47] It is a neat bit of architecture that has the initial turns regularly composed of greetings, one of the very few sequence types ("good-byes" is the other one I can think of) which do not have alternative second parts. Thereby, a gap after the first does not reflect on trouble in selecting which of the alternative seconds will be done, or temporarily delay a dispreferred second. Indeed, one would have thought that nothing could be more uncomplicated than finding the return to a greeting; the same item returned will do the trick. (And, indeed, that underlies the possibility of deception.) Nonetheless, as we have seen, first greetings are followed by delays, and recognition trouble turns out to be the issue. The underlying organization surfaces in the greeting sequence.

There does, therefore, appear to be an organization operating here, not identical with, nor merely a special instance of, the other organizations—of turn-taking, of sequences, etc.—always operating side by side in conversation. What happens in the first turn might be substantially accounted for by virtue of the fact that it is in second position in a sequence, and thus subject to the constraints of the sequence type in which it is placed. Even so, the turn components used there are not standard items for second parts of summons-uptake sequences. In any case, it will clearly not do to treat the second turn, which follows completion of a sequence, as free to be any of a range of next sequence starts. In fact, we find a concentration among a few types. More important, across even that variation one underlying theme predominates, and the sequence type initiated in second turn governs third turn only if that underlying theme has *its* requirements met. And third turn will be as much involved in showing that as in meeting the other sequence-type constraints (if any) set by second turn. Can anything systematic be said about the kind of organization operating here?

Several constraints preclude the systematic description of an organizational structure here. First, the appropriate organization almost certainly operates for the domain "openings" (if not for the yet larger domain, "overall structure of the conversation"), and not for its identification/recognition component alone. Second, as noted early in this paper, throughout conversation, but with special density in openings, a great many jobs and a great many organized resources are compacted into any turn. The considerations developed here about the turns that occupy the beginnings of these conversations need to be examined together with an analysis of the various other jobs these turns are occupied with; a systematic description that did not take such "interaction effects" into account would almost certainly pack into one organizational box the fruits of different trees. But it is possible to offer some systematically ordered features which seem to underlie many of the phenomena we have been examining, which seem to be candidates for inclusion in a description of an organization which engenders them.

1. Identification of other by each party is relevant.

2. Identification of other is relevant at first opportunity. (I.e., in co-presence, it is relevant pre- the beginning; on the telephone, not relevant until talk starts, but "I wonder who that is" can precede picking up the phone).

3. If recognitional identification of/by other—as one already known —is possible, it is preferred.[48]

4. Recognitional identification, if relevant and possible, is preferred where identification is relevant (and not, for example, as an additive form, subsequent to some other type of identification).[49]

5. Recognition as an interactional accomplishment has two components: a recognition source (composed of various of the resources from which recognition can be achieved), and a recognition solution (composed of the various resources by which the achievement of recognition by other can be claimed, displayed, evidenced, etc.).

6. Preferredly, recognition is "effortless," i.e., the recognition solution occurs next after the witnessing of the recognition source, or after the witnessed witnessing of the recognition source (i.e., when A has seen B seeing him see B).

7. If the recognition work is done wholly in turns to talk, it may occupy turns addressed to it, or it may inform turns occupied with some other sequential work (the "vehicle" or "host").

8. If the recognition work is done wholly in turns to talk, the recognition solution should occur in the turn after the recognition source, and should occur contiguously, with no gap.

9. Separation of source and solution exhibits trouble or failure to accomplish the recognition from the resources supplied in the source. Trouble or failure warrant repair.

10. A recognition solution terminates the sequence, unless trouble preceded the solution, in which case a turn component, turn, or sequence of turns diagnostic of the trouble may be added by the speaker of the recognition solution involved. (This theme has not been discussed in this paper, though the phenomenon has occurred in some of the segments cited.)

11. A recognition problem, once solved, is normatively solved for the duration of the conversation. What may be a recognition resource before

solution, loses that character after solution, and its recurrence (e.g., "voice") does not reoccasion recognition solution each time. But recog-nition/identification may be reopened when occasioned by evidence of misidentification.[50]

12. Two types of resources serve as recognition sources: "inspect-ables" and "self-references." Inspectables include appearance, voice sample, and behavior (e.g., talk) not directed to securing recognition which may include self-identificatory clues, as well as other possible resources. Self-references include most notably name (in the varieties in which name may be used: first name, title + last name, etc.) and self-description.

13. The recognition resources are graded. The basic recognitional resource is self-identification by name, the sort of name (first name, first name + last name, title + last name) being sensitive to recipient design for current recipient. Other resources are graded as "less than" or "more than" the basic resource. "Less than" resources may themselves be graded, from the minimal small voice sample devoid of other "clues," to more extended or multiple voice samples, to talk which adds to the voice sample self-identificatory clues (e.g., an address term, joke, first topic clues, distinctive recipient-designed intonation production, dis-played knowledge of other such as "you're home," etc.). "More than" resources may also be graded, from fuller forms of name than that which constitutes the recipient-designed basic resource, to recognitional de-scriptions (i.e., descriptions that allow recipient to find who it is that they already know, e.g., "what you know about me," "where you know me from," etc.). There is a "maximum recognitional resource" which is recipient-specific; it is that resource, or set of resources, beyond which speaker will not go. Should it not achieve recognition from other, identi-fication of other may be reviewed for possible misidentification (see #11 above). Frequently, the maximum is first name + last name when the basic resource is first name.[51] These grades are variable ethnographically and situationally, but "basic," "less than" and "more than" are more robust.

14. Recognition from least possible recognition resources sensitive to recipient design is preferred. Thus, recognizable should select lowest graded resource he can suppose can secure an "effortless" recognition solution.[52]

15. Should trouble or failure to recognize be displayed (see #9 above), recognizable may offer, or recipient request, supplementary resources. Regularly, supplementary resources are higher graded than previously offered resources, except when these have reached the "maximum" or when the provision of an additional voice sample is itself exploited as the

upgrading. The present provision may apply recurrently upon recurrent display of trouble, until the "maximum" is reached (see #13), until recognition is achieved, or until its irrelevance is warranted.

Several observations may be made from this list of probable elements of a systematic organization for the work of recognition:

a. Given that, on the whole, on the telephone, the answerer speaks first,[53] recognition of answerer by caller is the first recognition problem posed. It is posed at that point (unless the turn-type done there is such as displays recognition to be not oriented to) by virtue of the occurrence of a voice sample. A recognition solution is, therefore, relevant in next turn, T2. Since T2 is caller's first turn, it supplies a recognition resource, whose solution should be in next turn, T3. T1, T2, and T3 are, thus, the basic loci for the identification problem of the recognition type: T1 for the initial recognition source, T2 for the initial recognition solution and second recognition source, and T3 for the second recognition solution. "Hello" "Hi" "Hi" (see #42–45 above) realizes this sequence, and is very frequent. It, and much of what occurs in the other forms of sequence through which recognition is worked out, can be derived from the elements sketched above.

b. Aspects of the list of elements above are skewed in the direction of the caller-identification problem as central. Most notably, the selection of initial recognitional resource by recipient design is a tack callers can take, operating as they do after recognition of answerer.

It should be noted that the grading of recognition resources is a grading in information relevant to recognition; the higher graded resources are richer in clues that enable recognition. The lesser the resources provided, the greater the recognition claim. The recognition resources are thereby differentially discriminating; the import of recipient design is partially that an order of relationship can be defined by the resources needed, and supposed by other to be needed, for recognition. Those who can recognize from a "hi," or who would presume to be recognized from one, constitute a bounded population. And the preference for use of least possible resources tests the boundaries of that population, and any given person's membership in it for some interlocutor, on each occasion of such an interaction.

It must be recalled, however, that, whereas caller can select between the basic recognitional resource and a "less than" resource by reference to his suppositions about a particular, already identified recipient, in T1 answerer must select between the same classes of recognition resources—self-identification and what amounts to a voice sample, "hello"—but has that selection organized on other grounds. These grounds concern classes of putative callers, not particular, recognized ones. When recognizability is not expectable between answerer and caller, self-identification is regularly used in the first turn. But when it is, by reference to the setting, expectable, "hello"—a voice sample, a minimal resource—is employed.

Callers, therefore, routinely find themselves confronted with a discriminating recognition resource to work with. In T1, the discriminating recognition resource is used indiscriminately. It is not tailored to the supposed capacity of a particular caller to recognize from it, as it is tailored by callers for particular answerers. It should therefore come as no surprise that the incidence of uncertainty-marked recognition solutions is substantially greater among callers' recognitions of answerers than among answerers' recognitions of callers; that is, there are more interrogative names (leaving aside the clear pre-self-identification cases) in T2 after the T1 "Hello" than there are in T3 after a T2 "hello" or "hi." Nor should it be surprising that trouble and equivocation on the caller recognition problem is more volatile, sensitive, worthy of diagnosis, and implicative for the relationship.

c. Partially related to the preceding point: the voice is a variable instrument. Its use is at least partially socially organized, on the one hand for the organization of expression, and on the other because the impact of certain voice variations is treated as different in part by reference to sequential locus. Consider the following segment:

M:	Hullo?	
→ R:	(Hi.) Did I wake you up?	
M:	No̱:	
	(0.8)	
R:	Are you sure,	
	(1.5)	
M:	(Well,) hhhuh huh huh ˙hh	
	(0.5)	
→ R:	's this Marcia?	
M:	Yeah.	(98)
R:	(Howayou,)	
M:	Yeah. You did not wake me up	
	Reah.	
R:	Oh your voice sounds different.	
	(0.8)	

```
R:      (    )
M:      Gee everybody's been saying that
        lately.
R:      It's lower.
        (1.0)
M:      Huhh
R:      Sounds   better. = Sounds. .like
        you're happier.
M:      I  am.  I'm  taking  a  leave  of
        absence. . .
                            (MDE, Supp.)
```

Here, the voice of the answerer is heard first for "just current state" ("Did I wake you up?"), then for its recognition relevance ("'s this Marcia?"), and then for "general mood" ("Sounds like you're happier"). Voice can be inspected for any of these types of categories; of course, elsewhere in the conversation, quite other ones might be involved; these are regular to the opening. Voice quality can vary through a considerable range later in the conversation, and be subject to varying interpretations—emphasis, anger, attitude, mood, interest, excitement, etc.—relating the variation to some sequentially local event(s) in the conversation. It is very rare, if it happens at all, for voice quality, once "into" the conversation, to occasion a review of who is talking. But the same variation in the first turns can make trouble for caller's recognition of answerer. Added to the indiscriminate use of the discriminating recognition resource—voice sample—in T1, the problem is potentially formidable.

It is therefore worth noting the substantial standardization of first turn production by individuals.[54] That is, persons regularly do a standard-for-them "Hello" in first turn, which serves as a signature of sorts. This standardization seems at least partially to contribute to the usability of voice as a recognition resource for the range of callers for whom recognition is relevant by narrowing the range of voice type and quality employed in that sequential position, however much voice variation is used in immediately following turn. Correlatively, in view of the restriction on voice variation in first turn by reference to its use as a recognition resource, the importance of the solution of the recognition problem in the first turns may be appreciated to include that the resources of voice variation are thereupon freed for other uses (see point 11 above), uses especially and subtly exploited in the opening. Consider as well the achievement of getting first turn to display excitement, depression, sleepiness, etc., while nonetheless allowing recognition; a tightrope is walked between restriction of the voice for recognition purposes, and expressive variations in its use.

d. Finally, it should be noted that the list of elements omits mention of the recognition solution resources. As was noted in the previous two sections, these also are differentiated, partially fitted to the recognition resources they follow, partially recipient-designed. But they are especially sensitive to the articulation of the turns which address the recognition problem with the rest of the opening, and therefore especially require treatment within the context of a systematic account of the organization of the opening section as a whole.

VI

When examining a large number of openings, it is striking that some run off quite straightforwardly, in a very nearly, if not totally, standardized way, while others look and sound idiosyncratic—almost virtuoso performances. But it is worthwhile keeping in mind that the "special" cases are variants engendered by a systematic sequential organization adapted and fitted by the parties to some particular circumstances; the outlines of the organization's "standard product" are discernible through the variations of the particular case. At the same time, the standard-looking cases may be nonetheless special to the parties for their local circumstances. I shall close by examining these two themes in turn.

Consider the following segment:

```
M:     Hello::,
A:     Hello Margie?
M:     Ye::://s,
A:     ˙hhh We do pai:nting, a:ntiquing,
M:     I(hh) is that ri:ght.
(A):      eh!hh//hhh: : : : :
M:     hnh hnh hnh
A:     nhh hnh hnh! ˙hh                                    (99)
M:     ˙hh
A:     -keep people's pa'r too:ls,
M:     Y(hhh)! hnh//hnh
A:     I'm  sorry  about  that//that//I  din'
       see that-
              (NB, #119)
```

A is calling to apologize for keeping overlong some power tools borrowed from M.[55] It is an interactionally delicate task, which she brings off with considerable skill by building it into a joke, constructed in the form of a list, the fact that the joke list is a vehicle for an apology not becoming evident until the end, when laughter is already in progress. It is a virtuoso performance in a potentially embarrassing situation. Among the many interests this segment has, its bearing on openings, and on identification/ recognition is not prominent. Yet what is being brought off interactionally in the segment depends deeply on the organization of identification/recognition in telephone openings, and the outlines of one of that organization's standard sequences is apparent in it.

The segment is based on the sequence type described in section IV above. In T2 the caller uses a pre-self-identification, though M and A stand in a relationship which could well have a T2 greeting sufficient to secure recognition. The T2 pre-self-identification projects a self-identification in T4, and, indeed, T4 is built in the form of a self-identification. But the turn, and the form, are used to package a mock self-identification (like "This is your friendly goddess"). The mock self-identification is a joke, but its appreciation as a joke turns on M having already recognized who the caller is, and what is involved in that caller describing herself in this way, a recognition allowed to be in hand from the beginning of T4 by the voice sample in T2; it might well not have worked to begin "We do painting. . ." in T2; besides which, the mock self-identification takes a "business" form, and would be (were it real) placed in a fourth turn, preceded by an interrogative address term. With all the special circumstances involved here, the shape of a standard sequence is visible, and depended on for the special interactional job being done.

On the other hand, what appear to be standard identification/recognition sequences can have quite idiosyncratic and special status. Since for the most part those for whom recognition is relevant have talked before, any next opening—and recognition sequence—can have a prior history of such sequences informing it. By reference to such a history, a standard-appearing opening can be for the parties quite special. Thus,

A:	Hello,
B:	Mr. Lodge,
A:	Yes,
B:	Mr. Ford.
A:	Yes. (100)
B:	Y'know where Mr. Williams is?
A:	What?

B: hhhahhah
A: Do I know where who?
B: Leo is.
A: No.
B: Oh. Okay.
                (HS, #207)

Here, the standard appearing sequence is a joke; the parties are "on a first name basis"; the joke, indeed, interferes with A's recognition of the friend being referred to.

For parties to be "on a first name basis" can take doing. There is likely to be an historical development, in which the parties may first use T2 interrogative names with first name + last name self-identifications, then drop the last name, then perhaps one starts displaying evidenced recognition after the T2 interrogative name. Finally a greeting alone, perhaps in a distinctive intonation, would be sufficient. The first occurence of any of these will look like a standard sequence; to its parties it may be a minor event of sorts, a small *rite de passage* between phases of a relationship. In any case, the development is one through a series of standard, organizationally produced sequence types, as is the reverse direction, when, as noted earlier, a caller may supply more recognition sources after a long hiatus between conversations than had otherwise been the practice with some particular recipient.

The "practice" between a pair of persons can come to be a signature. A special form can come to be used by a caller for a particular recipient. Above, we noted a case in which a "joke" interfered with recognition. In other cases, the absence of a joke in favor of a standard "serious" procedure may be special, and may interfere with recognition. The segment, earlier treated in some detail, between the "friendly goddess" and her sometime boyfriend is a case in point. A number of conversations between these two are included in the corpus, and in nearly all of them in which she is the caller, she employs a "joke" of some form as her T2 turn-type; a number of the illustrations of joke T2s in section II above are hers. Whatever was involved in her not using that form in the second turn of the call which was examined in section III, the fact that she did not appears connected to C's failure to recognize her from the T2 she used. That she herself might have supposed that this was so may be reflected in her use, in T4 after the "who's this," of a joke form. And when she uses the joke form, she is recognized.

Recipient design can work over time to set a form "for us," and this standardized "for us" form will be incorporated into the grading scale that is otherwise operative for recognition resources. For C and his friendly goddess, the special recipient-designed form is "joke"; in other cases, other forms can be given the same status, most notably, special inflections given to otherwise standard items, such as greetings.

In any particular case, such idiosyncratic particulars may be operative, but they are made operative as local adaptations of an independent organizational format, and work the way they do by virtue of it. Particular cases can, therefore, be examined for their local, interactional, biographical, ethnographic, or other idiosyncratic interest. The same materials can be inspected so as to extract from their local particularities the formal organization into which their particularities are infused. For students of interaction, the organizations through which the work of social life gets accomplished occupy the center of attention, and whatever of their materials can be extracted and related to such organizations should be. For those whose lives are being led in interaction, those organizations are always filled out by the locally relevant details, the organizations by reference to which that detail is relevant receding into an unnoticed background.

Whatever a telephone conversation is going to be occupied with, however bureaucratic or intimate, routine or unusual, earthshaking or trivial, it and its parties will have to pass through the identification/recognition sieve as the first thing they do. The contingencies of its organization thus have a pervasive relevance, a relevance inherited from less specialized settings of interaction and adapted to a technological innovation, by which it is made more prominent. As a result, what was associated in the mythic past of the West with heroes and elders—recognition when identity is partially masked—has become democratized. Writ incomparably smaller, it has become anyone's everyday test.

NOTES

1. See Sacks, Schlegloff, and Jefferson (1974).
2. See Schegloff, Jefferson and Sacks (1977)
3. Schegloff and Sacks (1973); Sacks, Schegloff and Jefferson (1974)
4. Schegloff (1968); Sacks, Schegloff, and Jefferson (forthcoming), chapters 2 and 3; Sacks (1974); Schegloff and Sacks (1973); and Jefferson (1973).
5. See Sacks, Schegloff and Jefferson (forthcoming) chapter 3.
6. For a review of some of the relevant studies, see Wilson (1975), pp. 203-206, *passim*; and Wilson (1971), chapter 14.
7. Sacks and Schegloff, This Volume.
8. Goffman (1963), chapter 7.
9. For example, Goffman (1963) and Kendon (1973).

10. See Goffman (1963), pp. 112-113.
11. *The Odyssey,* Book 19; see also Auerbach, (1953), chapter 1.
12. Genesis 27.
13. Wilson, (1971)p. 272.
14. Openings are organizationally and interactionally very "dense." In them, and in the very short turns of which they are generally composed, are compacted the treatment of many issues central to the organization of interaction, and to the shape of any particular interaction getting underway. Accordingly, each turn is partially implicated in a number of different organizational issues, and the treatment accorded some turn or sequence of turns when addressing a particular organizational issue will almost necessarily be only a partial treatment of those turns. Further, since the various organizational issues and their solution in particular openings are concomitant and interact, even our understanding of a single issue being addressed will likely be partial until the full range of issues is at least somewhat surveyed, and the way particular sequences integrate and reconcile the requirements of different organizational structures is appreciated. (See note 7 for a discussion of a reconciliation of competing organizational preferences.) For example, in the data to which this paper is addressed, running parallel to the issues of identification on which I focus is the issue of the length and shape of the opening as it bears on the allocation of first topic and the displayed priority it should have. In sum, the paper is preliminary not only for a larger study of openings, but for its own narrower topic.
15. Title + Last Name can be distinct type, as will be seen below.
16. This telephone call, from a radio station to a bank where a robbery was in progress, with the robber answering the phone, was kindly made available to me by Mr. Sam Surrat, archivist of CBS News.
17. Self-identification occurs overwhelmingly in combination with other components.
18. In Sacks, Schegloff and Jefferson, (forthcoming) chapter 3.
19. A cause for considerable resentment on the part of those who frequently find themselves in this position; for example, wives answering the phone when husbands' colleagues, often met at social occasions, are calling.
20. There *are* sequentially relevant differences between the forms in each group, but they do not bear on the present discussion.
21. The best description based on recorded (in this case, filmed) data I know of is Kendon's (1973) account of greetings in the setting of a party.
22. An outcome which Goffman, in his discussion of greetings as access rituals, treats as marginal. See Goffman (1971), chapter 3, and p. 79 in particular.
23. Goffman (1971), notes urban/rural differences in this regard, rural folk offering greetings to strangers as well. It seems likely, however, that some aspect(s) of the first turn(s) will display some discrimination between recognizables and others (e,g., in the form of greeting used, the adding of an address term to it,or some less familiar variation).
24. I have argued elsewhere (Sacks, Schegloff and Jefferson, forthcoming), chapter 3, that first turn "Hello" is, sequentially, not fundamentally a greeting.
25. See Schegloff and Sacks (1973) pp. 295-298; Sacks, Schegloff, Jefferson (1974) pp. 716-718. Question-answer, request-grant/rejection, and the like are instances of types.
26. This paragraph sketches in a nontechnical way our current understanding of some aspects of this area based on the work of several investigators, but not yet published. Much of this work was reported by Sacks (1973). See A. Pomerantz (1974), which provides an illuminating discussion of these matters and more for "assessment sequences.
27. See Schegloff, Jefferson, Sacks, (1977).
28. See Sacks, Schegloff, Jefferson (1974), p. 715.
29. See Schegloff, Jefferson, Sacks (1977). The most familiar NTRIs are the various one-

word questions ("Huh?", "What?", "Who?"), whole or partial repeats of the trouble source in prior turn, and others. "Who's this" does not otherwise appear as an NTRI (except as an expanded variant of "who?"); it is, then, an NTRI specialized for use in openings for the identification/recognition issue, and is rarely found outside the first several turns.

30. Her "conversion" of C into source of the trouble is marked, as well, by her repeat of his question at the beginning of her turn. As stated in note 29 and in the paper cited there, repeats of all or part of the prior turn are one form of NTRI, the repeat marking the trouble source. Here it is not fully exploited as an NTRI, no room being left after it for its recipient to do a repair.

31. Schegloff and Sacks (1973) pp. 313-317.

32. This refers to the type of call under consideration here, in which the first turn is "Hello." In calls whose first turn is a self-identification, self-identification in the second turn is much more frequent. It is because of the different sequential consequences of "Hello" and self-identification in the first turn, directly reflected in the second turn, that these constitute different types.

33. Gail Jefferson (personal communication) has proposed that an address term without greeting in the second turn may operate similarly to foreshorten the opening. Initial examination of my materials lends some support, but to my mind leaves the issue open.

34. The sequences develop in this manner:

```
        C:    Hello:.
        M:    Miz Parsons?
        C:    Ye:s,                                        (a)
        M:    Fay Martin, Arthritis Foundation, the
              volunteer service,
        C:    Um hm.
                    (JG,#73a)
        I:    Hello,
        C:    Uh H'llo Mrs. Davis?
        I:    Yes.                                         (b)
        C:    Yeah = Hi, this is Diane from Mr. Eds.
        I:    Oh: great. . . .
                    (ID,#262)
        I:    Hello:,
        T:    H'llo Missiz Thomas?
              (0.4)                                        (c)
        I:    uh no. Who is speaking please,
        T:    uh This is Tasha Mann, from Southern
              Nevada Music Company . . .


        IL:   Hello:,
        T:    Hello, Is this Missiz Thomas,
        IL:   Ye:s.                                        (d)
        T:    Hello this is Tasha Mann. = I'm calling for:
              Southern Nevada Music // Company.
        I L :                              Y e a h .
                    (ID, #295-295a)
```

Note that the self-identification is regularly more than first name: First Name + Last Name, or supplemented by descriptions and/or affiliations. When no recognition occurs or is relevant, the self-identification may be followed not with a greeting, but with an "uh huh"—as in segments (a) and (d) cited above.

Title + Last Name does not always project the nonrelevance of recognition. It can be the recipient-designed appropriate address term, by virtue of relative age, status, degree of acquaintanceship, etc. For example:

```
F:    ((Hell))o,
B:    Hello Missiz Fineman,                           (e)
F:    Hi Bonnie.
              (ID, #237)
S:    Hello,
I:    uh Dr. Santos?
S:    Yes.                                             (f)
I:    Inge. Hi. =
S:    = Hi Inge.
              ID, #273)
M:    ((Hello))
P:    Mr. McDougal?
M:    Yeh sir                                          (g)
P:    This ih Mr. Perkins.
M:    Hi::ya Mr. Perkins. How ya doing.
              (JG, #50)
```

Still, for convenience, I will exclude the Title + Last Name cases from the data considered in the main text.

35. Another possibility should be mentioned here for the turn after a T2 greeting, intermediate between reciprocal recognition and "who's this," and that is an "uncertainty marked" reciprocal recognition, a guess. For example:

```
        M:    Hello.
        P:    Hehlo.
              (1.2)
———▶ M:    Pe:t?
              (JG, #43)

        M1:   Hello.
        M2:   Hello.    ((intonation echo))
              (1.0)
———▶ M1:   This Sid?
              (LL, #32)
```

36. Terasaki, (1976)

37. Schegloff (1968), and Sacks, Schegloff, Jefferson (forthcoming) chapter 2.

38. Sacks and Schegloff, this volume.

39. Ibid.

40. This counterpreference is evidenced in those seqments, cited later, in which caller self-identifies even though recipient has responded to the pre-self-identification with a recognition token.

41. The try-marker can also be applied to self-identification by name in the caller's second

turn when the speaker's supposition that the recipient can recognize from name is uncertain. As will be seen below, other of the procedures used in T2 are used in T4 as well.

42. Indeed, deception may be clear to the caller, if the answerer has not used the correct, recipient-designed greeting—i.e., the greeting in characteristic intonation which "that one" always uses "to me." The issue of recipient-designed opening components, although important, cannot be entered into here.

43. This segment is striking on a number of counts. L's interrogative "yeah" seems clearly nonrecognitional, following as it does a gap of 0.5 sec. Still, E does not self-identify after it. Nor does she supplement the greeting with self-identification when a gap develops after it. Finally, we find in L's third turn another evidence of deceptive recognition display, in a different locus from that discussed before, but similarly placed sequentially—after an invitation to recognize from les than self-identification. Her guess—"Erin?"—after the greeting shows the latter to have claimed a recognition that had not been fully achieved.

44. It may appear contradictory to say that the switchboard request defers or eliminates the relevance of recognition, when it is noted at various points that "who's this" is not uncommon in next turn. But it should be noted that the "who's this" that follows other T2 turn types and displays recognition-trouble is regularly preceded by a gap, whereas the "who's this" that occurs in the turn following a switchboard request hardly ever does. It is less a reflection of failure of recognition than a self-arming by first answerer for the potential question from the one who will be called to the phone, "who is it?" It is not the first answerer's recognition interest that is being served, in that case, but the intended answerer's. In those cases in which the first answerer "guesses" the callers identity, it may be treated as an "extra."

> M: Hello?
> K: Hello. Uh: is Tina there?
> M: Yes she is. I'll call her.
> K: ₍Thanks*
> M: ˡIs it-* 's this Karen?
> K: Yeah. Hi:.
> M: Hi Karen, I recognized your voice. This time.
>   Here's Tina.
>   (MDE, Supp.)

45. Note that in all three cases, T2 uses the try-marker, reflecting a doubt about voice recognition, and that in all three cases, the next turn is an interrogative "yeah?", indicating possible trouble.

46. The crux of the matter is this: Callers seek recognition because they suppose themselves to be, for the current recipient, "recognizables." However, answerers do not treat the recognition-of-caller problem as one involving a search of all those they know, or all recognizables, to find which one this is. Rather, it appears, answerers are oriented to a set of "potential callers." It happens that the two sets—"recognizables" and "potential callers"—are not identical for answerers. One familiar class of persons who are members of the former set but not of the latter is that of friends and nonimmediate kin who live "far away," and are not often "heard from." When they offer a voice sample, even with clues, from which to be recognized, they seek recognition as "recognizables," and often fail to get it because the answerer does not search that set to "find" them, but rather searches the set "potential callers," of which they are not members. "First name" may fail on these grounds as well. It is members of this class of persons who sometimes offer the challenge, "You'll never guess who this is," for that is one way of displaying that, while

recognizables, they are not potential callers. When recognized, however, they get the "big hello," and the talk is briefly occupied with the specialness of hearing from them, as happens in both calls here, as well as in #48 (the "Yolk" call) earlier cited. "Non-potential-caller" callers are another major source of self-identifications in T2, when they decline to initiate a recognition test from lesser resources.

47. This result is familiar from the study of third-person reference, where we found that when the preferences for recognitional reference and sequential minimization could not be satisfied simultaneously, the former took precedence (See Sacks and Schegloff, this volume). Several themes of that investigation recur here, with the same results. Indeed, the identification/recognition issue, and sequences examined here, are central to the domain of person reference, being the site at which the "I" and "you," which are used for "speaker" and "recipient" throughout the conversation, are grounded. I have preferred not to develop that theme here, but to reserve it for a paper on the organization of reference to persons in conversation, in preparation.

48. Two sorts of evidence on this point not previously adduced may be mentioned here. One is the occurrence of mid-turn repair, from a nonrecognitional identification in the process of being produced to a recognition try, if possible. See #97, and the switch from "Is Mrs.-" to "Marcia?". A second is the persistence of the attempt to secure recognitional identification even when it is prohibited by formal rule, and embarrassment when apparently recognized, though one had obeyed the rule. The materials are drawn from a radio call-in show, one of whose official rules was "no self-identification by name." The program had several "regular callers," who apparently felt themselves to be "recognizables" to the "host." A number of these calls have at T4 or T6 a turn beginning "I called you X amount of time ago about. . . .'", many of which seem to be self-identifications by recognitional description in lieu of the forbidden name, but could as well be treated as prefaces to the reason for the call, which is, in many cases, a continuation of an earlier conversation. Some, however, are unequivocally recognitional self-identification. For example:

> A: Good evening, W.N.B.C.
> B: Alrighty Brad.
> A: How uh you sir.
> B: Ah fine. How's yerself.
> A: Mhhm?
> B: Listen I uh call' you a couple a' weeks ago
>   an' yuh hadda cut me short because a' the
>   Pueblo uhhh:
> A: Yah.
>   (BC, Red, 159)

B goes on to talk about Mayor Lindsay and taxes. His T6 seems designed to replace a nonrecognitional identification as "call-in participant" by a recognitional identification, so as to be recognized. In another call, the caller does no such self-identification, but describes his problem, a six-month suspension of his driving license. Then:

> A: . . .wha'diyuh do, fer a living.
> B: Eh : m I woik inna driving school.
> A: Inna dri:ving school,
> B: Yeah. I spoke t'you menny ti:mes.
>   (BC, Beige, 20)

What B hears is a dawning recognition of him by A, not a noticing of the special comedy and tragedy of a driving instructor having his license suspended. (It turned out that B was not a driving instructor.)

49. The import of this point: organizational self-identification (e.g., "American Airlines") or nonrecognitional self-identification by name (e.g., "Ms. Jones speaking") can show that recognition is not expectably relevant by occupying, with a nonrecognitional component, the position at which a recognition-relevant turn would be done, and done preferredly, if relevant. If recognition were not relevant where identification is relevant, the nonrecognitional component could be a routine first phase, a preliminary, leaving the relevance of recognition still an open question. To be sure, caller can override this display of irrelevance for recognition in next turn, and show that, although not organizationally expectable, in *this* call recognition *is* relevant. But in doing this, he is transforming the incipient type of the call, and the resources for doing it are shaped accordingly. For example, a T2 "Hi" is rarely found in this sequential environment. Such "transformations" are discussed in a chapter with that name in Schegloff (1967).

50. Consider, for example, #58 above. M1 (the answerer) has apparently achieved and displayed recognition of M2 (the caller) at T3, from the voice sample at T2. At T9, he reidentifies him as someone else, occasioned by some trouble engendered by a recipient-designed inquiry. But two turns by M2 have intervened which might have allowed reidentification if the issue was still open, and the voice, for example, treated as a voice sample for recognition purposes on a continuing basis. The same is true in #97, where there is initial difficulty in "recognizing Marcia" from voice. Once done (incorrectly, as it turns out), further voice uses by "Marcia" do not occasion review of the recognition; that occurs only when "Marcia" fails to recognize caller.

"Voice" is initially treated as "voice sample," while recognition is a relevant issue; once solved, it is no longer attended to in that way.

51. For example, in #97, caller first uses the "basic"—first name ("This is Linda"); when it does not secure recognition, she adds a "more than"—last name ("Rubin"). When recognition is still not achieved, it turns out that she has reached her maximum for the recipient she means to be talking to. She does not upgrade further, e.g., to a recognitional description, but initiates a review of her identification/recognition of recipient.

52. But recall, other sequential organizational interests are concurrently relevant here, and may modify the selection. Thus, a move to shorten the opening section may lead to selecting the basic form even when "less"might be supposed to be adequate, as in #65 above.

53. Schegloff (1968); Sacks, Schegloff, Jefferson (forthcoming)

54. Independently noted by Gail Jefferson (personal communication).

55. I merely allude here to a rich and elaborate analysis of this segment by my late colleague, Harvey Sacks, included in various sets of lectures of his, hopefully to be published at some time in the future.

REFERENCES

Auerbach, Erich. (1953). *Mimesis.* Garden City, New York: Doubleday Anchor.

Blount, Ben, and Sanchez, Mary (eds.) (1974) *Ritual, Reality, and Innovation in Lanuage Use.* New York: Seminar Press.

Goffman, Erving (1963). *Behavior in Public Places.* Glencoe: Free Press Macmillan.

———— (1971). *Relations in Public.* New York: Basic Books.

Jefferson, Gail (1973). A case of precision timing in ordinary conversation: over-
lapped tag-positioned address terms in closing sequences. *Semiotica.* 9, 1.
Kendon, Adam, and Ferber, Andrew (1973). A description of some human greet-
ings. in Michael and Crook (1973).
Michael, R.P., and Crook, J.H. (eds.) (1973). *Comparative Ecology and the Behavior of Primates.* London: Academic Press.
Pomerantz, Anita (1974). Second Assessments. Ph.D. dissertation, School of
Social Sciences, University of California, Irvine.
Sacks, Harvey (1973). On the preference for agreement in conversation. Unpublished lecture, Linguistic Institute, University of Michigan.
_____ (1974). Everyone has to lie. In Blount and Sanchez (1974).
Sacks, Harvey and Schegloff, Emanuel A. Two preferences in the organization of
references to persons in conversation and their interaction, this volume.
Sacks, Harvey, Schegloff, Emanuel A. and Jefferson, Gail (1974). A simplest systematics for the organization of turn-taking for conversation. *Language* 50,
4.
_____ (forthcoming). *Studies in the Sequential Organization of Conversation.*
New York: Academic Press.
Schegloff, Emanuel A. (1967). The First Five Seconds: The Order of Conversational Openings. Ph.D. Dissertation, Department of Sociology, University
of California, Berkeley.
_____ (1968). Sequencing in conversational openings. *American Anthropologist*
70, 6.
Schegloff, Emanuel A. and Sacks, Harvey (1973). Opening up closings. *Semiotica* 8, 4.
Schegloff, Emanuel A., Jefferson, Gail and Sacks, Harvey (1977). The preference for self-correction in the organization of repair in conversation. *Language* 53, 2.
Terasaki, Alene (1976). Pre-announcement sequences in conversation. Social Science Working Paper #99, School of Social Science, University of California,
Irvine.
Wilson, Edward O. (1971). *The Insect Societies.* Cambridge: Harvard University
Press.
_____ (1975). *Sociobiology.* Cambridge: Harvard University Press.

A Technique for Inviting Laughter and its Subsequent Acceptance Declination

Gail Jefferson

Jefferson has extended the study of conversational interaction to laughter. She has worked out transcription procedures and notational symbols which have enabled those working with tape recorded materials to advance their analyses based on high quality transcriptions. Examination of her essay on laughter will show that basic to the study of laughter is such a well-developed and precise transcription and notational system. Prior to Jefferson, no studies of the organization of laughter in interaction can be found in the literature. It is clear that the close attention to and hearing of tape recorded interaction gives the analyst access to previously unnoticed regularities.

The paper focuses on one of several ways in which a participant may invite laughter, the placement, by the speaker, of a laugh upon completion of an utterance. Subsequent activities are examined to discover how the recipient may accept or decline the invitation to laugh.

In looking at laughter in conversation, I have used a collection of transcripts which capture some of laughter's details. In this paper laughter is considered as an activity to which one participant may invite another or others—an invitation which may be accepted or declined. I shall focus on one of several techniques by which laughter is invited—*a post-utterance completion laugh particle* by that utterance's speaker—and recipient activity subsequent to that particle will be examined for its acceptance/declination import.

Initially we can suppose that an utterance can have a range of possible responses, and for some utterances laughter may be among them. We can observe that some utterances which we might intuitively understand to be candidates for subsequent laughter get laughter, and get it in a particular way: *speaker himself indicates that laughter is appropriate, by himself laughing, and recipient thereupon laughs.* It is this sort of sequence of events which I'm pointing to with the formulation "invitation to laugh and acceptance."

The following two fragments are dramatic instances of such a sequence of events, since in each an utterance reaches completion, there is a pause, at some point in the pause prior speaker offers laughter and recipient thereupon laughs.

(1)
Dan: I thought that wz pretty outta sight didju
          hear me say'r you a junkie:
          (0.5)
Dan: hheh heh
Dolly: ⌐hhheh-heh-heh

(2)
Joyce: Cuz she wz off in the bushes with some
          buddy, tch!
          (0.7)
Joyce: ehh⌐hhhhhhh!
Sidney: ⌐Oh(hh)h hah huh!

In the following fragment a similar invitation/acceptance sequence is produced without a pause. Speaker starts to laugh just after utterance completion, and recipient thereupon laughs.

(3)

Ellen: He s'd <u>well</u> he said <u>I am</u> <u>cheap</u> he said,
           'hh about the <u>big</u> things. he says but not
           the <u>liddle</u> things, hhhHA HA⌐HA HA HA
Bill: ⌐heh heh heh

To get a sense of the interaction which can be involved in laughter's occurrence we can contrast these fragments to one in which laughter is produced on a *volunteer basis* by recipients. And we can observe in that fragment a source and warrant for the volunteer laughter's occurring just where it does—a source which is also present in fragment (3). In fragment (3) there is a straightforward contrast pair available: "the big things"/"the liddle things." In this next fragment there is also a contrast pair available: "git outta dih mood"/"git outta dih cah." In this next fragment that contrast pair is used as a locus for recipient laughter; i.e., given the unit that has gone before ("git outta dih cah"), the occurence of the subsequent unit ("git outta dih cah") is recognized and responded to as it is being announced—the point of the joke is clear at that moment and laughter is volunteered then and there.

Preceding the utterance we'll focus on there is a story being told. The transcript is simplified here, displaying only the story components:

Mike: There's Rastus settin'the ca:r . jis fro:ze.
           yihknow? ... She sz. <u>Ra::z</u>'s whutsa
           <u>mattuh</u> witchoo. ... She sid- you better
           hurry on up. Fore I git outta de <u>mood</u>.
           She says.

Then:

(4)

Mike: He says. I gotta git outta dih <u>mood</u> befo'
           I c'n git outta d⌐i⌐h ca:::h
Gary: ⌐A⌐h ha ha
Curt: ⌐U-huh-huh

The point at which these recipients have placed their response is not random; it has elsewhere been described as a *recognition point* (see Jefferson 1974), and is a legitimate and expectable place for recipient to respond in the course of an ongoing utterance.

Given the possibility of systematic recognition-point response, a place for such an activity can be located in fragment (3), roughly somewhere in the vicinity of ". . . but not the liddle. . . ." This can then be treated as a locus for recipient response and recipient can be observed as maintaining silence through that space, specifically in contrast to responding then and there.

Furthermore, we can look at fragment (3) in comparison to fragments (1) and (2) and see that, similar to those cases, recipient does not start up upon utterance completion but upon prior speaker's laughter. And if it is noted that prior speaker's laughter starts as a breath which is equivocal as to its character—i.e., may be a laugh onset or may be simply a postutterance exhalation ("[hhh]HA")—fragment (3) begins to approach fragments (1) and (2) in terms of the presence of a postutterance pause. A display which does not treat the breath as an interactional event looks very much like cases (1) and (2).

> Ellen: . . . but not the liddle things.
>
>   (•)
>
> Ellen: HA HA‚HA HA HA
> Bill: └heh heh heh

Clearly, then, a recipient laugh which follows utterance completion and a pause and laughter by the prior speaker is quite a different matter than a volunteer, recognition-placed laugh. While the latter has no explicit interaction between speaker and recipient, the former has a little sequence in which the speaker invites laughter and the recipient accepts the invitation; i.e., the laughter is generated at some distance from and independent of the utterance itself.

Another technique for inviting laughter can be briefly examined. Speaker constructs a laugh-specific recognition point by inserting particles of *within-speech laughter* into his utterance. And the recipient can treat such a particle as providing a recognition point, a locus for recipient laughter, and can accept the invitation to laugh then and there. Three fragments will be shown, each of which has an additional feature: the party who will be recipient of the within-speech laughter is, until that point, observably in serious pursuit of topical matters, and that pursuit is abandoned at the moment within-speech laughter occurs and recipient produces laughter. (Utterance parts subsequent to laughter are deleted.)

(5)

K: But going <u>sou</u>::th.
F: Et the end of Harbor
          Bouleva(HH)rd⌜
K: ⌐⌐⌐⌐⌐⌐[ahh ha::ha::ha::

(6)

M: I, Edna you know I didn't—
M: ⌐You know—
E: [[Hell <u>you</u> know I'm on
          ret(H)i⌜
M: ⌐⌐⌐⌐[ehh ye(h)hhmh˙hmh˙hmh

(7)

B: Dju watch by any chance Miss International
          Showcase las'night?
E: N:no I didn'⌐I wz reading my-
B: [You missed a really great
          pro(H)⌜
E: ⌐⌐⌐⌐[O(hh)h i(h)t wa(hh)s? =
E: =ehh heh heh heh!

Now recipients of a candidate laughable utterance do not always laugh.
A question is, how do they *not* laugh, since, for one, silence at a recognition point, at completion, post completion, or in some pause after completion, does not foreclose the possibility of laughter, but instead may
systematically generate a pursuit of laughter by speaker, a pursuit that
may eventuate in recipient laughter. One intuitive warrant for such a pursuit by speaker is that recipient may specifically be *awaiting* an invitation
to laugh, may find that the utterance itself is equivocal as to its
laughability and may require a warrant by the speaker, an assurance that
laughter is appropriate here, so that recipient may indeed go ahead and
laugh.

It appears, then, that the order of alternative responses to a candidate
laughable is not organized as freely as one might suppose; i.e., the issue
is not that *something* should occur, laughter *or* whatever else, but that
laughter should occur, on a volunteer basis *or* by invitation. In order to
achieve a no-laugh response to a prior utterance, the recipient must do
more than refrain from laughing at any "now," but must act, at some
"now" to terminate the relevance of laughter.

An obvious solution is for recipient to start talking at a "now" in which he might otherwise be laughing or awaiting an invitation to laugh. Talk will observably *replace* both laughter and the silence which may be awaiting an invitation. Crucially, talk can revise the order of alternatives present so far. It is not that, having so far not laughed voluntarily, recipient may now be brought to laugh; other matters altogether are relevant and operative. And, routinely, the "other matters" are pursuit of topical issues present in the candidate laughable utterance.

That is, recipient does not simply refuse to laugh, but, while declining to take up one aspect of the utterance (its status as a candidate laughable), he does take up another aspect (its topical import). Roughly, the utterance is not killed off, it is served as a *sequentially implicative* object and turns out to have generated subsequent activity, although perhaps not the activity intended by its speaker. The order of relevant alternatives, then, is revised from [Volunteer Laughter. . .or. . .Invited Laughter] to [Laughter. . .or. . .Topical Pursuit].

At this point I'll focus on pursuit of topic as a technique for terminating laughter's relevance; specifically as a technique for dealing with an invitation to laugh that has been offered just post-utterance completion.

Here is a series of fragments in which an utterance reaches completion without recipient laughter and speaker appends an object which is either clearly or equivocally a particle of laughter—i.e., is clearly or equivocally a postcompletion invitation to laugh. For each we can observe that recipient starts to talk, and to talk by reference to topical matters in the prior utterance, and does so immediately after speaker clearly or equivocally starts to laugh.

(8)

James: I don'<u>mind</u> eh pullin'em but he comin at <u>me</u>-dat <u>nee</u>dle's what I can't stand. HAH

Vic: [[]Use- Tellim <u>ga</u>:s.

(9)

Gene: So that shook the old (h)house(h)hold up fer a(h)whi(h)le heh

Patty: [[]Oh <u>yes</u> I c'n <u>im</u>agine.

(10)

Mike: Wud is dat. ((The astrological sign Sag-
           gitarius))
                    (0.9)
Vic: Uh::::ih-ah-ih guy widda bow'n arrow
           enna half en a:sss. ˙hh A half en a:ss of
           a ho::sss.he˙h
Mike: ⌜Yeh but wuddih they call it

(11)

Natalie: U(h)nfortunately he lives in Van Nuys,
           ehhm.⌜
Edna: Izzee unencumbered?

(12)

Bee: So the nex'cla: ss hh!˙hh fer an hour en
           f'fteen minutes I sat there en I watched
           his ha:n(h)ds hh hh⌜
Ava: ⌜Why what's the
           matter with him.

(13)

Natalie: en there I sit with all these (h)young
           fellas, I fel'like a den mother. ˙hhh⌜
Edna: ⌜Are
           you the oldest one'n the class?

In each fragment, whether the utterance is intuitively a candidate
laughable or contains markers by speaker (such as within-speech laugh
particles), recipient does not start to laugh within or at completion of
that utterance. Furthermore, the laugh-declining speech which recipient
does provide occurs at a very slight but observable distance from the
utterance's completion point. It should be noted that recipients/next
speakers can and do start up directly upon an utterance's completion
point, and, for example, that such startings are a routine locus of overlap; that is, at a possible completion point a recipient starts to respond,
and it turns out that that point was merely a *possible* completion point,
not the actual completion point, current speaker continuing the utterance
with syntactically fitted next utterance components. (See Sacks, Schegloff, and Jefferson, 1974). The product can be a collection of at-com-
pletion "false starts" by recipient.

(14)

Penny: An' the fact is I- is- I jus' thought it was
         so kind of stupid =
Janet: ═⟦ Y-
Penny: ═⟦ I didn'even say anything =
Janet: ═⟦ Eh-
Penny: ═⟦ when I came ho:me.

Or for example, routinely "tag terms" (questions, address terms, etc.) are overlapped by recipient/next speaker starting directly on the utterance's otherwise obvious completion.

(15)

Bert: Uh you been down here before havenche.
Fred: ⌊Yeh.

(16)

Desk: What is your last name Lorraine,
Lorraine: ⌊Dinnis.

That is, while speech can and does start up directly upon completion point of an utterance, in the fragments pertaining to declined invitations to laugh (8-13), speech starts up just a bit after completion. And it may not be just somewhere just a bit after, but specifically after the speaker of the prior utterance has recognizably started to laugh, or at least made a sound which might potentially turn into laughter.

James: ... can't stand. + HAH
Vic: ⌊Use ...

Gene: ... fer a(h)whi(h)le + heh
Patty: ⌊Oh yes ...

Vic: ... of a ho::sss. + he h
Mike: ⌊Yeh but ...

Natalie: ... in Van Nuys, + ehhm.
Edna: ⌊Izzee ...

Bee: ... his ha:n(h)ds + hh hh
Ava: ⌊Why ...

Natalie: ... den mother. + ·hhh
Edna: ⌊Are you ...

Now a speaker can have grounds to suspect that recipient is disinclined to laugh (e.g., if the utterance contains some markers and/or specific invitations to laugh and recipient has bypassed them), and can produce his postcompletion invitation attending the possibility of recipient's declining. The fragments shown initially for recipient's positioning of utterances which contain no laughter and which address topical matters in candidate laughables will now be examined for speaker's work vis-a-vis his just-started pursuit of laughter.

A speaker can be prepared to relinquish pursuit if recipient does not immediately accept. For example, in fragment (9) the speaker who has appended a laugh invitation turns out to have appended but a single laugh particle which stops simultaneously with the onset of recipient's declination/pursuit of topic. The invitation is a mere suggestion, following a series of within-speech laugh particles recipient has bypassed.

> (9)
> Gene: So that shook the old (h)house(h)hold
>   up fer a(h)whi(h)le heh⌐
> Patty: ⌐ᴸOh yes I c'n
>   imagine.
> Gene: Y'know, a:nd uh I think Jill's, realized
>   thet hell maybe . . .

Note that all pursuit of laughter is abandoned and prior speaker now follows recipient's pursuit of topic with more topical talk.

On the other hand, speaker can be prepared to counter recipient pursuit of topic with pursuit of laughter. The following two fragments occur in a multiparty setting, which can be relevant to speaker's pursuit of laughter; i.e., there are others present who might take it up even if this sequence's co-participant/recipient does not.

> (8)
> James: . . . dat needles what I can't stand.
>   HAH⌐HAH⌐ H⌐AH HAH!⌐
> Vic: ⌐ᴸUse⌐- ⌐ᴸTellim ga:s. =
> James: ·hh Huh?
> Vic: Tellim gass.
>   (0.4)
> James: Uh- No I don't go with gas
>   y' know I wi- I will take it.

(10)

Mike: Wud is dat.
               (0.9)
Vic: Uh::::: ih-ah-ih guy widda bow'n arrow
          enna half en a:sss. 'hh A half en a:ss
          o f a ho::.sss. =
Mike: [Is that-]

Vic: =he h -he:h (h)uh w(h)uddevuh
Mike: [Yeh but wuddih they call it] =

Vic: duh hell 'e i(h)::s,
Mike: what izzit the ra:m?] =

Vic: 'hhh!
Mike: =[[Saggitarius's uh ra:m?
                 (•)
Vic: No. Ra:m is, ram is uh:: a ram.Yihknow
          wid ho:rns.

In each of these competitions held in multi party settings, speaker and recipient engage in competitive overlapping talk and the competition terminates with no other parties joining the laughter and with speaker relinquishing the pursuit of laughter and taking up topical talk in response to the recipient.

An alternative consequence for multi-party settings is that others will join in the laughter. The following fragment has as an additional feature the fact that there are two separate topics under way: (1) placing bets on the weekend's football games and (2) diagnosing a rash. A participant of the football talk breaks off to do a joke about the rash. The post completion invitation to laugh is quickly countered, not by serious talk about the rash, but by serious talk about the football bets, by the other participant to that topic. The fact of two ongoing topics will be simply asserted, and the transcript will start at the point one member of the football conversation places a remark about the rash.

(17)
Bill: Yeah Mom. <u>Di</u>aper rash.
                    (•)
Bill: ──► hh⌐hnhh
Sam: ──►⌐I'll give yih th' ⌐Gi⌐ants-
Bill: ─────────────────────►⌐ I ⌐bet it
Gloria: ⌊HEH HEH

Bill: ⌐is!
Gloria: ⌊HUH· HUH⌐HE:H⌐HE:H HA:H A:HH-'hh⌉
Lorrie: ⌊heh heh ⌐he:h⌉   ⌉
Bill: ⌊'hnh⌋he::h heh 'hnnhhhh ⌋

One nice detail here: although Bill's pursuit of laughter competes with
the attempt to set up a bet, it uses the language of that topic: "I bet it
is!"

This case contains an instance of a postcompletion invitation to laugh
which is in the first place equivocal. Such objects, while they are
recognizably not speech and while they contain some of the characteristic
sounds of laughter, are not definitively laughter but could be: a breath
(exhaled or inhaled), a throat-clearing, a cough-onset, etc. Should reci-
pient(s) accept the invitation, *then* these sounds can be followed by
sounds which retroactively formulate the initial sounds as having indeed
been the start of a laugh. Such minimal-equivocal invitations are routinely used, both by current speakers and by a first-responding recipient in
multi-party conversation. For example:

(18)
Roger: <u>You</u>:: are what dey refer to in rougher
         circles as a chick'n shit. =
Roger: = hhh⌐hhehh
Ken: ⌊heh:heh heh

(19)
Jeff: en Ramsbach's in there lyin there with a
         smoke,
                  (•)
Jeff: 'hh⌐hh ehhhh
Vana: ⌊aaahhh!

(20)
Al: better getta good price fer me.
           (0.6)
Ken: hhh hheh heh heh
Louise: hehhh heh heh heh

(21)
Ben: "Pwitter O'Toole."
           (•)
Bill: ˙hh hh hheh heh
Ellen: eh heh heh

Should others decline to laugh, then the equivocal sound may be terminated, and remain just a breath, throat-clearing, etc., or may be
followed by more sound which retroactively formulates the prior as
definitely not laughter. The remainder of the fragments initially shown
to illustrate recipient starting to talk just after an invitation or possible
invitation to laugh has begun, are, as well, instances of minimal-
equivocal invitations.

(12)
Bee: So the nex'cla:ss hh!˙hh fer an hour en
           f'fteen minutes I sat there en I watched
           his ha:n(h)ds hh hh ˙hhh
Ava: Why what's the
           matter with him.
           (•)
Bee: ˙hh t!˙hhh He keh- he doesn' haff uh-full
           use uff hiss hha-fin:gers

(13)
Natalie: en there I sit with all these (h)young
           fellas, I fel'like a den mother. ˙hhh hh
Edna: Are
           you the oldest one'n the class?
           (•)
Natalie: Oh:: w- by fa:r.

Some small vestige of the fact of actual competition, although it has been reduced in its displayed features, is the occurrence of the token-of-special-interest "Oh::". Massively, such tokens and other expressions of special interest in another party's talk appear at resolution of competition for the floor and/or for the direction the talk will take, and are part of doing the relinquishing of a heretofore competitive act. Here are two examples:

(22)

Louise: How s- How s-( )-
Roger: Theh wantuh git me in the r-swing a'thing hnh
(•)
Louise: How-How old were you wny'first went.
Roger: By th'time I'm nineteen'm a genuine neurotic. heh!
(•)
Louise: How old were you when y'first went,
(•)
Roger: → Oh:: I'd say about, thirteen,

(23)

Natalie: Course I don't know whether it's that, er just thet we're just- completely bogging down et work, ˙hhhhm =

Natalie: = er what a waytuh- waytuh ta:::ke,
Edna: Oh::::::: well evrybody's sa:d.

Natalie: my finals?
(•)
Natalie: hhh! huh huh ˙hhh!
Edna: finals. Oh:::! Howjuh do with yer

In our final instance, speaker not only produces an equivocal invitation, but after recipient's declination via serious pursuit of topic, further reduces the possible formulation of the postcompletion noises as an invitation to laugh. This she does by producing a phrase which, although subsequent to completion of recipient's utterance, ties back to and is continuous of her own prior utterance. Thereafter she responds to recipient's utterance.

(11)
Natalie: U(h)nfortunately he lives in Van Nuys,
           ehhm.⌐
Edna: ⌐Izzee unencumbered?
               (•)
Natalie: ‚works out there, =
Natalie: = Yes, he's living, with his aunt . . .

We might see this fragment as a version of a particular overlap-remedial technique: a party who has been overlapped and has dropped out, starts to talk again at completion of the overlapping utterance, and provides a continuation of the overlapped talk from the point it was cut off. For example:

(24)
Roger: ⏐ happen tuh wear buloo jeans
         constantly.
                  (0.3)
Ken: Well,
            (•)
Roger: ⟶ Even⸢in-
Ken: ⌊So do ⏐ now,
            (•)
Roger: formal occasions, y'know? hheh hh!

Furthermore, a party can successfully propose that an utterance was interrupted although there was no overlap involved, by constructing a continuation of the otherwise completed utterance. For example:

(25)
Louise: Twelve and a half years old and I- seven-
          teen and a half and we look the same.
                  (2.0)
Ken: You know, my brother and I have come
          to one a- mutual agree=
Ken: ⌐ment that- that we-
Louise: ⌊She's taller than I am, too.
                  (•)
Ken: She is? She's taller'n you?

And note another version, here, of the competition-relinquishing token of special interest.

That is, in fragment (11), the one who offered a minimal-equivocal invitation to laugh which was overlapped by serious pursuit of topical talk, retroactively proposes that recipient's pursuit of topical talk was "interruptive" of speaker's own intention to go right ahead and pursue topical talk.

Conclusion

Laughter can be managed as a sequence in which speaker of an utterance invites recipient to laugh and recipient accepts that invitation. One technique for inviting laughter is the placement, by speaker, of a laugh just at completion of an utterance, and one technique for accepting that invitation is the placement, by recipient, of a laugh just after onset of speaker's laughter.

Declination of an invitation to laugh is not achieved by recipient silence, but can generate a pursuit of laughter by speaker, that pursuit eventuating in recipient laughter.

In order to terminate the relevance of laughter, recipient must actively decline to laugh. One technique for declining a postcompletion invitation to laugh is the placement of speech, by recipient, just after onset of speaker's laughter, that speech providing serious pursuit of topic as a counter to the pursuit of laughter.

Speakers can expect, and can collaborate in or compete with the declination to laugh, and it appears that the distinction between two-party and multi-party conversation can be relevant for speaker's treatment of a recipient's declination; i.e., in two-party conversation decliner is the only potential co-laugher, while in multi-party situations there are others present who may take up laughter.

Crucially, whether recipient accepts or declines and whether speaker collaborates or competes, the fact of a preferred invitation and its subsequent treatment does not, in these materials, emerge as a conversationally explicit issue in its own right, as it always potentially can and occasionally does. For example:

(26)
Roger: Well it struck me funny.
                        (1.0)
Al: HA, HA-HA-HA
Ken: hh
Roger: Thank you.

(27)
Bill: That wz a jo:ke people,
                        (•)
Bill: That‚wz-
Ellen: ᴸYeh.
                        (•)
Bill: That- En yer spoze tuh smi:le.

REFERENCES

Jefferson, Gail (1974). A case of precision timing in ordinary conversation. *Semiotica* 9: 56–59.

Sacks, Harvey, Schegloff, Emanuel A. and Jefferson, Gail (1974). A simplest systematics for the organization of turn-taking in conversation. *Language* 50, 4, 696-735.

Data Sources

I produced all the transcripts which appear in this paper, and where noted, others worked with me. In those cases where a collector is named, special appreciation is marked.

The materials are described by instrument-type (in person or telephone), by number of parties (two- or multi-party), age and sex of participants, general situation, and place and year collected.

Fragment

(1) Two-party in-person, young man and woman, neighbors, after an interchange with two young men. Philadelphia, Pa., 1973. Collected and co-transcribed by Dan Rose.

(2)   Two-party telephone, elderly woman and young man, former neighbors. Orange County, California, 1970.

(3)   Multi-party, family. In this fragment, mother and son. Newport Beach, Ca., 1970. Collected by James Schenkein.

(4)   Multi-party, three young men with their wives and children at a backyard picnic. Ohio, 1973. Videotape. Collected and co-transcribed by Charles and Marjorie Goodwin.

(5)   Two-party telephone, young man and woman whose children are friends. Newport Beach, Ca., 1968.

(6)   Two-party telephone, middle-aged woman and young woman friend. Newport Beach, Ca., 1968.

(7)   See (3) above.

(8)   Multi-party, a group of men gathered at a neighborhood upholstery shop. Brooklyn, New York, 1970. Collected and co-transcribed by Richard Frankel.

(9)   Two-party telephone, a divorcee and a married boyfriend. Los Angeles, Ca., 1968. Collected by JoAnne Goldberg.

(10)   See (8) above.

(11)   Two-party telephone, middle-aged woman and young, recently divorced woman friend. Same extended corpus as (6) above.

(12)   Two-party telephone, two college girls, formerly close friends. New York City, N.Y., 1970.

(13)   Two-party telephone. Same participants as (11) above, but different phone call.

(14)   Two-party telephone, two middle-aged women, second of three consecutive calls about a possibly interesting event. Los Angeles, Ca., 1967.

(15)   Two-party telephone, two men. Same extended corpus as (6) above.

(16)   Two-party telephone, fire department personnel and young woman caller. Anchorage, Alaska, 1964.

(17)   Multi-party, family. Santa Barbara, Ca., 1975. Collected and co-transcribed by Michelle Weiner.

(18)   Multi-party, teenage therapy group. Los Angeles, Ca., 1964.

(19)   Multi-party, interview with high-school kids. Philadelphia, Pa., 1973. Collected by William Labov et al.

(20)   See (18) above.

(21)   See (3) above, this fragment includes father.

(22)   See (18) above.

(23)   Same extended corpus and same participants as (11) above, but different phone call.

(24)   See (18) above.

(25)   See (18) above.

(26)   See (18) above.

(27)   See (21) above.

The Interactive Construction of a Sentence in Natural Conversation

Charles Goodwin

Charles Goodwin uses another technical source of data for the study of interaction, videotape recordings. His collection of materials inccludes several videotape recordings, segments of which are discovered to contain instances of the phenomenon he describes. A sentence, as Goodwin is able to show, can be shaped and re-formed in the process of its utterance. In face-to-face interaction it can be affected by such matters as the direction of glances (which indicate attention to the speaker by the recipient) and the relationship of the parties to each other. Thus, Goodwin opens for further consideration by interactional analysts the question of what a sentence is by showing that it may not be understandable as a unit apart from the situated occasion of its production. The implications for linguists and others who work with this unit of utterance are manifold.

Sentences emerge with conversation.[1] However, in traditional linguistics it has been assumed that the analysis of sentences can be performed upon examples isolated from such an interactive process.[2] In opposition to such a view it will be argued here that sentences in natural conversation emerge as the products of a process of interaction between speaker and hearer and that they mutually construct the turn at talk.

Two ways in which the collaborative process of constructing the turn might lead to the modification of the speaker's emerging sentence will be examined. First it will be proposed that the speaker can reconstruct the emerging meaning of his sentence as he is producing it in order to maintain its appropriateness to its recipient of the moment. It will then be argued that the accomplishment of other interactive tasks, such as the negotiation of an appropriate state of mutual orientation between speaker and hearer, may require changes in the length of the turn being constructed. To make the turn longer the speaker can change the sentence he is producing by adding to that sentence new sections, in the form of words, phrases, and clauses.[3] Both the length and the meaning of the sentence eventually constructed within a turn at talk can thus emerge as the products of a dynamic process of interaction between speaker and hearer.

For clarity, analysis will focus upon the following sentence: "I gave up smoking cigarettes one week ago today actually." Though only a single sentence is being investigated, the process of its construction will provide the opportunity to examine in detail some of the more basic interactive tasks posed in the construction of the turn.

This sentence is taken from a videotape of an actual conversation,[4] a dinner in the home of John and his wife Beth attended by their friends Ann and Don.[5]

The actual production of the sentence is accomplished in two different turns separated by a recipient's "yea:h":

G.26:(T)8:50

John: I gave, I gave up smoking
        cigarettes::. =
Don: = Yea:h,
        (0.4)
John: I-uh: one-one week ago t'da:y.
        acshilly,

However, irrespective of any such division, John's talk produces only a single coherent sentence. The manifest coherence of his utterances as a single sentence constitutes both an initial observation about their organization and a warrant for analyzing this talk as a single unit.

Within the coherence of this single unit it is, however, possible to locate subunits. In producing this talk the speaker directs his gaze to three different recipients over three different sections of the utterance. Specifically, his gaze is directed to Don during "I gave up smoking cigarettes," to Beth during "one week ago today," and finally to Ann during "actually."[6]

The relationship between the movement of the speaker's gaze and his utterance can be displayed more precisely through use of a simple transcription system.[7] The gaze of the speaker is marked above the utterance. A line indicates that he is gazing at some particular recipient. The precise point where his gaze first reaches that recipient is marked with a left bracket. A series of dots indicates that the speaker is moving his gaze toward some recipient, while commas mark a movement away from some recipient.

Applying this transcription system to John's utterance:

John: . . , , ... [Don, ,   [Don_____
        I gave, I gave u[p smoking ci[garettes::. =

Don: = Yea:h,

John: . . . [Beth_____ . . .[Ann_____
        I-uh: [one-one week ago t'da:[y. acshilly

In brief, by plotting aspects of the speaker's gaze it is possible to divide his sentence into three separate sections during each of which the speaker gazes at a different recipient.

The question now to be investigated is what relevance, if any, the speaker's gaze direction has to the accomplishment of tasks facing him in constructing a turn at talk.[8]

One possible rule that would implicate the speaker's gaze in the construction of the turn might be the following:

> *Rule 1:* The gaze of a speaker should locate the party being gazed at as an addressee of his utterance.

It will now be argued that this rule is in fact operative and that the speaker's orientation to it produces characteristic phenomena within the turn.

In the first section of his sentence John tells his recipients that he has given up smoking cigarettes. Sacks (1973, p. 139) has noted the operation in conversation of a "general rule that provides that one should not tell one's co-participants what one takes it they already know."[9] This rule is implicated in the organization of a range of different types of *informings,* including announcements, stories, and reports.

In constructing the first section of his sentence, John is thus proposing a criterion for an appropriate recipient to it.[10] namely that such a recipient does not yet know that he has given up smoking.

For convenience, a possible recipient not expected to know about an event being reported by a speaker will be referred to as an *unknowing recipient* while a possible recipient already informed about that event will be referred to as a *knowing recipient.*

Don and his wife Ann are the dinner guests of John and his wife Beth. Neither has seen the speaker for some period of time before the present evening. John thus has reason to suppose that Don has not yet heard the news he is now telling[11] and, he would thus be an appropriate recipient of the announcement. It is to Don that John directs his gaze during this section of his utterance. Insofar as the party being gazed at can be seen to satisfy the criterion proposed for a recipient of John's statement, Rule 1 is satisfied.

At least one party present at the dinner would not be an appropriate recipient of the first section of John's sentence. Beth, the speaker's wife, has been living in the same house with him for the past week and knows that he has given up smoking. Further, this is something that the speaker knows that she knows and indeed the others present can also legitimately see these things.[12] Insofar as John's initial statement is appropriate to an unknowing recipient and Beth is a knowing recipient, the present line of analysis implies that the event described to Don should not be reported to Beth.

This raises the possibility of investigating more systematically in this data the properties of Rule 1. The speaker's active orientation toward this rule could be demonstrated if when he shifted his gaze to another recipient who did not satsify the criterion proposed by his action, he then simultaneously reshaped his emerging utterance so that it was made appropriate to the current object of his gaze.

For the next section of the sentence, "l-uh: one-<u>one</u> week ago t'<u>da</u>:y.", John switches his gaze from Don, an unknowing recipient, to Beth, a knowing recipient.

With the addition of this section to the sentence, the news that John has stopped smoking cigarettes is transformed into a different piece of news: that today is an anniversary of that event. Such an anniversary is a new event that none of the parties present, including Beth, need be expected to know about.

The structure of an anniversary makes it particularly appropriate as a solution to a problem such as that faced by John. An anniversary is constructed via the lamination[13] of events at two separate moments in time, an original event which becomes the object of celebration, and the anniversary itself. The two are related by the occurrence of some regular period of time between them.[14]

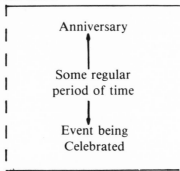

An anniversary is an appropriate object to call to the attention of someone who shared experience of the event celebrated by it with the speaker. More precisely, interest in the anniversary is contingent upon interest in the event being celebrated by it.[15] However, a party who knows of the original event need not be aware of the fact that a period of time appropriate for the location of an anniversary has passed. The laminated structure of the anniversary thus integrates items of common experience with novel information in a way particularly suited for the inclusion of a knowing recipient, such as Beth, in John's utterance.

Such a laminated structure also maintains the relevance of this section of the sentence for its original recipient. First, the initial report to him is incorporated within it as the lowest layer of the lamination. Second, the report of the anniversary continues to perform an action relevant to an unknowing recipient, the description of that original event. In particular, it specifies the time at which the event occurred, an item that a recipient persumed to be ignorant of that event would not be expected to know. Thus, though this section of the sentence is made appropriate to a new type of recipient, it maintains its relevance for its original recipient:[16]

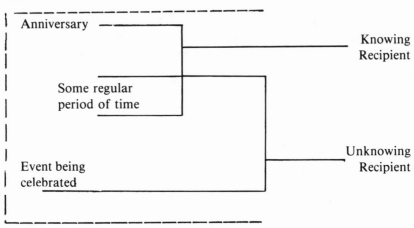

In essence, each layer of the lamination locates an alternative type of recipient. Some demonstration is here provided that a cultural object emerging through a turn at talk might be selected for presentation at a particular moment because its structural properties permit the solution of interactive problems posed in the construction of the turn.

Other features of John's utterance provide support for the argument that he is reshaping his sentence in order to make it appropriate to a new type of recipient.

First, an alternative to the section of his sentence actually produced at this point is begun and abandoned:

John: I-uh: one-<u>one</u> week ago t'<u>da</u>:y.

The word beginning, "1-", plus the hesitation, "uh:", plus the second word "one" correspond to what Jefferson (1974a, p 186) has described as the Error Correction Format. The word begun by the initial fragment[17] constitutes an alternative to the second word, which corrects it. "Last week" and "last Monday" are possible alternatives to the section actually produced. An expression beginning with "last" in this position would do more than simply specify the time the event occurred. It would argue for the status of the speaker's statement as news to an unknowing recipient by explicitly telling the recipient that it happened since they were last in contact with each other.[18] In view of Don's "yea:h," which neither acknowledges the newsworthiness of the event[19] nor requests elaboration of it, warranting what has just been said in this fashion may be a relevant act for the speaker to perform.

Such a section differs, however, from the one eventually selected in that it does not construct an action appropriate to a recipient already informed about the event being described. The rejection of such an alternative provides further support for the argument that John, faced with the task of making his utterance appropriate to a new type of recipient, reshapes the event being described through the utterance.

Other evidence that the anniversary, which redesigns the sentence for its new recipient, was not projected as an element of the sentence from its beginning is provided by the speaker's intonation, which locates surprise at the beginning of the section and places stress on the revelation of the anniversary:

John: I-uh: one-<u>one</u> week ago t'd<u>a</u>:y.

The discovery intonation at the beginning of the section is placed in contrast to a possible beginning without such stress. Specifically, the first and second "one" differ most noticeably in their intonation so that the change in intonation is marked to be heard as the warrant for the restart. Such a structure both announces that something unanticipated has been discovered and locates where that discovery occurred. Recipients are thus informed not only that some new basis for listening is being offered but that this new information was discovered after the first section of the utterance. Such an announcement would be particularly important for a party, such as Beth, who has been located as an unlikely recipient to the speaker's sentence by its first section.

One further issue relevant to the anniversary can be briefly considered. Though the discovery of the anniversary solves the problem of including a knowing recipient in the turn, it is not in fact the characteristic way that speakers solve this problem. More precisely, the situation of a speaker in the simultaneous presence of both a knowing and an unknowing recipient is one that recurs regularly and systematically in conversation,[20] and speakers have available to them some standard procedures for dealing with the structural problems generated by it. For example, speakers moving their gaze from unknowing to knowing recipients regularly display uncertainty about some detail of the event being described to the unknowing recipient and request that the knowing recipient verify its accuracy.[21] Such a standard solution could have been employed in the present case. For example, on turning to Beth John could have produced the time that the event took place (as he indeed began to do at the beginning of the section) but indicated that it was problematic by pronouncing it with rising intonation, i.e., "last week?" or "last Monday?" In a certain sense a solution of this type would have been simpler than the one actually used, since it would have involved less modification of the emerging utterance. John's choice of an atypical procedure for including a knowing recipient in his turn, and further a procedure that is not the most simple availabled for performing the tasks posed, invites speculation as to why his particular solution was chosen.

One other aspect of this data might be relevant to the speaker's seeing that a regular period of time, appropriate for the location of an anniversary, has passed. Sacks and his colleagues have shown that one feature implicated in word selection in conversation is punning relationships of various types.[22] Several utterances after John completes the sentence being examined here, he states that he is taking a course on how to stop smoking. Concerning the course Beth says, "Yeh, it wz like Seventh Day Adventist." The regular time relationship necessary for the discovery of the anniversary, seven days, is thus available in the scene being described.

Once the anniversary has been found it has a preferred status for being told, since it is the latest news, the original event being news that is already a week old.

The turn until this point thus provides some demonstration that the gaze of a speaker locates the party being gazed at as a recipient of his utterance. Evidence has also been provided that a speaker in natural conversation has the capacity to modify the emerging meaning of his sentence as he is producing it in accord with the characteristics of its current recipient. Through use of such procedures the appropriateness of the utterance for its recipient of the moment can be maintained and demonstrated. Though the sentence originally begun proposed that its recipient had no knowledge of the event being described within it, by transforming that event and locating a new piece of news the speaker was able to make the sentence appropriate to one who shared experience of it with him.

In constructing his turn the speaker thus demonstrates precise orientation toward the particularities of his recipient. However, within conversation sentences are not just addressed to a recipient but constructed to be actually heard by a hearer. Therefore it might be expected that the speaker would also be attentive to his recipient's orientation toward him.

One possible feature of the hearer's behavior toward which the speaker might direct his attention is the hearer's gaze, perhaps in terms of whether or not the hearer is gazing toward the speaker. However, the analytic problem is not simply to propose categorizable variations in the hearer's gaze, but rather to demonstrate the relevance of specific alternatives. not for the analyst. but for the participants themselves, who are engaged in the task of constructing the turn.[23] Further, even the most casual examination of actual conversation reveals that in the course of a turn hearers regularly look both at the speaker and away from him, changing their gaze as the turn progresses. Given the presence of both alternatives within the turn it seems difficult to establish the special importance of either.

The work of Sacks and his colleagues on the sequential organization of conversation provides analytic resources with which these problems might be addressed. Sacks (1972) observes that—

> Certain activities not only have regular places in some sequence where they do get done but may, if their means of being done is not found there, be said, by members, to not have occurred to be absent.
>
> For example, the absence of a greeting may be noticed. . .
>
> Observations such as these lead to a distinction between a "slot" and the "items" which fill it, and to proposing that certain activities are accomplished by a combination of some item and some slot.
>
> The notion of slot serves for the social scientist to mark a class of relevance rules. Thus, if it can be said that for some assertable sequence there is a position in which one or more activities properly occur, or occur if they are to get done, then: The observability of either the occurrence or the nonoccurrence of those activities may be claimed by reference to having looked at the position and determined whether what occurs in it is a way of doing the activity. (p. 341)

If the turn at talk provides a slot for the hearer to gaze at the speaker then the problems stated above could be solved. First, the fact that the hearer looks both toward and away from the speaker during the course of the turn would pose no particular analytic difficulty. Rather than searching the turn as a whole one could look at that particular slot to see whether the hearer is gazing at the speaker. Second, the presence of such a slot within the turn would establish the relevance of this event so that one could locate its nonoccurrence as well as its occurrence, while yet providing places in the turn where the hearer could gaze elsewhere than at the speaker without failing to bring about this event. Third, such a slot would establish the relevance of this action for the particpants themselves. The presence or absence of the hearer's gaze in this slot would constitute different events for the parties with different consequences for the subsequent course of their interaction and the construction of the turn.[24]

The following will be proposed as a rule describing where in the turn a hearer should be gazing at the speaker.

> *Rule 2:* When a speaker gazes at a recipient he should make eye contact with that recipient.

Complete discussion of the operations and implications of this rule is beyond the scope of this paper.[25]

However, one feature of it relevant to the construction of the utterance being examined in this paper will be briefly noted. A speaker can request the gaze of a recipient by producing a phrasal break, such as a restart or a pause, in his utterance. After such a phrasal break nongazing recipients regularly bring their gaze to the speaker.[26] Consider the following, where a speaker who gazes at a nongazing recipient immediately produces a phrasal break just after which the recipient begins to move his gaze to the speaker.[27] (The gaze of the hearer is transcribed in the same way as the gaze of the speaker, but plotted below the utterance.)

G.50:(T)05:30

```
Clacia:      . . ̟X _____ , , ,
             'N he cˡa- he calls me a ̟Vassar sno:b.
Dianne:               . . . . . . ˡX _____
```

G.26:(T)18:45

```
Beth:        . . . ̟X _____
             Michaeˡl- Daniel's faˌscinated with elephants.
Ann:                       . . . . ˡX _____
```

Lee: . . . . . . ₍X ———————————
Can you brin⌐g-? (0.2) Can you bring
Ray: . . . .

Lee: ———————————
me here that nylo⌐n?
Ray: . . . . .ˡX —

The fact that the speaker will initiate a remedy if the situation described by Rule 2 does not occur provides some demonstration of the orientation of the participants themselves to the features specified by the rule.

The application of Rule 2 to the construction of John's utterance will now be investigated, beginning with its first section:

John: . . , , ... ⌐Don , , , . ⌐Don
I gave, I gave u⌐p smo⌐king ci⌐garettes::. =
Don: . .ˡX ———————————

Don is the recipient toward whom John gazes during the production of this section. At one point within it the conditions specified in Rule 2 are not satisfied as the speaker gazes at a nongazing recipient. When this happens John quickly withdraws his gaze, returning it to Don only after Don has begun to gaze at him. The act of actively moving gaze away from a nongazing recipient is consistent with the argument that the speaker is oriented toward the features of Rule 2.

This section also contains a restart. While that restart fails to immediately secure Don's gaze, the expectation that it would may be one reason why John brings his gaze to Don shortly after its production. Some evidence that this might be the case is provided by the speaker's pattern of gaze (marked with dots and commas) over the restart. Just before the restart John, who had been moving his gaze toward Don, begins instead to move it away from him. Immediately after the restart his gaze once more starts to move toward Don.

For the next section of the sentence John moves his gaze from Don to Beth. According to Rule 2 a speaker should expect to gaze at a gazing recipient. However, the structure of the utterance until this point provides no basis for John to expect Beth to be gazing at him, and indeed some reason to expect that she is not doing so. As was seen earlier in this paper Beth was not located as an appropriate recipient to the sentence by its first section.

As John moves his eyes to Beth he produces a standard request for the gaze of a recipient, a phrasal break, "1-uh:". It may be noted that the production of this fragment occupies the precise time it takes the speaker to move his gaze from one recipient to the other so that the next section of the sentence begins just as the gaze of the speaker reaches his new recipient. Such precision may not be accidental but rather seems to be achieved through the speaker's choice and control over the sounds he produces. The initial part of the fragment ends in a glottal stop, a sound of limited duration that could not be extended to occupy the entire time it takes the speaker to produce his head turn. However, to this sound is added another, "uh:", which has no fixed length of time for its production but rather can be pronounced for variable lengths of time. The speaker's production of this sound is noticeably long (as indicated by the transcriber's colon after it), this extra length providing the means to extend the fragment until the head move has been completed. This suggests that the speaker has the ability to precisely control events even within the production of a single phonetic unit in order to accomplish social tasks posed in the construction of the turn.[28]

However, when John's eyes reach Beth he finds that, despite his phrasal break, she has not even begun to turn her eyes toward him. The first word John produces in this situation is terminated with a glottal stop and made the first part of a restart, "one-one", producing another phrasal break. Beth still does not bring her eyes to John and when the end of this section of the utterance arrives, remains involved in the task of eating:

> John: . . . ₍Beth _____
>   ˡ
> I-uh: ˡone-one week ago t'da:y.
> Beth:

Despite John's careful and precise work to redesign his utterance for Beth, and to signal that her gaze is needed, Beth's failure to bring her gaze to John means that he does not make eye contact with her as specified in Rule 2. Instead the speaker is gazing at a recipient who is not gazing at him.

If Rule 2 is to be satisfied the speaker should now work to change the existing situation to one in which his utterance is being addressed to a recipient who is gazing back at him.

Though the restart does not secure Beth's gaze, another party, Ann, does begin to attend the turn at this point. During the initial sections of John's sentence, and indeed for some time previous to it, Ann has displayed lack of orientation to the conversation, staring to her side with a fixed middle-distance look. However, shortly after the restart Ann abruptly raises her head and moves her gaze to the recipient of the present utterance, Beth:

John:

    . . . ┌Beth_____

I-uh: └one-one week ag‿o t'da:y.

Beth:

Ann: . . . . Beth

Ann's abrupt movement of her gaze occurs in the standard position for a next move to a signal that the gaze of a recipient is being requested, i.e, shortly after a restart. However, Ann does not direct her gaze to the speaker but instead to another participant, Beth. Several features of John's utterance are relevant to Ann's choice of Beth over John as the appropriate object for her gaze. First, as was seen above, the sentence at this point is being addressed to a knowing recipient, Beth, rather than to an unknowing recipient such as Ann. By the time Ann begins to move her gaze this has been displayed in a number of ways: by the replacement of "1-" with "one", by the discovery intonation of the second "one" and by the projection of an object to be recognized by a recipient provided by "one" week. . . ." as opposed to "a week. . ."or "last week. . .", which propose no such recognition.[29] Ann has thus been provided with resources permitting her to locate not only that she is not the current addressed recipient of the utterance but also who that addressed recipient is. Second, John's sentence is projected to come to a possible completion point rather soon after Beth brings her gaze to the turn. "I gave up smoking cigarettes one week ago today" is an adequately complete sentence and, especially in view of the idiom used to construct the anniversary, such a unit could be projected at the point Ann brings her gaze to the turn. Ann's gaze reaches Beth one word before the completion of this unit. If the floor were to pass to the speaker's addressed recipient at this point Ann would be positioned to be gazing at the new speaker.

Two different parties, John and Ann, are now gazing at Beth, who is returning the gaze of neither. If these two parties were gazing at each other instead of Beth the conditions specified in Rule 2 would be satisfied: the speaker would be gazing at a gazing recipient. Because of Beth's repeated failure to bring her gaze to him John might now be prepared to seek the gaze of another party. Ann, who has just displayed her orientation to the turn by bringing her gaze to its field of action, is a possible candidate. However, while the task of securing a gazing recipient might lead John to switch his gaze from Beth to Ann no comparable motivation exists for Ann to move her gaze from Beth to John, especially since she is not his current addressed recipient.

Less than a syllable after Ann begins to move into orientation John withdraws his gaze from Beth. He then brings it to Ann, reaching her after she has demonstrated her co-participation in the field of action constructed through his turn by gazing at Beth, but before the turn has reached its next projected completion. Note that the time required to reach this completion point has been extended through the elongation of a sound within "t'da̲:y":

```
John:    . . . ┌Beth _____, , . . ┌Ann
         I-uh: └one- one week ag┌o t'da: └y.
Beth:                           [
Ann:                 . . . .    └Beth_____
```

Though John is now gazing at Ann rather than at Beth he is still gazing at a recipient who is not gazing at him. His move has, however, made it relevant for Ann to bring her gaze to him. As she is the party being gazed at by the speaker, Rule 2 now applies to her rather than to Beth.

Features such as those described in Rule 2 not only provide guides for the participants' action but also resources for viewing and appropriately interpreting the scene in which they are engaged. The viewings provided by such a structure are available to all relevant parties. Thus the opening part of this section provides Ann with the resources to see that Beth is its addressed recipient. However, when she looks at Beth she as well as the speaker can see that Beth is not prepared to take the floor at that point. When the speaker then brings his gaze to Ann this same structure enables her to see not merely where the speaker is gazing but where she herself should be gazing. The possibility of such recognition and interpretation makes nonconformity to the rule a meaningful event capable of organizing subsequent action.

John's shift in gaze thus permits Ann to recognize that she should bring her gaze to him. However, no time is left within the turn for Ann to perform this action. As indicated not only by its grammatical structure but also by its falling terminal intonation (indicated in the transcript by a period), John's utterance has come to a recognizable completion.

If the length of the turn could be extended, Ann might have the time to move her gaze from Beth to John. However, providing the turn with such time for maneuvering requires that the sentence being constructed through it be extended past the completion point presently proposed for it.[30]

Ann is given time to bring her gaze to John through the addition of the word "actually" to his sentence:

```
John:    . . . ┌Beth                  , , . . ┌Ann
         I-uh: └one- one week ag ┌o t'da: └y. acshi ┌lly,
Beth:                            └Beth                    └
Ann:              . . . . └Beth  , . . . └John
```

The features specified in Rule 2 are thus achieved by the collaborative action of speaker and hearer. While hearer brings her gaze to the speaker, speaker provides time in his turn for her to accomplish this task by adding a new word to his sentence. The turn now reaches completion with the speaker gazing at a gazing hearer.

An event that does not occur at this point is also relevant to the addition of this segment. "Acshilly" is not overlapped by any talk from Beth though a turn transition point for the section of the utterance addressed to her has just been passed. Her lack of action here provides some validation of the readings made earlier about her participation in the turn. From this perspective the addition of a new segment to John's sentence can be seen not only as a way of providing time within the turn for Ann to move but also as a means of avoiding the gap that would result from Beth's failure to take the floor from John.[31]

When John moves his gaze from Beth to Ann, the task of reconstructing his utterance so that it is made appropriate to his recipient of the moment is posed a second time. Unlike Beth, but like Don, Ann did not share with John experience of the event he is describing. Thus, a constraint on the segment to be added to the sentence to provide for her inclusion is that it make the proposed recipient of the sentence an unknowing recipient.

"Acshilly" accomplishes this task. Through its addition the discovery of the anniversary is transformed into a report about it. Rather than being asked to recognize the anniversary the recipient is told that in fact the event being marked by it did occur a week ago. The addition of "acshilly" thus again reconstructs the emerging meaning of John's sentence so that once more it becomes appropriate to its recipient of the moment.

A state of appropriate mutual orientation between speaker and hearer having been achieved, a no gap-no overlap transfer of the floor to the recipient obtained through this process occurs:

```
John:    I gave, I gave up smoking cigarettes::. =
```

Don: = Yea:h,

John: I-uh: one-<u>one</u> week ago t'<u>da</u>:y.
        acshilly,

Ann: Rilly? en y'quit fer good?

In the course of its production the unfolding meaning of John's sentence is reconstructed twice, a new segment is added to it, and another is deleted prior to its production but replaced with a different segment. The sentence eventually produced emerges as the product of a dynamic process of interaction between speaker and hearer as they mutually construct the turn at talk. The fact that a single coherent sentence emerges, and that this was apparently the sentence being constructed all along, is among the more striking features of this process.

The turn at talk provides an area where nontrivial social, linguistic and cultural phenomena, as well as such nonvocal phenomena as gaze, can be analyzed as elements of a single integrated process. Such an integrated perspective upon this field of action might be not only valuable but necessary for the accurate description of the phenomena under analysis. For example, in traditional linguistics it has been assumed that the analysis of sentences can be performed upon examples isolated from the process of interaction within which they naturally emerge. The analysis presented here has argued, to the contrary, that the sentence actually produced within a particular turn at talk is determined by a process of interaction between speaker and hearer. Their collaborative work in constructing the turn systematically modifies the emerging structure of the sentence, adding to it, deleting from it, and changing its meaning. Insofar as this is the case, the procedures utilized to construct sentences are, at least in part, interactive procedures.

NOTES

1. The present line of inquiry is directly motivated by the research of Sacks, Jefferson, and Schegloff into the structure of human conversation. Not only has their work on turn taking (1974) prepared the ground for the investigation of the interactive organization of the turn itself, but they also have provided and continue to provide illuminating analyses of the internal structure of the turn. See for example Schegloff, Jefferson, and Sacks (1977) and Jefferson (1974b).

I am most grateful to Harvey Sacks and Gail Jefferson for a critical reading of an earlier version of this analysis which led me to substantially change it. My deep indebtedness to them extends, however, to their work, ideas, and teaching, in general and in detail, without which my own attempts to analyze the present phenomena would not even be possible. I alone am responsible for the problems with the present analysis that remain.

2. For example, Lyons (1969) states that—

> linguistic theory, at the present time at least, is not, and cannot, be concerned with the production and understanding of utterances in their actual situations of use....but with the structure of sentences considered in abstraction from the situations in which actual utterances occur. (p. 98)

See also Chomsky (1965, pp. 3-4). Curiously enough, some researchers interested in the sequencing of turns (though not Sacks and his colleagues) have also argued that the interaction of speaker and hearer is irrelevant to the construction of the turn itself. Thus Coulthard and Ashby (1975) state:

> The basic unit of all verbal interaction is the exchange. An exchange consists minimally of two successive utterances: one speaker says something and a second says something in return. Anything less is not interactive. (p. 140)

3. In linguistics a distinction is frequently made between utterances and sentences and it is argued that "sentences never occur in speech" (Lyons 1972, p. 61). Rather:

> As a grammatical unit, the sentence is an abstract entity in terms of which the linguist accounts for the distributional relations holding within utterances. In this sense of the term, utterances never consist of sentences, but of one or more segments of speech (or written text) which can be put into correspondence with the sentence generated by the grammar. (Lyons 1969, p. 176)

Such a distinction may be useful analytically. For example, in the following the word "put" occurs twice in the stream of speech but only once in a unit on another level of organization necessary for properly understanding that stream of speech:

Clacia: He pu:t uhm, (0.7) Tch! put crabmeat
            on th'bo::dum.
                    [G.50:03:45]

The processes being examined in this paper change, in Lyon's terminology, both the utterance and the underlying sentence abstractable from it.

4. All data consists of videotapes of actual conversations recorded in a range of natural settings. Though the present paper focuses upon a very few illustrative examples to demonstrate particular processes, the total corpus for this analysis consists of over fifty hours of tape recorded jointly by myself and Marjorie Goodwin. Tape G.26 was recorded by George Kuetemeyer and I am indebted to him for permitting us to use it.

The reference cited for each example, i.e., "G.26:(T)8:50," provides (1) the tape number from which the example was taken, and (2) the place on the tape (measured from an arbitrary zero point either in minutes and seconds or in counter revolutions) where the example is found.

Data cited in the present paper is drawn from the following sources:

G. 26
(1/28/73, West Philadelphia)

Dinner conversation
of two young couples.

G.50
(7/4/73, suburban Pittsburgh)

Conversation between
two middle-class women
during a Fourth of July
block party.

G.75
(8/12/73, central Michigan)

Conversation between
several families at a
picnic thrown by a lodge of
the Loyal Order of the
Moose.

G.85
(7/29/73, central Ohio)

Conversation between three
young couples at a backyard picnic.

5.   John and Beth's two children, Allen and Ben, are also present. Their actions will not
be considered further in the present analysis. This should not be taken to imply, however,
that their actions are in no way relevant to the events being examined.

6.   The route taken by the speaker's gaze as it moves from Don to Beth to Ann can be
seen most clearly with a simple diagram. The participants are seated around a circular
table.

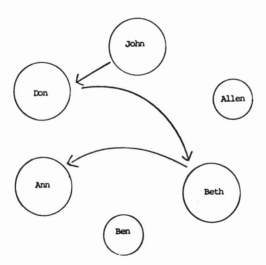

The patterns regularly utilized by speakers to move their gaze from recipient to recipient in conversation have not yet been systematically investigated. It is, however, perhaps relevant in this data that the movement of John's gaze does not follow a single direction, i.e., moving from right to left, or clockwise or counterclockwise, pausing at each recipient en route. Rather, a marked change in direction is found. He gazes to his right to look at Don but then to his left to look at Beth and then Ann. Were a single direction or clearly recognizable order utilized, that might project from early in the turn that other recipients would eventually be gazed at in a particular sequence. Such recognizable projection would enable future addressees to orient to both the sequence as a whole and their approaching place in it. (For some consideration of how the structure of 'rounds,' as found for example in introductions, might provide organization for the activity of all present, including those not yet reached in the sequence, see Sacks 1966, Fall Quarter, Lecture 1, p.2.) The unavailability of such a recognizable pattern in the present data might be relevant to the fact (to be examined later in this paper) that neither the second nor the third addressee is gazing at the speaker when his gaze reaches them.

7.   The data is transcribed according to a notation system for utterances developed by Gail Jefferson and a system for coding gaze direction developed by myself. The symbols most important to the analysis in the present paper are provided in Appendix II. I am indebted to Gail Jefferson for audio-transcribing the tape from which John's utterance is taken.

8.   Strong empirical demonstration of the relevance of gaze to face-to-face communication is provided by the work of Kendon (1967), Goffman (1963, 1967), Argyle and Cook (1976), Scheflen (1974), Ekman and Freisen (1974) and Exline (1974).

9.   Ways in which the analysis participants make of each other's information states are relevant to the organization of conversation have received considerable study. See for example Schegloff 1972, Sacks 1971 (especially his class lectures of 10-19-71 and 10-22-71), 1974, Sacks and Schegloff this volume, Jefferson 1973, Labov 1970, Labov and Fanshell 1977, Goffman 1974, and Terasaki 1976.

10.   Sacks, Schegloff, and Jefferson (1974) have noted that "perhaps the most general principle which particularizes conversational interaction [is] that of RECIPIENT DESIGN."(p. 727). For further consideration of this issue see Garfinkel 1967.

11.   What is at issue is not the actual state of Don's knowledge but rather the speaker's analysis of what is known by his recipient. Further, participants in conversation have access to systematic resources for affirming, denying or negotiating that analysis (on this issue see works cited in note 9). For detailed study of specific ways in which participants analyze what their co-participants know, display that analysis to each other, and utilize that analysis in the detailed production of their talk, see Schegloff 1972.

12.   Sacks (10-19-71) notes that tellables and news of various types are organized so that one should tell particular others about some piece of news at the first opportunity. This accounts in part for the phenomenon that a party can be asked about someone that he hasn't just seen and nevertheless state that the asked-about party is "all right." If some major event had occurred the assumption is that one would have been called and told about it. For spouses the class of events that one member of the couple should tell the other is extremely large, and in fact if a spouse tells others some piece of news that he could have told his partner but didn't, this can constitute grounds for complaint:

Indeed, pretty much anything you would properly tell anybody else, you will have or should have told your spouse on the first occasion you could have—which will characteristically be

before you've had occasion to, in public with your spouse, be
telling someone else. It would plainly be bizarre, seeing your
spouse everyday, to, on a Saturday night in the company of
others, announce that you got a raise on Wednesday. She
might well figure that something is up in that you didn't tell her
that. (Ibid:7-8)

Sack's analysis makes explicit some of the structures enabling all participants in the present
data to legitimately see that Beth should know that John has given up smoking cigarettes.

This analysis also provides a systematic basis for the co-presence of knowing and
unknowing recipients. Speakers regularly find themselves telling a story to unknowing recipients in the presence of a knowing recipient, their spouse. The rules for telling events to
relevant others thus run into conflict with the general rule that one should not tell someone
something they already know. This leads to

a modification of the general rule "don't tell someone what
you've already told them," a modification for spouses, which
says "in the presence of a variety of people, relax the don't-tell
rule in the case of spouses," i.e., you can tell a story to a variety of people including your spouse that you've already told
only your spouse. (Ibid:9)

The simultaneous presence of both unknowing and knowing recipients is thus a systematic
product of particular conversational structures. Despite the fact that the rule that a speaker
shouldn't tell his recipient something that the recipient already knows can be relaxed in
such cases, this situation poses particular problems for the interaction of the participants,
some of which are being examined in the present data.
13.   The analytic notion of lamination as a structural feature of events and actions is
discussed in Goffman (1974, pp. 82, 156-157).
14.   An interesting discussion of how measurements producing "round numbers" can
construct distinct cultural phenomena (a "four-minute mile" for example) is provided by
Lotz (1968). Jefferson (1973, pp. 65-66) provides some analysis of how participants in conversation orient to and utilize this phenomenon in the construction of their talk. Gusfield
(1976, p. 20) notes how numbers that are recognizably not round, such as percentages given
in decimals, may be employed by a scientist to demonstrate "meticulous attention to
details. . .thereby avoiding a judgment by the reader that he has been less than
scrupulous."
15.   For example, few other than a particular couple have any interest in the anniversary
of their meeting.
16.   Sacks (1966, Fall Quarter Lecture 1:18-19) notes that in multi-party conversation in a
nonaddressed recipient is not expected to behave as an overhearer to the exchange between
the speaker and his addressed recipient but rather can be held responsible for knowing what
happened in that exchange.
17.   Jefferson (1974a, pp. 185-186) provides evidence that participants in conversation do
orient to such fragments as word-beginnings and analyzes the procedures utilized for such
recognition.
18.   On this issue see Sacks (1974, p. 341). The alternative in fact produced at this point
also has this relevance. Sacks (1-15-70:31) provides some analysis of the use of the word
"today" in reports and announcements. He notes that this term does not simply stand in

contrast to other names for days as a way of specifying a time reference but rather warrants the report as news.

19. The relevance of a recipient's acknowledging the newsworthiness of an event and ways in which this is done have been investigated by Terasaki (1976, pp. 4-9).

20. Some structural reasons for why this should be the case were noted in note 12.

21. For a more complete examination of this process see Goodwin (1977).

22. See for example Sacks (1973), Jefferson (1974a, pp. 189-190) and Sack's first three Fall 1971 class lectures.

23. On this issue see Sacks 1963, Schegloff 1972, Schegloff and Sacks 1973 (especially p. 290), Garfinkel 1967, and Sudnow 1967.

24. With respect to these issues see also Schegloff's analysis (1968, p. 1083) of the property he refers to as "conditional relevance":

> By conditional relevance of one item on another we mean: given the first, the second is expectable; upon its occurrence it can be seen to be a second item to the first; upon its nonoccurrence it can be seen to be officially absent—all this provided by the occurrence of the first item.

25. The operation of this rule is more completely described in Goodwin 1977. Among other things, the rule provides the participants with different rights to look at each other within the turn, with the speaker being expected to gaze only at a gazing hearer, while the hearer may gaze at both a gazing and a nongazing speaker. This distribution of permissible lookings may account in some measure for the repeated finding that hearers look at speakers more than speakers look at hearers (see for example Exline 1974, p. 74; Argyle 1969, p. 107; Allen and Guy 1974, pp. 139-140; Kendon 1967, p. 26; and Nielsen 1964). Rule 2 also establishes a preferred sequencing for the gaze of the parties at turn beginning, with the hearer expected to bring his gaze to the speaker before speaker brings his gaze to hearer. Sequencing in the opposite order produces a situation where the speaker is gazing at a nongazing hearer. This implication of the rule is consistent with the finding of Kendon (1967, p. 33) that a speaker looks away at the beginning of his utterance, while the hearer gazes toward the speaker there.

26. The actions of speaker and hearer constitute a type of summons-answer sequence. Schegloff (1968) has provided detailed analysis of such sequences and how they are employed to open conversations. Though the present sequence occurs within the turn, rather than at the beginning of a whole conversation, it possesses the properties described by Schegloff. For example, the absence of an answer from a hearer is a relevant event which may provide for recycling of the speaker's summons, and the speaker has the obligation to produce further talk after the summons is answered by the hearer. For more detailed examination of the present sequence see Goodwin 1977. The fact that a sequence originally analyzed as operative in the exchange of turns is also found to organize phenomena within the turn would seem to indicate that the structures notes and analyzed by Sacks and his colleagues operate quite generally and organize a very wide range of phenomena in conversation, and perhaps in human interaction in general.

27. The structure of this process raises doubts about the validity of such arguments as the following: "While. . .hesitations mark speaker uncertainty they have little utility for the listener" (Martin and Strange 1968, p. 474).

Hesitation phenomena, such as restarts and pauses, have received considerable study from psychologists. In such research, phrasal breaks are assumed to result from processes entirely internal to the speaker, such as anxiety, cognitive difficulty, or problems in encoding the utterance (see for example Goldman-Eisler 1961, p. 19; Boomer 1965, p. 148; Dittman 1974, p. 179; Henderson 1974, p. 122; Mahl 1959, p. 110). The present data raises an alternative possibility, specifically, that the actions of the hearer as well as the speaker might be relevant to the production of phrasal breaks by the speaker. It certainly cannot be argued that processes internal to the speaker are irrelevant to the production of phrasal breaks or that the hearer is implicated in the production of all phrasal breaks. However, in cases where the speaker's phrasal break is coordinated with specific actions of the hearer it would seem inadequate to attempt to specify either the distribution of phrasal breaks within the utterance or the processes providing for their occurrence without reference to the actions of the hearer. The present work thus complements a particular line of research in psychology by investigating interactively phenomena which have there been investigated from an individual perspective.

The general organization of repair in conversation has received considerable study from Sacks and his colleagues (see for example Schegloff, Jefferson, and Sacks 1977, Sacks, Schegloff, and Jefferson 1974, Jefferson 1972, Schegloff 1972, Jefferson 1974a, and Sacks 1974).

28. Another example of this phenomenon is found at the end of the first section of John's sentence, where a no-gap transition to Don's "Yea:h," occurs in part because the final sound of the word "cigarettes::" is lengthened. Sacks, Schegloff, and Jefferson (1974) note that the end of a turn constructional unit "is in fact a consequential locus of articulatory variation" (p. 707), and indeed provides one systematic basis for the occurrence of overlap.

29. These alternatives differ also in their length. The sentence could have reached completion after "ago" if the speaker had begun this section of it with "a" rather than "one" ("I gave up smoking cigarettes a week ago"). However the idiom begun with "one" projects the inclusion of a specific time reference such as "today" after "ago." The speaker also might have specified the time with a still shorter phrase such as "last week" (and indeed, as was seen above, the cut-off "l" at the beginning of this section provides some indication that such an alternative was in fact begun but changed). If this is in fact the case the speaker in this example, faced with the task of securing a new recipient's gaze in this section has gone from a short unit ("last week"), skipped the next longest ("a week ago"), and found a longer one ("one week ago today"), providing more time in his sentence for his task to be a accomplished. I am indebted to Gail Jefferson for bringing this progression to my attention.

30. The turn-taking rules of Sacks, Schegloff, and Jefferson (1974) explicitly provide for the possibility of a sentence being extended past its initial point of possible completion, and Sacks and his colleagues have provided considerable analysis of this phenomenon.

31. Jefferson (1973) has described

> 'utterance lengtheners' which indicate to the recipient that the utterance can have been completed so that he may begin to talk, while as well providing that the ongoing speaker has not stopped talking. This may be seen as a technique for specifically 'avoiding' . . . . a pause between the utterance containing the problematic component and the recipients' response. (p 69)

REFERENCES

Allen, Donald E., and Guy, Rebecca F. (1974). *Conversation Analysis: The Sociology of Talk.* The Hague: Mouton.

Argyle, Michael (1969). *Social Interaction.* London: Methuen.

Argyle, Michael, and Cook, Mark (1976). *Gaze and Mutual Gaze.* Cambridge: Cambridge University Press.

Boomer, Donald S. (1965). Hesitation and grammatical encoding. *Language and Speech* 8:148-158.

Chomsky, Noam (1965). *Aspects of the Theory of Syntax.* Cambridge: M.I.T. Press.

Coulthard, Malcolm, and Ashby, Margaret (1975). Talking with the doctor. *Journal of Communication* 25:140-147.

Dittman, Allen T. (1974). The body movement-speech rhythm relationship as a cue to speech encoding. In *Nonverbal Communication,* ed. Shirley Weitz, pp. 169-181. New York: Oxford University Press.

Ekman, Paul, and Friesen, Wallace V. (1974). Nonverbal leakage and clues to deception. In *Nonverbal Communication,* ed. Shirley Weitz, pp. 269-290. New York: Oxford University Press.

Exline, Ralph V. (1974). Visual interaction: the glances of power and preference. In *Nonverbal Communication,* ed. Shirley Weitz, pp. 65-92. New York: Oxford University Press.

Garfinkel, Harold (1967). *Studies in Ethnomethodology.* Englewood Cliffs, New Jersey: Prentice-Hall.

Goffman, Erving (1963). *Behavior in Public Places: Notes on the Social Organization of Gatherings.* New York: Free Press.

_____, (1967). *Interaction Ritual: Essays in Face to Face Behavior.* Garden City, New York: Doubleday.

_____, (1974). *Frame Analysis: an Essay on the Organization of Experience.* New York: Harper and Row.

Goldman-Eisler, Freida (1961). A comparative study of two hesitation phenomena. *Language and Speech* 4:18-26.

Goodwin, Charles (1977). Some Aspects of the Interaction of Speaker and Hearer in the Construction of the Turn at talk in Natural Conversation. Ph.D. dissertation, Annenberg School of Communications, University of Pennsylvania, Philadephia, Pennsylvania.

Gusfield, Joseph (1976). The literary rhetoric of science: comedy and pathos in drinking driver research. *American Sociological Review* 41:16-34.

Henderson, Alan I. (1974). Time patterns in spontaneous speech—cognitive stride or random walk? A reply to Jaffe, et al. (1972). *Langauge and Speech.* 17:119-125.

Jefferson, Gail (1972). Side sequences. In *Studies in Social Interaction,* ed. David Sudnow, pp. 294-338. New York: Free Press.

_____, (1973). A case of precision timing in ordinary conversation: overlapped tag-positioned address terms in closing sequences. *Semiotica* 9:47-96.

_____, (1973). Error correction as an interactional resource. *Language in Society* 2:181-199.

_____, (1974b). In pursuit of laughter: onset sensitivity in invitations to laugh. Paper presented at the 73rd Annual Meeting of the American Anthropological Association, Mexico City.

Kendon, Adam (1967). Some functions of gaze-direction in social interaction. *Acta Psychologica* 26:22-63.

Labov, William (1970). *The Study of Nonstandard English*. Champaign, Illinois: National Council of Teachers of English.

Labov, William, and Fanshell, David (1977). *Therapeutic Discourse: Psychotherapy as Conversation*. New York: Academic.

Lotz, John (1968). On language and culture. In *Language and Culture*, ed. Patrick Gleeson and Nancy Wakefield, pp. 101-105. Columbus, Ohio: Charles E. Merrill.

Lyons, John (1969). *Introduction to Theoretical Linguistics*. Cambridge: Cambridge University Press.

_____, (1972). Human language. In *Non-Verbal Communications*, ed. R.A. Hinde, pp. 49-85. Cambridge: Cambridge University Press.

Mahl, George F. (1959). Exploring emotional states by content analysis. In *Trends in Content Analysis*, ed. Ithiel de Sola Pool, pp. 89-130. Urbana: University of Illinois Press.

Martin, James G., and Strange, Winifred (1968). Determinants of hesitations in spontaneous speech. *Journal of Experimental Psychology* 76:474-479.

Nielsen, G. (1964). *Studies in Self-Confrontation*. Copenhagen: Munksgaard.

Sacks, Harvey (1964). Sociological description. *Berkeley Journal of Sociology* 8:1-16.

_____, (1966). Unpublished class lectures.

_____, (1970). Unpublished class lectures.

_____, (1971). Unpublished class lectures.

_____, (1972). On the analyzability of stories by children. In *Directions in Sociolinguistics: the Ethnography of Communication*, ed. John J. Gumperz and Dell Hymes, pp. 325-345. New York:Holt, Rinehart and Winston.

_____, (1973). On some puns:with some intimations. In *Report of the Twenty-third Annual Round Table Meeting of Linguistics and Language Studies*. ed. Roger W. Shuy, pp. 135-144. Washington, D.C.: Georgetown University Press.

_____, (1974). An analysis of the course of a joke's telling in conversation. In *Explorations in the Ethnography of Speaking*, ed. Richard Bauman and Joel Sherzer, pp. 337-353. Cambridge:Cambridge University Press.

Sacks, Harvey, and Schegloff, Emanuel A. (1978). Two preferences in the organization of reference to persons in conversation and their interaction. This volume.

Sacks, Harvey, Schegloff, Emanuel A. and Jefferson Gail, (1974). A simplest systematics for the organization of turn-taking for conversation. *Language.* 50:696-735.

Scheflen, Albert E. (1974). *How Behavior Means*. Garden City, New York: Doubleday.

Schegloff, Emanuel A. (1968). Sequencing in conversational openings. *American Anthropologist* 70:1075-1095.

Schegloff, Emanuel A. (1972). Notes on a conversational practice: formulating place. In *Studies in Social Interaction,* ed. David Sudnow, pp. 75-119. New York: Free Press.

Schegloff, Emanuel A., and Sacks, Harvey (1973). Opening up closings. *Semotica* 8:289-327.

Schegloff, Emanuel A., Jefferson Gail, and Sacks, Harvey (1975). The preference for self-correction in the organization of repair in conversation. *Language* 53: 361-382.

Sudnow, David (1967). *Passing On: The Social Organization of Dying.* Englewood Cliffs, New Jersey: Prentice-Hall.

Terasaki, Alene (1976). Pre-announcement sequences in conversation. Social Science Working Paper 99. School of Social Sciences. Irvine, California: University of California.

Formulations as Conversational Objects

J. C. Heritage and
D. R. Watson

Heritage and Watson focus on a specific feature of conversations, namely, that as conversations proceed, members may "formulate" what it is they have been saying. Conversations are not unambiguous, even for those who are engaged in their production. The introduction of a formulation enables co-participants to settle on one of many possible interpretations of what they have been saying. They may thus be provided with the sense that they were indeed involved in a colloquy which was self-explicating, i.e., which contained and subsequently revealed its sense to them (and presumably could do so for others). Formulations are shown to be important methods used by members for demonstrating that, among other things, the conversation has been and is ongoingly self-explicating.

A central focus of ethnomethodological work is the analysis of the practical sociological reasoning through which social activity is rendered accountable and orderly. Assumed by this concern is the notion that all scenic[1] features of social interaction are occasioned and established as a concerted practical accomplishment, in and through which the parties display for one another their competence in the practical management of

123

social order. As analysts, our interest is to explicate, in respect of naturally occurring occasions of use, the methods by which such orderliness can be displayed, managed, and recognized by members.[2] While many aspects of the seen-but-unnoticed management of conversational order have been uncovered and described by Sacks and his collaborators[3] in a series of published papers and mimeos, our interest in this paper is to focus on some instances in which the achievement of conversational order becomes for participants, albeit temporarily, a topic in its own right. Such occasions, we believe, routinely emerge when members engage in conversational formulations. In developing this line of inquiry, we have started from the observation, furnished by Garfinkel and Sacks, that—

> A member may treat some part of the conversation as an occasion to describe that conversation, to explain it, or characterize it, or explicate, or translate, or summarize, or furnish the gist of it, or take note of its accordance with rules, or remark on its departure from rules. That is to say, a member may use some part of the conversation as an occasion to *formulate* the conversation. . .

and subsequently,

> . . .along with whatever else may be happening in conversation it may be a feature of the conversation for the conversationalists that they are doing something else; namely, what they are doing is saying-in-so-many-words-what-we-are-doing (or what we are talking about, or who is talking, or who we are, or where we are).
>
> We shall speak of conversationalists'practices of saying-in-so-many-words-what-we-are-doing as formulating.[4]

In this paper we seek to describe some of the properties of a specific subclass of formulations. This subclass may be delimited by noticing that speakers may formulate matters which are conventionally understood as in the first instance known to them. Alternatively, speakers may formulate matters presented to them in, for instance, the delivery of stories, reports, and announcements[5] or, more generally, *news*. These conventional understandings concerning the distribution of knowledge among conversationalists may be marked in a variety of ways. For example, formulations by *news recipients* may be more tentative than formulations by *news deliverers.* Moreover, the receptions of formulations produced by news deliverers may embody different turn-shapes as compared with receptions to formulations produced by news deliverers. The example below illustrates both types of formulation.

Example 1[6]

1. E: Hullo:
2. C: Hello = is eum (0.3) ˙hhh Ilene there?
3. E: Ye::h this is Ile:ne
4. C: Oh hi, = this is Charlie about th'trip tih Syracuse?
5. E: Yeah, (hi)mh
   ( )
6. C: Hi how ya doin'.
7. E: Goo::d,
8. C: ˙ hhheh heh ˙hhh I was um: (o.3) I wen' u- (˙) I spoke t'
9. the gir- I spoke to Caryn. (0.2) ˙hh andum (˙) i' w'z really
10. bad because she decided of all weekends for this one to go away
    (0.6)
11. E: What?
    (0.3)
12. C: She decided to go away this weekend. =
13. E: = Yeah
14. C: ˙hhh (˙) So that (˙) y'know I really don't have a place ti'stay
15. E: ˙hO:::h.
    (0.4)
16. E: ˙hh So you're not gonna go up this weekend?
17. C: = Nu:h I don't think so =
18. E: = How about the following weekend

It may be noticed that line 14, produced by C, is clearly a formulation in terms of Garfinkel and Sacks' discussion. It formulates materials which are conventionally ascribable as (1) known to C and (2) formulated by him as part of his delivery of news. By contrast, E's line 16 formulates materials furnished to her as a news recipient. In this paper, our interest will be focused upon formulations which are produced by news recipients or which are produced concerning materials which are developed over the course of a conversation by both or several parties. That is, our interest is in formulations which characterize states of affairs already by him as part of his delivery of news. By contrast, E's line 16 formulates materials furnished to her as a news recipient. In this paper, our interest will be focused upon formulations which are produced by news recipients or which are produced concerning materials which are developed over the course of a conversation by both or several parties. That is, our interest is in formulations which characterize states of affairs already described or negotiated (in whole or in part) in the preceding talk. In setting out some of the properties of this subclass of formulations, our interest is to indicate some of the work which conversationalists can do through these properties with respect, in particular, to the ongoing management of conversational order. Before proceeding to this task, however, we will note in a gross way some of the problems which face co-conversationalists in the practical management of conversation as an orderly achievement.

In respect of naturally occurring, naturally situated conversation, the practical management of social order is problematic from two *analytically* distinguishable points of view.

1.   The turn-taking system for natural conversation operates on a turn-by-turn or utterance-by-utterance basis and thus works on the level of single transitions at a time: it is, in short, a local management system which is interactionally administered by the co-participants.[7] Additionally, the slots which are created through the turn-taking system should preferably contain items (or utterances) whose selection can be found by co-conversationalists to be nonrandom and thus tied to occasioned aspects of "the talk thus far." In natural conversation, therefore, members must ongoingly monitor utterances for possible turn-transition-relevant points; similarly, with the items which come to fill what will be preceding turns or slots, members must ongoingly both search for the methodic basis of their selection and locate the prospective consequentiality of such selections for future talk.

2.   The stretches of talk which fill conversational slots are overwhelmingly made up of indexical expressions whose "for-all-practical-purposes" definiteness of sense can only be assured, for participants, by tacit reference to the contextual features of the interaction (including, of course, those established in and through the conversation itself as an ordered phenomenon), and by ad hoc reference to tacitly held-in-common background understandings and expectancies (commonsense knowledge of social structures). Thus in their practical task of recognizing order and coherence both in stretches of talk and in the settings of such talk which reflexively document one another, members are constantly and unrelievedly informed by tacitly held background understandings. Members' incessant monitoring of these held-in-common understandings

is a crucial feature of their procedures of practical reasoning in retrieving or repairing the context-dependent features (indexical particulars) of conversational settings in such a way as to render them orderly-for-all-practical-purposes.

This gross consideration of some of the central issues in the practical management of conversational order can yield us two general points concerning the properties of formulations.

1. Insofar as conversational formulations are grossly oriented to by members as conversational actions of a recognizable type, their properties may be sensitive to the basic parameters of the turn-taking system for natural conversation. For instance, they may be organized with regard to potential first utterance completion points, etc. In particular, analysis of the sequentially organized properties of formulations may indicate that formulations are treatable, by analyst and layman alike, as cases of a conventionally given class of serially organized utterances whose operation is sensitive to these basic parameters. Such sensitivities have already been isolated and explicated with respect to such conversational activities as greetings, closings, questions, invitations, and the like. In each case, the activity in question has been found to be conventionally organized in two parts (e.g., greeting-return greeting, question-answer) in which the second part of the pair of conversational actions is placed immediately after the provision of the first pair part. This adjacency pair[8] organization of the above mentioned conversational activities is finely sensitive to the turn-taking organization of natural conversation and also constitutes, for such activities, a constraint on the potential flexibility of the turn-taking system as a locally managed organization. One possibility then, is that formulations may, upon inspection, prove to be organized in a similar way so as to constitute an oriented-to constraint which is sensitive to the local management of talk.

2. We can observe that, insofar as formulations are themselves made up of indexical expressions, they cannot constitute a once-and-for-all solution for the practical problems of achieving definiteness of sense. In fact, as Garfinkel and Sacks observe,

> the very resources of natural language assure that doing formulating is itself for members a routine source of complaints, faults, troubles and recommended remedies, *essentially*.[9]

A part of our task, then, will be to examine how the achievements of formulations—together with their alternatives (e.g., complaints, faults, troubles, and recommended remedies)—are managed within the conversational context of turn-taking in general and adjacency pairing of utterances in particular. Given the problems inherent in the practical management of descriptions—problems summarized by Garfinkel and Sacks in the observation that

> a description,. . .in the ways that it may be a constituent part of the circumstances it describes, in endless ways and unavoidably elaborates those circumstances and is elaborated by them[10]

—it is clear that formulations can do no more than gloss[11] the circumstances they describe, where the practical achievement of such glosses is itself premised for members in the assurance that they can mean, and count upon meaning, "more than they can say in so many words." Formulations thus essentially preserve or reestablish the problems inherent in the practical management of descriptions. It can, therefore, be no part of their work to finally terminate, or provide "time out" from such problems. On the contrary: a generic conventional feature of the work of doing formulations consists of the involvement of members in a reflexive consultation of the conversation thus far and/or some naturally bounded segment of that conversation. Put another way, formulations—as a part of the conventional apparatus usable for the generation of conversational order—occasion a collaborative inspection of conversational materials, particulars, mentionables, etc. that have been furnished in the conversation thus far. As a class of glossing practices, formulations are treatable as embedded in such materials.

In Garfinkel and Sacks' terms then, the status of formulations as "proper glosses" may be adjudged by members through a retrospective consultation of, and a reliance upon, "accountable texts" furnished in the conversation in progress. It is in this sense that members may, via the production of formulations, be seen as engineering a "folding back"[12] of the conversation upon itself. Such inspections themselves unrelievedly rely upon the reflexive or self-explicating (i.e., describable) properties of the materials consulted. Thus the very embeddedness of formulations constitutes a crucial aspect of their immense practical utility. Such embeddedness or contextuality is thus the very antithesis of a liability or defect.

The uses of formulations are multiplex. As we shall see, they may be used to address an immense variety of matters, these matters being, in their most specific terms, heavily embedded in the specific stretches of talk in which they occur. Nor is it the case that formulations are resorted to only on occasions when members orient to a conversation as being in-some way troublesome as regards sense or as regards some more specific practical issue as given by the relevances in a particular segment of talk.[13]

With this said, however, it can be suggested that while the problem of multiple accounts (e.g., discrepancies, however small, in what the participants have monitored as "the sense of the conversation so far") is relevant in a general way to formulating work, the manifest and specific relevance of multiple discrepant accounts as an explicitly oriented-to issue varies with the occasion under inspection.

In sum, on a given occasion of formulating, participants may not explicitly orient to (or treat as problematic) the possibility of competing readings of the conversation: : indeed, members' relevances on an occasion of formulating may well be primarily geared to the specific practical interactional tasks to be achieved in and through that occasion. However, it can be claimed that *as analysts* we can work from members' specific orientations to the general and more abstract relevance of multiple accounts to "formulating work." A warrant for the analyst's "working back" in this way may be found in members' own background understanding that for the performance of any activity there are multiple (though not equally preferred) accounts extractable from that performance. We may also note in a prefatory way that the apparatus mobilized during the doing of formulating work operates in the same way (and is analyzable in the same terms)—irrespective of whether the issue of discrepancies in sense is explicitly attended to by conversationalists.

An Initial Characterization of Formulations by Type

We can start with the general observation that understanding is a practical achievement in conversation and that there may be junctures in and items of the conversation where the business at hand is manifestly and specifically to exhibit participants' understanding.[14] A second observation is that repeat utterances are equivocal as demonstrations of understanding, and that unequivocal displays of understanding can be achieved by producing a transformation or paraphrase of some prior utterance.[15] Such paraphrases preserve relevant features of a prior utterance or utterances while also recasting them. They thus manifest three central properties: preservation, deletion and transformation. These features are readily detectable in the following sequence in which a solicitor is being interviewed on a radio program:

Example 2[16]

S: The inescapable facts are these, er in nineteen thirty
    two when he was er aged twenty three mister Harvey
    was er committed to Rampton hospital under something
    called the mental deficiency act nineteen thirteen which
    of course is a statute that was swept away years ago
    and er he was committed as far as I can er find out on an
    order by a single magistrate er sitting I think in private.
I: How long did he spend in Rampton
S: Well he was in er Rampton and Mosside hospitals er
    alternatively er until nineteen sixty one
F———▶I: That's the best part of <u>thirty</u> years
S: That's right. Now in nineteen sixty one . . .

In this example, the interviewer's formulating utterance: "That's the
best part of <u>thirty</u> years" exhibits these three properties. Specifically, it
preserves the length of time Mr. Harvey was in hospital whilst simultaneously *deleting* such information as: the names of the hospitals involved, the Act of Parliament under which Mr. Harvey was committed,
what subsequently happened to the Act, the circumstances of his com-
mittal and so on. At the same time, the interviewer's utterance *transforms* some of the information furnished to him (i.e., that Mr. Harvey
entered hospital in 1932 and left in 1961) and re-presents this information
as the outcome of an arithmetical operation: "That's the best part of
<u>thirty</u> years." In furnishing the formulation, the interviewer re-describes
or re-references parts of the information already delivered to him, thus
preserving them 'in other words.'

Bearing these features of preservation, deletion and transformation in
mind, we now present a gross characterization of two types of conversational formulation produced by news recipients: gists and upshots.

1. Members may, on occasion, formulate the sense or gist achieved
thus far either in a conversation *in toto* or in some foregoing section of
the conversation. Such formulations may, and frequently do, come to
constitute clarifications, or demonstrations of comprehension or in-
touchness with the talk thus far. The following extracts exhibit this type
of formulation.

Example 3

(Extract from a telephone conversation between a crisis intervention center staff member (S) and a male caller (C) whose request to be put in
touch with a marriage bureau has been unsuccessful)

107. S: Yeah, well the only thing I can suggest is
       th- unless you try and
108.   join s-s- some of these clubs or- I know
       there's plenty of Irish
109.   clubs in the city you know where they have
       dancing/ and stuff
110.   like this er- I I if
111. C: (yes yes yeah yes I know what
112. S: you know what I mean (.....) I mean these
       are the only places I can sug-
113. C: you mean yes)
114. S: -gest to you Sean / I mean er there's all
       sorts of other other kinds
115.   of girls
116. C: huhum huhum
G——►117. S: you know, but-er she (these're) not the
       type you're wanting you're
118.   wanting- to meet a girl so that you might
       settle down one day and get
119.   married
120. C: that's right sir yes

Example 4

(Extract from a telephone conversation between a crisis intervention center staff member and a female caller)

G——►187. C: (...)It's a terrible cruel world, you just don't
188.   want to hear about it
189. S: No I haven't said that I don't want to hear
       at all Mrs. N.
190. C: You have I can tell you have and nobody
       wants to know .....

Example 5

(Extract from a face-to-face interview with the "Slimmer of the Year" relayed on radio)

27. S: You have a shell that for so long pro-
          tects you but sometimes
28.   things creep through the shell and then
          you become really aware
29.   of how awful you feel. I never ever felt
          my age or looked my
30.   age I was always older-people took me
          for older. And when I was
31.   at college I think I looked a matronly
          fifty. And I was completely
32.   alone one weekend and I got to this
          stage where I almost jumped
33.   in the river. I just felt life wasn't worth it
          any more - it hadn't
34.   anything to offer and if this was living I
          had had enough
G→35. I: You really were prepared to commit
          suicide because you were a
36.   big fatty
37. S: Yes, because I   - I just didn't see
          anything in life that I had to look for-
          ward to. . . . . . .

Example 6

(Extract from a face-to-face interview with a parent of an I.R.A. suspect believed to be on the run in England)

12. P: Margaret couldn't possibly have been in
13.   England for we were in touch with her as
          my husband has said constant for the
14.   past two years. em- one of the reasons
          why I'm almost certain she wasn't
15.   in England was anybody who leaves
          Northern Ireland for the safety
16.   of er- the republic so to speak em- they
          could be arrested in

17.		England and for that reason they probably would never have gone
18.		to England and the-he one of the reasons why she almost certainly definitely didn't go to England
20.	I:	What exactly was her fear about what might happen to her living
21.		here?
22.	P:	Most er- people here are - families certain families are harassed
23.		to the extent that er- they'd probably be interned // (........)
24.	I:	because they're
25.		republican families
26.	P:	Because they're republican families they'd be interned and detained
27.		and things like that and she'd thought it was better to go somewhere
28.		like the Republic of Ireland where she wouldn't come in for that
29.		harassment
30.	I:	But you say that she's had nothing to do with sectarian activities
31.	P:	None-so whatsoever. She left here after she left school and took
32.		a job in the Republic
33.	I:	What sort of a girl is she? Can you describe her to me
34.	P:	(Interview continues)

G ⟶ 30.

Example 7[17]

(Extract from a group therapy session—approximately one hour after its commencement—which a session member G is being questioned about differences in his eating habits while at home and in public. Between lines 1 and 77, it has been discovered that he will eat food which upset his stomach in public places whereas at home he will leave the food.)

1.	Dr:	How are you <u>eat</u> -ing.
2.	G:	I've eten everything since I've been 'ear
3.	Dr:	Heh heh h(h)ave you.

4. G: Bu//t - when I'm at home I pick and
          choose.
:   ::   . . . . .
:   ::   . . . . .
77. P: Would - why why doesn't he just lea:ve
          it: (0.5) (   ) =
78. G: = Which I don't like leavin it in com-
          pany with people around
79.   me (0.5) cos I always have that feeling
          that their sayin
80.   oh well (1.0) he:s just a (   ) pickin it
G——▶81. Dr: So what you'r saying is that you'r self
          conscious
82. G: Uhm
83. Dr: In company: =
84. G: = Ye//s
G——▶85. Dr: You   -you don't have the confidence
          (1.0) to do your thing (0.5)
86.   You conform for the sake of con:formity
87. G: With me:als?
88. Dr: Yes =
89. G: = *Yes//uhm
90. Dr: You see. (1.5) Why do you do this?

2. Members may simply move directly to the formulation of upshots,
which presuppose some unexplicated version of gist, as in the following
examples:

Example 8

(Extract from a radio interview with Mr. John Gouriet (G) after his successful application to the Court of Appeal for leave to take out an in-
junction against a boycott of mail to South Africa planned by the Union
of Post Office Workers)

I: If occasion -if occasion 'rises again will
      you take similar action?
G: Well we have never hesitated so far to er take
      action where er freedom is being abused.
U——▶I: So there might be another occasion on which
      you will use the law against unions

G: Not necessarily against unions but against
any body or which has become over mighty
er and is abusing its responsibilities er if that
happens to be a trades union so be it but we're
<u>not</u> I repeat <u>not</u> er looking out er for trouble to
bash the trades union er the unions have their
proper role to play and I believe that to be not
in the political field

Example 9

(Extract from a telephone conversation between a crisis intervention
center staff member and a caller who is in the process of completing a
lengthy description of someone who has absconded from the caller's hotel
without paying the bill)

19. C: now a: red 100 came for her and I think
she phoned you before it
20.   came, would you have any record - of it
you know?
21. S: er well I'm sorry but we just can't divulge
any information at all
U──▶22. C: you can't do anything
23. S: I'm sorry I can't no
24. C: no:
25. S: I think your best plan . . . . . .

Example 10

(Extract from a telephone interview with Dr. Conor Cruse O'Brien
relayed on radio)

12. O'B: The Dublin government is extremely
concerned er- especially
13.   about the growth in political sectarian
murders er- in Northern
14.   Ireland and the er-government is anx-
ious that all possible steps
15.   er- be taken and to try to control this
situation we realise the
16.   extreme difficulty er- in doing it and
the government is prepared

17.   er- to cooperate in every way in the er-
           pulling down of the various
18.   violent er- organisations and gangs
           which exist on both sides of
19.   the border
U→20. I: You'd support Mr. Rees if he decided
           on er- tougher security than
21.   he is instituting at present
22. O'B: In general, yes. We the government
           has publicly welcomed. . . . . .

In this paper, our central concern is with formulations of conversational gists and, to a lesser extent, with formulations of upshots. Our aim is to discuss the particular significance of the reflexivities of conversational formulations of gists and to explicate some of the interactional work which can be achieved in and through such reflexities.

Some General Features of Conversational Formulations of Gist

In this section we address ourselves to a general consideration of the special claims that can warrantably be made as to the specific significances of the reflexivities of conversational formulations of gists. Perhaps we can begin to establish these significances by reiterating that formulations cannot constitute once-and-for-all solutions to the problems of the practical management of sense. Similarly, the fact that formulations may turn the sense accomplished in a conversation into a topic in its own right does not imply that formulations are the only self-descriptive features of a conversation that could otherwise remain non-self-descriptive or nonreflexive. On the contrary, all talk is essentially reflexive or self-descriptive in that the resources being mobilized in establishing the sense of the conversations are also being invoked or consulted as part of assembling of sense. In this sense the conversation can be said to constitute a "self-explicating colloquy."[18] With this point in mind, a preliminary inspection of our materials would suggest the following.

1. We can begin to indicate the significance of formulations of gist by suggesting that since formulations invoke and initiate a consultative "reflection" on the whole, or some part of the "rest" of the conversa-

tion, they can work to establish the members' fact that the conversation *has been* a self-explicating colloquy, a collaborative unfolding of interpretive resources. In that formulations involve members in the collaborative redemonstration of the sense of gist of a conversation, they occasion an "instanced fixing" or "reading" or "redemonstration" of the self-descriptive properties of conversation.

2. In the introductory section we outlined two analytically distinguished points of views from which the practical management of conversational order might be viewed as a routine source of troubles. The first point of view provides that the sequential organization of conversation is itself an artful accomplishment for which there exist conventional devices[19] which may be used to effect "repairs" in the event of some perceived breakdown in the achievement of sequential organization. Similarly, the second point of view provides that members have a potential "descriptions problem," though the potentially problematic element may not always be actualized or manifested in the specific practical relevances addressed by members on particular occasions. The potential descriptions problem resides in the tacitly oriented-to fact that for every description furnished using the resources of natural language, a for-all-practical-purposes definiteness of sense must be established through the use of contextual resources in ad hoc ways. The ad hoc character of the consultation of contextual resources may result in different readings for utterances, stretches of talk, or even conversations as a whole. A corollary of this is that conversations or stretches of conversations may, on occasion and in strictly occasioned ways, prove amenable to multiple glosses providing, in turn, for the possibility of multiple or multi-implicative gists or upshots.

In sum, multiple readings may, on occasion, prove extractable from stretches of conversation and, by the same token, members may thus be oriented to the occasioned multifaceted quality of their conversational productions with a view to establishing preferences among available readings. Thus, given that it is not the case that members can invariably treat stretches of conversation as automatically unproblematic from a descriptive point of view, it is clear that a concerted arrival at a "determinate, for-all-practical-purposes" reading of a stretch of conversation may, on occasion, be treated as problematic and hence in need of repair.

3. Whereas the above comments are intended to address the possibility that conversational activities may be mutliply accountable or multi-implicative, we do not intend to imply that the production of formulations is invariantly and manifestly addressed to this potential multiple accountability or multi-implicativeness. Much of our data indicates that formulations are commonly used during the routine course of

specifically unproblematic conversations or stretches of talk. In such un-problematic occasions, formulations may be used to address practical matters in which the multiple-readings issue is, for members, no more than a nonmanifested part of the taken-for-granted background understandings informing the production and monitoring of these for-mulations.

4. Insofar as a routinely produced formulations may be judged by a recipient to be defective or nonpreferred, it may occasion a retrospective inspection of conversational materials which is addressed to the multiple accountability of such materials.

5. The point that formulations may be varyingly addressed to the mutliple readings extractable from some self-explicating stretch of talk, rather than to failures of comprehension or attention, can be exemplified by the following observation: lapses of understanding or attention with regard to some stretch of talk may be expressed by the provision of a "misapprehension marker" (such as "questioning repeats") which works to elicit corrections as in the following "statement-misapprehen-sion-correction" sequence:

(1)   But the air's gotta come in there, and the air
      is sorta infiltrated with little uh pixy dust.
      ..   ....
(2)   "Pixy dust"".?
      ..   ..
      ..   ..
(3)   "Radioactivity" I think is what he means.[20]

In contrast, the provision of formulations regularly involves the provi-sion of some "candidate reading" for a preceding stretch of talk whose adequacy or preferredness may subsequently be decided upon, e.g.,

(1)   . . . I just felt life wasn't worth it anymore - it
      hadn't anything to offer and if this was living
      I had had enough
(2)   You really were prepared to commit suicide
      because you were a big fatty
(3)   Yes, because ....

By contrast, then, with sequences of talk whose business is to demonstrate some form of failure to understand and to solicit remedies for such failure, we may grossly say that the primary business of for-mulations is to demonstrate understanding and, presumptively, to have that understanding attended to and, as a first preference, endorsed.

6. Thus formulations of gist are not the junctures of conversation where it becomes a self-explicating colloquy. Instead, formulations constitute a members' method for providing that the conversation *has been* and is *ongoingly* a self-explicating colloquy: a specific instanced sense of the colloquy being retrievable *as part and parcel of this demonstration.*

Formulations and Conversational Structure

In this section, we address some properties of formulations and some aspects of the conversational work which can be achieved in and through them. We address these matters through a consideration of three orders of conversational organization outlined by Sacks and Schegloff, namely, speaker turn or utterance-by-utterance organization, topical organization, and organization at the level of the unit "a single conversation". Before we proceed, we note an important caveat with respect to this enterprise (and with respect to our previous analytic distinction between achieving sequential and descriptive order), that while such analytic isolations of conversational orders or general issues relating to conversational construction may prove useful from an analytic point of view, the production and monitoring of the orderliness of conversation is charactèristically achieved through the simultaneous and integrated treatment of utterances in terms of all orders and with respect to the solution of all problems in maintaining conversational coherence.

(a) Utterance-by-Utterance Organization

In the introductory section of this paper, we noted that a universal issue in members' ongoing management of conversation is the requirement that members discover the basis for the selection of items which fill just-completed slots. For every about-to-be-produced next utterance, members must locate a methodic basis for the previous utterance's production and assess the prospective consequentiality of that basis for the production of a next utterance. Similarly, for many just-produced utterances, a methodic basis for their selection may be found in some relationship to an immediately preceding utterance. There is thus a sense in which some preceding utterance may be said to provide a constraint on the production of some next utterance: indeed if this were not grossly the case the sequential analysis of conversation would prove impossible and it would be hard to find a rationale for referring to some sequentially ordered collection of utterances as "a conversation".

In achieving methodic solutions to the pervasively relevant "why that now" issues in terms of which items can be found to be selected nonrandomly for slots, and in producing.further sequentially appropriate utterances in line with such solutions, members may be said to be displaying for one another their "receptions"[21] of utterances and their orientation to the prospective consequentiality of such receptions. While, for many utterances, receptions may be produced in relatively unconstrained ways (in that the display of a reception may be achieved through a wide variety of utterances types), in those cases where utterances are analyzable into specific, sequentially implicative actions, a constraint on their reception will consist in the requirement to produce some sequentially appropriate next action. For many such actions, receptions may be achieved through a variety of sequentially appropriate next actions. Thus "wisecracks" may have their reception established through "laughter" or "retorts".[22] Similarly, complaints may have their reception established through such sequentially appropriate activities as "apologies", "expresions of sympathy", "excuses", "justifications", and so on, but not, for instance, by "laughter". To the extent that receptions of such acts are found to be noticeably absent and such absences may be inspected for their "motivated"character, it is legitimate to speak of such acts as constraining the items which may fill subsequent slots. Thus, while a wisecrack may be transformed into a misapprehension as in the following:

A: ...I shave around Saturday night y'know.
     cause going out Saturday night. hhh
B: You- you know- The rest of the week you don't
     shave but Sa(h) turday night.
A: No, I mean I usually shave in the morning ex-
     cept on Saturday when I shave at night.[23]

To the extent that B's utterance can be found to be a wisecrack independently of A's reception of it as a misapprehension, i.e., from its relation to A's first utterance, A's reception of it (and hence transformation of it) can be inspected to find, for instance, that he has no sense of humor. Similarly, failure to respond in a sequentially appropriate way to a complaint can be inspected for evidence of a lack of sympathy, or even—where the complaint is directed against a co-conversationalist —may be found to constitute an "aggravation" or an expression of hostility.

The most sequentially constraining of all utterances are the first pair parts of what Sacks and Schegloff[24] term "adjacency pairs," where the production of a first pair part requires that a next speaker produce (1) adjacently, (2) a second pair part, (3) of the pair type previously selected by a first speaker. Thus greetings require returns, questions require answers, and offers require acceptances or rejections (or, more generally, decisions).

An inspection of our data indicates not merely that formulations occasion receptions and hence that they are oriented to in adjacent utterances, but also that the character of their receptions is sharply constrained to confirmations or disconfirmations or, more generally, decisions. E.g.:

F	S:	you know, but-er she (these're) not the type you're wanting you're want- to meet a girl so that you might settle down one day and get married
D +	C:	that's right sir yes
F	C:	...... you just don't want to hear about it
D −	S:	No I haven't said I don't want to hear at all Mrs. N.
	C:	You have I can tell you have and nobody wants to know....
	S:	I just felt life wasn't worth it anymore - it hadn't anything to offer and if this was living I had had enough
F	I:	You really were prepared to commit suicide because you were a big fatty
D +	S:	Yes, because ......
F	I:	But you say that she's had nothing to do with sectarian activities
D +	P:	None-so whatsoever ......

Given that formulations involve the provision of candidate readings for the sense established in preceding stretches of talk and thus involve some demonstration or marking of that sense in an instanced way, we may warrantably assert that they are deeply implicative for subsequent talk. It is this sequential implicativeness which, in turn, requires the adjacency pair format for the "formulation-decision" pair. Sacks and Schegloff[25] note that the value of the close ordering embodied in the adjacency pair format derives from that format's assured provision for some desired event, in this case, a decision, to happen next; they conclude that—

> By an adjacently placed second, a speaker can show that he understood what a prior aimed at, and that he is willing to go along with that. Also by virtue of the occurrence of an adjacently placed second, the doer of a first can see that what he intended was indeed understood, and that it was or was not accepted. Also, of course, a second can assert his failure to understand or disagreement, and, inspection of a second by a first can allow the first speaker to see that while the second thought he understood, indeed he misunderstood. It is, then, through the use of adjacent positioning that appreciations, failures, corrections etc. can themselves be understandably attempted. Wherever then, there is reason to have the appreciation of some implicativeness made attendable, 'next utterance' is the proper place to do that, and a two-utterance sequence can be employed as a means for doing and checking some intendedly sequentially implicative occurrence in a way that a one utterance sequence can not.[26]

While the specification of "what we are talking (have talked) about" may be undertaken for a variety of contextually bound reasons, e.g., for underlining points, reestablishing previously mentioned mentionables for the construction of inferences, clarifying issues and the like, it is clear that formulations of gists, upshots, or activities are deeply implicative for the development of subsequent talk. Some of this implicativeness can be most clearly observed in the following step-by-step formulation of a problem and its solution.

Example 11

(Extract from a telephone conversation between a crisis intervention center staff member and a girl caller relating to "home troubles" and troubles relative to obtaining qualifications for a desired job)

F   173. S: No, at least you know that you
              want = what you want to do you're
    174.   rather keen to get into the civil
              service
D + 175. C: Yeah
    176. S: So you know you - because you
              know what you want to do
    177.   you're probably as well to wait
              another six or twelve
    178.   months and till you've got your
              other 'O' levels,
    179.   when do you actually take your 'O'
              levels?
    180. C: I take them in June
    181. S: In June
    182. C: Yeah
F   183. S: Yes so you know you will get the
              results and you could get a job
D − 184. C: (Well look) you see, it's not just
              that get's me down it - it
    185.   you know, because my mum's,
              she's she's a bit (. . .)

Given that the decision part of the formulation-decision adjacency pair consists of confirmations and disconfirmations, it is relevant to ask whether some preference exists with respect to the choice of a decision. A preliminary inspection of our data suggests that such a preference does exist with respect to formulations and that confirmations are massively preferred. Confirmations and disconfirmations of formulations them-selves form a subclass of agreements and disagreements which, as Pom-erantz has pointed out, form "a major co-ordinational system linking talk in adjacent turns."[27] Pomerantz also indicates that where agree-ments or disagreements constitute second assessments (that is, assess-ments produced by recipients of first assessments in adjacent turns), agreements—like confirmations of formulations—are massively pre-ferred.

To the extent that formulations of gist constitute candidate readings or redescriptions of stretches of talk, it is possible to locate a basis for the preference for confirmation of formulations in what Pollner has termed the presupposition of a world-essentially-known-in-common.[28] As we have indicated, formulations of gist describe materials which have been collaboratively furnished through an ongoing temporal sequence of talk for which appreciations of that talk's orderliness and sense have been routinely and accountably displayed and have subsequently been treated as a basis for subsequent talk. Disconfirmations of formulations may thus jeopardize the sense of "the talk thus far" as an accountable test which is available as an unequivocal resource for members' collaborative constructions. Hence to directly fault a formulation as a candidate reading for some talk with a "flat" disconfirmation may minimally terminate an ongoing stream of topical talk and initiate a search for a fresh basis on which concerted comprehension can be established—thereby bringing some stretch of talk "back to square one."

Additionally, to directly fault a formulation may come to constitute a criticism of a co-conversationalist's attention to what has been talked about thus far and, since appreciations of that talk will have been accountably furnished, such appreciations may retrospectively be found to have been routine, perfunctory, or even deceitful (as where the ritual "uh huh's" from behind a husband's newspaper are challenged by a wife's "you're not listening to a word I say" or "what have I just been talking about?"—challenges which are defeatable only by the provision of a proper gloss (i.e., a formulation) of the talk (thus far).

More fundamentally, the direct faulting of a formulation may imply a challenge to the formulator's membership: his capacity and competence in monitoring, cognitively processing, and reproducing these gists of talk. Conversely, inadequate responses to formulative utterances may stimulate an inspection of that inadequacy's motivation—an inspection which may culminate in a challenge to the responder's membership, e.g.;

Example 12[29]

(Extract from a face-to-face conversation in which a medical social worker (MSW) has repeatedly explained a set of arrangements for leaving hospital to an elderly female patient.)

> MSW: Oh I think well I think you can go any
>   minute now. I think
> F   we've got everything sorted out.

NonD   P: Do you
       MSW: Yes. Now can you remember what
             day you're going home on?
       P: No
             (2 seconds)
       MSW: It's Monday.
       P: Monday
       MSW: Would you like me to write it down/
             for you
       P: Oh (   )
             I was going to say I ought to put it
             down because I'm so stupid
       MSW: Okay . . . (Utterance continues)

Here the patient's nonprovision of a decision to the MSW's formulation initiates a fourth recapitulation of the arrangements provided for the patient's discharge from hospital, where the patient herself provides for her failure to assemble the conversation's mentionables in terms of her own stupidity (loss of short-term memory), a basis which in turn has previously been provided as a source of other failures in the conversation's sequential organization. The provision of nondecision to formulations may, upon inspection, prove warrantable, however, as in example 13 where a checking operation is interposed between a formulation and a decision.

Example 13

(Extract from a telephone conversation between a crisis intervention center staff member and a male caller concerning the arrangements made by the caller's girlfriend for putting the caller in contact with the center)

         19. S: pardon ((2 seconds)   ) well er!!!
                  do you keep having depressions?
         20. C: pardon?
         21. S: do you keep having depressions?
F   22. C: no oh sorry it's - it's been all mixed
                  up it must be
         23.   just a gag or something y'know
NonD 24. S: oh are you sure?
         25. C: must be yeah

D +   26. S: Okay I'm sorry about that Anthony
       27. C: okay then
       28. S: bye bye

(see also Example 7, lines 85-89)

Given that confirmations of formulations are preferred and that flat disconfirmations of formulations may occasion inspections of conversationalists' capacities and motives in monitoring and comprehending talk, it is not surprising that such disconfirmations of formulations as candidate readings are unusual and, as we shall see, specially accountable. In one of the few examples of flat disconfirmation of a formulations which we have to hand, the disconfirmation is apparently associated with the formulation's directly complaining or accusatory content (see also example 15) where the sequentially appropriate deniability of an accusation is used to override the preference for confirmation of the formulation in which the accusation is embedded.

F   C: .... you just don't want to hear about it
D −   S: No I haven't said I don't want to hear at
            all Mrs. N.
      C: You have I can tell you have and nobody
            wants to know . . .

However, even in this example where the disconfirmation is clearly accountable, we can see one serious consequence for communicative order in the flat disconfirmation of formulations, namely, that what we may call, following Pollner,[30] a conversational "reality disjuncture" is initiated in which mutually exclusive readings of the conversation are proposed and the character of the conversation as an accountable text becomes indeterminate. In such environments, the search for, and location of the motivated character of purportedly defective formulations stands or falls with the original reading of the conversation, and the provision of an (in principle) endless cycle of alternating readings (together with rejections of such readings as specially motivated) is potentiated. The flat disconfirmation of formulations, then, is fraught with problematic implications for the reassembly of a coherent conversational reality.

In view of the foregoing, it is not surprising that disconfirmations of formulations are regularly combined with confirmatory elements, e.g:

Example 11

F   S: Yes so then you know you will get the
         results and you could get a job
D – C: (Well look) you see, it's not just that
         gets me down . . .

Example 8

F   I: So there might be another occasion on
         which you will use the law against
         unions
D – G: Not necessarily against unions but
         against any body er which has become
         over mighty er and is abusing its re-
         sponsibilities . . .

Work on the characteristics of disconfirmations of formulations is continuing and cannot easily be summarized here. Such work indicated that
"seconds" to formulations which combine elements of confirmation and
disconfirmation may be usable for a variety of interactional tasks, and
that a central factor bearing on such tasks concerns the relative ordering
of the confirmation and disconfirmation components.

We have already indicated that formulations constitute members'
methods for demonstrating comprehension of sections of talk. However,
formulations are by no means the only technique for demonstrating such
understanding, nor are the demonstrations achieved in and through them
achieved independently of other aspects of the sequential analysis of
talk. For example, many formulations are constructed through the use of
pronomials and other pro-terms (for instance, what Sacks has called pro-
verbs-to be, to do, etc.—which stand for other verbs) and it is clear that
the interpretation of such utterances as formulating cannot, in any sense,
be independent of the analysis of the sequential emplacement of the pro-
terms used in constructing the utterance. While the large range of pro-
terms have a particular value in eliminating word repetition as a central
tying device in conversation and hence generate large-scale interactional
economies, the achievement of these economies necessitates considerable
collaborative close-order inspectional work on the sequential placement
of pro-terms so as to redress their indexicalities. The value and complexity of this work is only enhanced by considering those (frequent) cases
where the item in terms of which the pro-term is redressed itself contains

pro-terms that must themselves be redressed through establishing a tie to some preceding item.[31] In example 13, for instance, much of the formulating work of line 22-3 is achieved through the indexicalities—

F   22. C: no oh sorry it's-it's been all mixed
                    up it must be
         23.   just a gag or something you know
Non-D 24. S: oh are you sure?
         25. C: must be yeah
D+   26. S:·   okay I'm sorry about that Anthony

—of pro-terms whose referent (the character of the conversation thus far) has itself been established as "mixed up" through contrastive mappings of pro-terms. Similarly, line 25 ("must be yeah") "skip-ties" through the pro-term *be* to the first-part formulating utterance (lines 22-23) and in virtue of that, the pro-term *that* in the (line 26) decision utterance ties through the preceding utterance (line 25) to lines 22-23, thus tying the decision to the formulation across the two-utterance wedge which has been introduced into the adjacency pair format.

The use of tying terms then, in allowing co-conversationalists to exploit the special economies of their indexical properties, occasions close-order collaborative work, thus providing not only what Matthew Speier has metaphorically called "interactional cement" but also for the demonstration of understanding or misunderstanding. The understanding of formulations as such then is in no way independent of the many tying devices (of which pro-terms are an important subset) which contribute to the sequential orderliness of conversation. Indeed, to say that formulations are independent of these devices would be rather like saying that a seam is independent of its stitches. Instead, the role of the many tying devices located within formulating utterances attests to the embeddedness of formulations within the complex, finely grained structure of conversation. In short, we do not propose that formulations are independent of, or substitutes for, the conventional tying devices through which the sequential organization and sense of conversations are managed and achieved: we assert, in contrast, that formulations depend for their sense on their participation in and structuration by such devices.

In this section, we have sought to show that the provision of formulations is highly constraining on the form that an immediately subsequent turn of talk may take. Specifically, a formulation constrains a decision as an immediate next action; where the decision may address the adequacy or the preferredness of the candidate reading of gist embodied in the formulation. With respect to such decisions, confirmations are massively preferred. We have sought to provide a basis for this preference in the interactional implicativeness of disconfirmations of formulations. Such implicativeness may also be a factor informing the construction of disconfirmations using provisional acceptance tokens (such as, "well . . . .") or turn shapes which combine elements of confirmation and disconfirmation varyingly ordered. Finally, we have argued by reference to the example of pro-term tying devices that formulations are assembled for what they are in and through the complex of tying devices by which any serially organized array of talk is assembled for an inspection of its coherence. Thus formulations are not independent of such devices, nor can they act as substitutes for them.

(b) Organization at the Level of Topic

In a sense, all conversations can be seen as organized around topics in that topics are massively available to members as loci around which descriptions of "what has been talked about thus far" can be organized. In this connection it is instructive to note that the notion of topic is one regularly addressed by members as a matter for attention in its own right, for instance, where utterances are judged irrelevant to the topic at hand and their producers are requested to keep to the point.

Given that formulations of gist provide a gloss on "what we are talking about (or have talked about) thus far," their significance for topical organization in conversation seems manifest. As a starting point, we can observe that "first topic analysis," i.e., analysis of "what the conversation is about" or the reason for the conversation, is inseparable from the production of formulations. The making of formulations, then, is a built-in part of rendering conversations preservable and reportable, and it is in this sense that formulations may be said to "fix" what will have turned out to be a (the) topic.

Talking to topic, however, is an active achievement over its course in which the central "load" is borne by the sequential organization of turns at talk through which the parties' utterances build on and extend, and in so doing demonstrate their appreciation of, the orderly development of topical talk. By the same token it is grossly apparent from an inspection of conversational materials that topics may be established or concluded (or indeed "peter out") through the operation of the complex of devices which sustain the sequential organization of turns of talk. In face of these observations, it may legitimately be asked whether formulations have any particular or special role to play with respect to the solution of problems relative to the management of topical organization in conversation. In response to this issue, we may note the following points:

1. In many conversations, long sections of talk may be devoted to the descriptive unfolding of complex collections of matters. Where such a collection is available to one speaker but not to his or her co-conversationalists, the unfolding of that collection may involve the development of a turn pattern which consists of a series of lengthy turns by the knowledgeable speaker complemented by short turns by that speaker's recipients. Under such conditions, the production of formulations by recipients may serve to demonstrate understandings of the *cumulative* import of a previous string of utterances. This work cannot be achieved through the use of continuations (such as "uh huh" and the like), whose work is confined to the claiming of understanding for immediately preceding utterances. Some of our data is culled from conversations which involve the description of complexes of "troubles" whose characteristics are previously totally unknown to the recipients of such communications—communications which ordinarily involve the pattern of turn shapes described above. In such environments, the provision of formulations by news recipients may elegantly address the problem of preserving a sense of cumulative understanding of long stretches of talk.[32] The provision of formulations (or formulating assessments) by communicators of troubles or, more generally, by those who produce a series of long turns, may also address the problem of achieving cumulative sense.

2. Where it is a feature of topical talk that the sense of gist achieved has, over its course, been the object of contest or negotiation, the provision of formulations of gist may work to establish the outcomes of such contests or negotiations 'for another first time'. This use for formulations may be said to be extensively institutionalized in the routine provision for such procedures as "summings up" of meetings and the like. The importance of this role for formulations may be noted in the institutionalized distribution of rights to formulate, which may be held by chairpersons, judges, and the like.

3. Where understandings of gist are used to warrant the construction of some implicativeness, formulations of gist may be established as prefaces to or as part and parcel of the construction of some analysis of such implicativeness.

4. Where the gist of some section of talk involves matters regarded as being of special import or significance, formulations may be used (a) to reattend to such issues, and (b) to mark such gists.

5. The provision of formulations to mark newly arrived-at understandings of gist may, in turn, become a way to terminate talk to some topic prefatory to the establishment to some new topic-at-hand or indeed the termination of the conversation as a whole. In this respect, formulations may work to give a "signature" to a section of topical talk.[33].

6. Where the trajectory of some section of talk is directed to the achievement of some practical end, the provision of a formulation may work to reestablish the collaborative achievement of that end both as a first topic and as an outcome of the conversation's course. Through this means, the making of arrangements and other practical activities may come to formulate and provide a signature for a section of talk or for a whole conversation.

We have already noted that formulations serve to establish and demonstrate for members that a conversation (1) has been a self-explicating colloquy, (2) an instanced reading of which is retrievable as part and parcel of the demonstration, where (3) such an instanced reading may work inter alia to achieve the kinds of practical tasks itemized in 1 to 6 above. We now address the specific advantages which formulations may offer conversationalists in achieving these ends and which, therefore, might undergird the preferredness of formulations for these kinds of work.

A trivial solution to this issue would consist of the observation that an alternative measure, such as the provision of some utterance as, for instance, "we can sum up for a minute," or some similar utterance, might warrant an ascription of inattention from a co-conversationalist. Such a solution is trivial because it is precisely through the preferredness of formulations that the provision of such alternatives as the above may warrant a search for the basis of the nonpreferred alternative, a search which may eventuate in the decision that a co-conversationalist had failed to attend to a conversations' particulars, or that he implies that those particulars are sufficiently defective to be incapable of formulation. Thus it is to the technical basis of the preference for formulations that we must look for a solution to this question.

A beginning for a basis for the preference for formulations (by contrast, for instance, with sequences which work to elicit recapitulations or summaries of topical talk) can be located by observing that it is through the provision of formulations that, inter alia, understandings of gists can be displayed and checked, and discrepancies with respect to gists can be located and remedied. It is noticeable that where, for instance, the provision of a formulation constitutes a "side sequence" devoted to the checking of sense, its *duration* (if successful) reduces to a minimum of one utterance (plus a decision) which minimizes any break in the flow of topical talk, and indeed enables the checking procedure to be successfully embedded in that flow. Thus, although the provision of a formulation-may come to constitute a self-imposed "understanding test" with certain attendant risks and gains, the conversational economies of formulations would appear to be of overriding significance.

Moreover, just as formulations can work to minimize 'breaks' with respect to the flow of topical talk, they can also be used as an economical means to achieve other conversational ends, such as providing constructional materials for the establishment of implicativeness, underlining or marking significances, terminating topics, and incorporating other conversational activities (e.g., "making arrangements") in reassembling the sense of conversational materials. This "double duty" is not available to sequences which elicit recapitulations of conversational materials and this fact further vitiates their utility.

In sum, the provision of formulations is economical (by comparison with alternative sequences) in two respects: (1) if successful, it minimizes the period spent checking a reading without any loss of efficiency in that checking operation, and (2) formulating utterances can be made to do other interactional tasks without losing their simultaneously formulating character. In this sense, formulations may do "double duty" and this may in turn enable conversationalists to check on the sense of a conversation incidentally, casually or even covertly.

Bearing these points in mind, a second source for the economics of formulations may be located by observing that where the provision of a formulation is unsuccessful with respect to the achievement of its tasks (e.g., examples 4 and 12), the sense of "the conversation thus far" becomes an indeterminate matter whose reachievement becomes a first priority.[34] Thus in the utterance following the nondecision in example 12, the medical worker repeated many of the matters which had apparently been established during previous sections of the conversation. In short, the failure of a formulation may recycle entire sections of topical talk as matters now mentionable "for another first time." (Where the formulation comes off as an accusation and is rejected (as in example 4), this recycling of topical talk may become hearable as recrimination.) It is likely that requests for recapitulations or summaries may operate in similar fashion to renew the relevance of, and hence recycle preceding sections of topical talk. Such techniques would, therefore, involve more redundancy and less economy than the direct production of formulations. Moreover, such sections of talk, now (uneconomically) recycled, may once again come to stand in need of formulation and indeed, in principle at least, a potentially endless chain of requested and recycled topical talk may be initiated in this way and could proliferate indefinitely. Thus it is through the provision of formulations that a potentially endless recycling of topical talk may be economically forestalled with some measure of assurance.

Finally, the self-selection which frequently characterizes formulating activities provides an economical solution to issues of speaker selection in the provision of formulations which would routinely arise where utterances such as "can we sum up for a minute?" were used to elicit summaries of gists. This feature may additionally contribute to diminishing the level of technical competition over formulating slots.

In sum, formulations provide an economical basis for topical recapitulation which will normally obviate the possibility of recycling topical talk. In this connection, it is instructive to call the preference for confirmations of formulations noted in the previous section, as well as the tendency for disconfirmation to provide for the nonpreferred character of specific formulations. Disconfirmation of formulations which indicate their nonpreferredness are normally associated with the search for grounds for disconfirmation which may not (or even should not) be exclusively extractable from preceding sections of talk. Where disconfirmation of formulations are followed by (and warranted by) the provision of previously unmentioned mentionables as grounds for disconfirmation, the formulation-decision pair may come to constitute an economical basis through which topic-tying may be achieved, e.g.:

183. S: Yes so you know you will get the results
          and you could get a job
184. C: (Well look) you see, it's not just that
          gets me down it-it
185.   you know, because my mum's she's
          she's a bit. . . . (talk continues about
          mother)

From the above, it is clear that while formulations may provide an economical basis through which to achieve and demonstrate cumulative understandings of gist, with some measure of assurance that topics will not be recycled; their provision in no sense forecloses or determines a conversation's sequential prospects and possibilities. Formulations, like other conversational devices, constitute resources for the achievement of conversational ends rather than foreclosures of conversational possibilities.

(c) Overall Structural Organization of the Unit "A Single Conversation"

While so far we have emphasized that what a formulation will have achieved with respect to topical organization is a contingent matter, perhaps we can now begin to locate a major role for formulations in the achievement of "closings" as a feature of the overall structure of conversations. In particular, it is clear that formulations may come to stand as candidate preclosings[35], that is, as devices which work to set up the prospective relevance of terminal adjacency pairs. e.g:

Example 14

(A complete call between a crisis intervention center staff member (S) and a girl caller (C))

1. S: Hello, hello telephone companions. Can I help you.
2. C: Er good evening love I phoned you (') Friday night er Wednesday
3. S: Wednesday night yes
4. C: About me boyfriend.
5. S: Oh yes.
6. C: Well I couldn't get him to phone you that night
7. S: I see
8. C: So anyway I'm just meeting him now =
9. S: = Yes
10. C: Shall I get him to phone you.
11. S: Yes alright dear.
12. C: Is it alright.
13. S: Yes it'll be alright dear wait just a minute.
14. C: Pardon, co⌐(.....)
15. S: └What's your na- what's your name please love.
16. C: His name's er Arthur Jones.
17. S: Wha-what's your's though your first name love.
18. C: Er Felicity.
19. S: Felicity (') okay, who did you speak to.
20. C: Pardon.
21. S: Who did you speak to on Wednesday night (.......) remember

22. C: Oh well he's always on about committing suicide you know.
23. S: Oh yeh -y- your boyfriend is (ˈ) I see.
24. C: Yeah.
25. S: Okay
26. C: (So we) informed you (of your clo⌈ser to =
27. S: ⌊Yes

    = the) question ⌈(.........)
    =   ⌊Yes o- kay love.
28. S: I'll talk to him my name my name's Robert
29. C: Alright love.
30. S: Okay
G————▶31. C: So I'll tell him to ask for Robert and that's Arthur Jones.
32. S: Yes okay ⌈thanks very much bye
33. C: ⌊(..................) thank you
34. S: G'bye.
35. C: Bye-bye.

Our question now becomes: what special problems exist for members with respect to the closing of conversations that formulations can work to solve?

1.   Insofar as, as Sacks and Schegloff[36] have elegantly demonstrated, there exists for members the problem of collaboratively deciding upon a point at which terminal adjacency pairs may warrantably be inserted to terminate a conversation, the provision of formulations may prospectively warrant such insertions in two ways: (a) Just as formulations may work to close down a topic as a mentionable, so they may work to close down a conversation insofar as the topic thus closed down constitutes a "last" topic. (b) Moreover, in terminating some last topic, the introduction of an utterance which formulates the conversation as a whole (or its first topic) may work to establish a circular, rounded and concluded signature. This work in turn is achieved through:

2.   The reflexive properties of formulations which can work to establish those features of the conversation that are preservable and reportable as its sense, gist, upshot, etc. Where formulations are invoked as part of a closings sequence, they can provide the means through which the parties to a conversation can collaboratively establish its gist before the conversation is closed *and* as part and parcel of its closing. The "social order" of the conversation is thus built into its concerted closure as an integral feature.

3.   Through formulations, the preservable and reportable features of a conversation can be incorporated into such activities as marking sig-

nificances, reestablishing outcomes of negotiations or contests, making arrangements, and so on. As such, formulations may have a discernable value for single topic centered or business-at-hand based conversations and their closings. Indeed, it is through such uses of formulations that participants may establish that such conversations were in fact and "after all" business-based.

4. In respect of 1–3 above, formulations work to exhibit for members the fact that the conversation *has been* an understandable, coherent, decidable, preservable, and reportable—i.e. *orderly*—phenomenon. It is this feature of formulations which requires that the formulation-decision sequence must work on an adjacent utterance basis, and it is in this sense that the three orders of organization in conversation are not, for members, insoluble from one another.

Formulations as Analytical Objects

The sequential structure of natural conversation's character as an unfolding and self-explicating colloquy is a phenomenon of very great complexity whose features have only recently begun to yield to analysis. In this paper we have, firstly, addressed formulations as objects whose provision redemonstrates the self-explicating character of a conversation, and not as objects whose provision can substitute for that self-explicating character. To repeat, in no sense are formulations independent of, or substitutes for, the conventional devices through which the sequential organization and sense of conversations are managed and achieved.

Secondly, just as formulations depend for their sense and intelligibility on the multiplex tying devices which contribute to the sequential orderliness of conversation, so too formulations themselves may be located in utterances which achieve considerably more conversational work than formulating per se. Once again, it is clear that analyzing utterances into conversational activities is not an either/or matter. We have sought to show in this paper that it is precisely through their particular fixative conversational work that formulations may prove valuable in achieving larger conversational undertakings.

Thirdly, it is clear that formulations are not strictly separable from other types of utterances which share sequentially organized properties in common with them. Thus many closed-ended questions (such as "Are you over six feet in height?") require positive or negative decisions as their answers. Similarly, such closed questions can achieve semi-rhetorical status when preferences as to their answers are built into the format of the question, e.g., "you went downtown last night, didn't you?"

Given that these sequentially organized properties of this class of question are held in common with formulations, it is unsurprising that, on occasion, formulating utterances may achieve "questioning work"[38] as in the following examples:

F   30. I: But you say that she's had nothing to
              do with sectarian activities
D + 31. P: None-so whatsoever. She left here
              after she left school and took a job in
              the Republic.

F   35. I: You really were prepared to commit
              suicide because you were a
     36.   big fatty
D + 37. S: Yes, because I-I just didn't see any-
              thing in life that I had to
     38.   look forward to ....

It seems likely that this overlap between the sequential properties of formulations and those of the restricted class of questions mentioned above gives formulations a particular usability for interviewers in the broadcasting media, where formulations can be used to vary the question-answer format of such occasions and to underline aspects of news generated in such interviews as especially important.

Fourth, where formulating utterances are used to achieve larger conversational undertakings, the conventionally organized properties of these larger undertakings may override aspects of the properties of formulations. Thus, as we have already noted, where a formulating utterance achieves accusatory work, the sequential appropriateness of a denial as a second pair part to an accusation overrides the preference for an acceptance as a second pair part to the formulation in which the accusation is embedded. However, while aspects of the properties of formulations may, on occasion, be overridden in this way, it remains true that the majority of their properties remain operative. Thus in legal proceedings the careful, "step-wise" interrogation of witnesses may prove valuable in forestalling the kinds of reality disjunctures which arise when formulating accusations are rejected: indeed such interrogation may be held to be prospectively oriented to the generation of accountable texts whose status is, at least in part, independent of the fluctuating fortunes to which formulating accusations are subject. Some of the interpretive difficulties are posed in extreme form by the following extract:

Example 15[37]

(Extract from transcripts of the evidence to the Tribunal of Inquiry into Violence and Civil Disorder in Northern Ireland in 1969, Government of Northern Ireland; Day 91, 22nd October 1970. Tribunal counsel (C) cross-examining a witness (W), the Royal Ulster Constabulary Deputy Commissioner for Belfast)

139. C: Yes, we are coming to that shortly. I want to ask you about the

140.   phraseology there, "Ask people in Percy Street to go home as they

141.   can't stand there." Was that your message?

142. W: Yes, that is my message.

143. C: That was a rather polite way of addressing a mob who had burned and

144.   pillaged a Catholic area was it not?

145. W: I did not know that. The object of my message, if I may answer it this

146.   way, looking back, was that there was such heavy firing in particular

147.   areas that it was in the interests of saving life that this message

148.   of mine was sent.

149. C: What I am suggesting to you is that you had information or means

150.   of information that this mob had burned and petrol bombed Catholic property and Catholic people.

152. W: No

153. C: And that that was a rather polite way to address them or address the

154.   the command for orders as to how they were to be dealt with.

155. W: No, that is not so.

156. C: What did you think those people were doing there?

157. W: From experience. . . . . (evidence continues)

While the fact that the formulation (lines 149-151 and 153-154) of the evidence generated in the previous hundred lines of data is itself formulated as a "suggestion" (yet is and hearably does an "accusation") and generates analytic problems of immense scope, this scope itself testifies to the immensely multifaceted work achievable through such constructions. Moreover, the achievability of this work testifies in its turn to the multiply stratified character of conversational productions and their multiple—yet simultaneous and integrated—analysis by their recipients.

Conclusion

In this paper, we have sought to demonstrate that conversational formulations are a highly constraining conventional utterance type whose connection with their sequentially appropriate decisions is adjacently paired. We have argued as well that this adjacency pairing of the formulation-decision pair is associated with the crucial role of formulations as a means for the collaborative assembly, maintenance, and transformation of the sense of sections of talk, and that this role is also associated with the existence of certain preferences among second part decisions. We have sought to show that formulations afford major economies to conversationalists who are concerned to maintain concerted control over the cumulative sense and coherence of their collaborative conversational productions, and have introduced a number of complicating factors with respect to their production and properties.

A key area of ethnomethodological enquiry focuses on the topic of reflexivity. Our aim in this paper has been to demonstrate not only that conversationalists are oriented to the reflexive properties of natural language use, but also to demonstrate that they can and do use these reflexive properties as interactional resources. Given the ubiquitous and multifaceted character of conversational reflexivities, our account of formulations of gist has been necessarily rudimentary and schematic. We offer it in the hope of stimulating enquiry into ths field rather than as the precipitate of such an enquiry.

NOTES

1. By 'scenic,' we intend such oriented-to features of interactional settings as biographies, events, personalities, spatial and temporal locations, etc.

2. This general program is developed by Harold Garfinkel in a series of foundational writings collected as *Studies in Ethnomethodology* (Prentice Hall, 1967).

3. Of particular importance are H. Garfinkel and H. Sacks, "On Formal Structures of Practical Actions," in J.C. McKinney and E. A. Tiryakian (eds.), *Theoretical Sociology,* (Appleton-Century-Crofts, 1970), pp. 337-366; H. Sacks, "An Initial Investigation of the Usability of Conversational Data for Doing Sociology," in D. Sudnow (ed.), *Studies in Social Interaction* (Free Press, 1972), pp. 31-74; H. Sacks, "On the Analyzability of Stories by Children," in J. J. Gumperz and D. Hymes (eds), *Directions in Sociolinguistics,* (Holt Rinehart and Winston, 1972), pp.325-345; E. A. Schegloff and H. Sacks, "Opening Up Closings," *Semiotica* 8:289-327 (reprinted in R. Turner, (ed.), *Ethnomethodology* (Penguin, 1974); H. Sacks, "On Some Puns With Some Intimations," in R. W. Shuy (ed.), *Report of the Twenty-Third Round Table Meeting on Linguistics and Language Studies* (Georgetown University Press, 1972); H. Sacks, E. A. Schegloff, and G. Jefferson, "A Simplest Systematics for the Organization of Turn-Taking for Conversation," *Language* 50:696-735; H. Sacks, "An Analysis of the Course of a Joke's Telling in Conversation," in R. Bauman (ed.), *Explorations in the Ethnography of Speaking* (Cambridge, 1975), pp. 337-353; H. Sacks, "Everyone Has to Lie," in M. Sanches and B. Blount (eds.), *Sociocultural Dimensions of Language Use* (Academic Press, 1975), pp. 57-79; E. A. Schegloff, "Notes on a Conversational Practice: Formulating Place," in D. Sudnow (ed.), *op. cit.;* E. A. Schegloff, "Sequencing in Conversational Openings," *American Anthropologist* 70, No. 6, 1968; G. Jefferson, "Side Sequences," in D. Sudnow (ed.), *op. cit.;* additionally, Harvey Sacks' unpublished lectures, together with unpublished papers by Schegloff, Jefferson, Schenkein, Turner, and Pomerantz, have materially added to the stock of knowledge now generally available on the management of conversational order.

4. Garfinkel and Sacks, *op. cit.,* pp. 350 and 351.

5. Other aspects of members' orientations to conventionally understood distributions of information are discussed in Charles Goodwin, "The Interactive Construction of a Sentence in Natural Conversation," in this volume.

6. This data was kindly furnished by Anita Pomerantz.

7. Sacks, Schegloff, and Jefferson, *op. cit.,* pp. 724-727.

8. Schegloff and Sacks, *op. cit.,* p. 238. (Page references are to the reprinted version of this paper in R. Turner, ed., *op. cit.)*

9. Garfinkel and Sacks, *op. cit.,* p. 353.

10. Garfinkel and Sacks, *op. cit.,* p. 338.

11. In a personal communication, Professor Emanuel Schegloff has noted that the term "gloss" is often taken as implying such properties as defectiveness, inadequacy, superficiality and the like, as conveyed by the phrase "glossing over." In treating formulations as a class of glossing practices, we do not intend to foster the impression that we regard formulations as somehow less than adequate. We regard the issue of the adequacy of formulations as one which is exclusively decidable by members on each occasion upon which formulations are produced and monitored.

12. A. V. Cicourel, "The Acquisition of Social Structure: Toward a Developmental Sociology of Language and Meaning," in J. D. Douglas (ed.), *Understanding Everyday Life* (Chicago: Aldine Publishing Co., 1970).

13. As Professor Emanuel Schegloff observed at a seminar at the University of California, Irvine, it would be a dangerous strategy if one were to simply examine the occurrence of "troubles" in conversation in order to reveal in contrastive terms the nature of conversational organization. This is partly because there are features of conversational organization which work to deal with troubles as routinely as possible. "Repairs," for instance are routine and almost simultaneously mobilized systems-for-troubles. Thus to attempt to inspect the troubles themselves *in vacuo* is not to locate in simple terms some putative opposite of organization or systematicity in conversation. Moreover, without inspecting routine systems (including repairs), analysts are in no position to pinpoint or describe what the troubles are in the first place. By the same token, it would make little analytic sense to look at formulations simply by examining their use at troublesome junctures of the conversation without first inspecting their routine uses.

14. H. Sacks, Lecture 9, University of California at Irvine, March 5, 1969, p.2.

15. *Ibid.* ., p.4.

16. *Our* formulations of the conversational contexts in which the extracts occur are indicated in parentheses above the extracts. It may be noted that the analysts' perceived requirement to (and ability to) fill in such contexts testifies to the unrelievedly required competences which are mobilized in lay *and* professional analyses of formulations, and to the impossibility of sequestering formulations from more general conversational contexts. Appropriate letter headings indicate speakers, while indications of formulations are done by arrow and/or letter labeling where: F = formulation; G = gist; U = upshot; D = decision; D + = confirmation; D - = disconfirmation; and Non-D = non-decision. All names have been changed in the transcripts drawn from the crisis intervention center data.

18. This term is taken from Garfinkel and Sacks, *op. cit.*

19. E. A. Schegloff, G. Jefferson and H. Sacks, (1977). The preference for self-correction in the organization of repair in conversation *Language* 53, 2.

20. This example is taken from Gail Jefferson, "Side Sequences," in D. Sudnow (ed.) *op. cit.*, p. 316.

21. Schegloff and Sacks, *op. cit.*, p.241. The term "reception" is taken from Roy Turner's paper "Utterance Positioning as an Interactional Resource," *Semiotica*, forthcoming.

22. G. Jefferson, *op. cit.*, p.307.

23. Example from G. Jefferson, *op. cit.*, p.308.

24. Schegloff and Sacks, *op. cit.*, p.239-240.

25. Ibid.

26. Ibid.

27. A. M. Pomerantz, *Second Assessments: A Study of Some Features of Agreements/Disagreements*, Unpublished Doctoral Dissertation in Sociology, University of California at Irvine, 1975, p. viii.

28. M. Pollner, "The Very Coinage of Your Brain: The Anatomy of Reality Disjunctures," *Philosophy of the Social Sciences* 5:411-430.

29. This data was kindly furnished by John Harris. It is perhaps unnecessary to add here that the search for, and location of, bases for failures to treat formulations as such as a highly contextualized matter. Compare the inference from the utterance "is it?" in the following hypothetical conversation between a husband and his wife's lover.

> Lover: Let's cool off now, this conversation's going round in circles.
> Husband: (loudly) IS IT?
> Lover: Yes it is. Now don't start something you'll regret later on.

30. Pollner, *op. cit.;* see also Jeff Coulter "Perceptual Accounts and Interpretive Asymmetries," *Sociology* 9:385–396.

31. On tying terms and techniques, see various mimeo lectures by H. Sacks, especially *Lecture 11*, November 9, 1967, and lectures given on April 5 and April 7, 1971 (University of California at Irvine); see also M. Speier, *How to Observe Face to Face Communications: A Sociological Interpretation;* also D. R. Watson, *Calls for Help: A Sociological Analysis of Telephone Calls to a Crisis Intervention Center,* unpublished doctoral thesis in Sociology, University of Warwick, Coventry, England, 1975, especially Chs. 7 and 8: "Tying Down Misunderstandings and Other Interactional Uses of Pro-Terms," pp. 381–472.

32. In this respect, the production of formulations by news recipients may fulfill a role similar to that played by the production of second stories. See H. Sacks, *Aspects of the Sequential Organization of Conversation,* Ch. 1, mimeo, n.d.

33. The term *signature* is taken from Schegloff and Sacks, op. cit., p. 256.

34. This observation further underlines the utility of the adjacency pair format for formulations-decisions in ensuring the provision of a decision as an immediate next action.

35. On pre-closings, see Schegloff and Sacks, op. cit., p. 256.

36. Schegloff and Sacks, op. cit.

37. We are indebted to Paul Drew for the use of this extract. For further analysis, see P. Drew, "Accusations: The Occasioned Use of Members' Knowledge of 'Religious Geography' in Describing Events," *Sociology,* 1978, 12, 1.

Acknowledgments

We should especially like to thank Jeff Coulter and Anita Pomerantz for their friendly and extensive critical comments on earlier drafts of this paper. We also thank Max Atkinson, Dave Francis, Lena Jayyusi, Peter Halfpenny, and Julian Laite for their helpful comments on an earlier draft, and the participants at the Conference on Phenomenology and Social Theory, University of Durham, April 1975 and the participants at the Workshop on Ethnomethodology and Conversation Analysis, Boston University, June 1975 who also commented on earlier drafts. Jonathan B. Theobald gave assistance in initially transcribing some of the data, and J. Michael Newton gave invaluable technical assistance.

Beliefs and Practical Understanding

Jeff Coulter

Coulter merges the work of conversational analysts and ordinary language philosophers by exploring presuppositions which operate in common-sense reasoning. Presuppositions operate as resources for both speakers and hearers. Words, such as those which "claim" truth, are found to presuppose, on the part of speaker or hearer or both, the belief in something (i.e., a moral or normative belief that something is the case (i.e., a propositional belief), or both. That is, presuppositions are implicit in the use of these words by a speaker and in their interpretation by a hearer. Such uses can be found in discourse or in written materials. The explication of what presuppositions are made by those who speak/hear such words in particular contexts can reveal, among other things, differences in the ascription of meaning, the belief-commitments of the speaker/hearer, and certainty or uncertainty about the truth-value of another's claim. Thus, ascriptions of belief or knowledge to truth-claims made by others operate at the level of the implicit, unstated presupposition. The elucidation and analysis of presuppositions is an extension of the ethnomethodological approach to studies of practical reasoning as well as to studies of the organization of social interaction.

This paper offers a treatment of some selected issues involved in studying beliefs as social phenomena and exemplifies some ways of working on them. The observation and ascription of beliefs are usually considered to be problematic methodological issues for the analyst who is interested in making statements about what is believed by persons or collectivities. The perspective recommended here is informed by the obvious fact that *members,* conducting their affairs under the auspices of the practical attitude of everyday life, routinely avow, disavow, ascribe, invoke, and in other ways exhibit beliefs: for them, the observation or ascription of belief is not invariantly problematic. The analyst's task envisaged and developed here consists in providing some formal description of these modes of presentation of beliefs insofar as they exhibit orderliness and organization.

It is clear that this version of the analyst's task contrasts with the more orthodox sociological concerns with members' beliefs, in which some belief or set of beliefs are ascribed to some collectivity (with appropriate methodological modesty) and are then formulated as functions (or effects) of the social characteristics of that collectivity. The available discussions of "rationality"[1] and "ideology"[2] are typically preoccupied with furnishing accounts that purport to explain in some functionalist or deterministic manner the holding of beliefs considered by the analyst to be *false.* We may refer to this as the expression of an *ironic attitude* to lay beliefs. I shall say a little more about this before proceeding to discuss the alternative approach recommended here.

Members' Beliefs Treated As Competing Sociological Theories

Karl Mannheim extended Marx's conception of ideology and formulated a version of members' beliefs-about-society which argued that not only are they differentially located within a social structure, but that they are equivalently subject to analysis to determine to what extent they are a "function of the generally prevailing social situation."[3] This "total conception of ideology"[4] marked the transformation of the notion of ideology as used by Marx, in whose work it was a device for discrediting the beliefs which he claimed served the interests of the capitalist order and obscured its functioning, into a more general epistemological thesis. In this expanded version, not only one's adversary's beliefs but one's own as well become analyzable for socially induced distortions:

> With the emergence of the general formulation of
> the total conception of ideology, the simple
> theory of ideology develops into the sociology of
> knowledge. What was once the intellectual argu-
> ment of a party is transformed into a method of
> research in social and intellectual history general-
> ly. To begin with, a given social group discovers
> the "situational determination" of its opponents'
> ideas. Subsequently, the recognition of this fact
> is elaborated into an all-inclusive principle ac-
> cording to which the thought of every group is
> seen as arising out of its life conditions.[5]

For Marx, the rationale for relating *some* members' beliefs-about-
society to their social circumstances was to argue that such circumstances
provided them with interests which tacitly informed their beliefs. In
challenging them (for moral and political purposes), he sought to
relativize them; the beliefs he discussed were treated as *faulted com-
petitors* with the version of history and the social order he was developing.[6] For Mannheim, the rationale for relating *any* members' beliefs-
about-society to their social circumstances was a quasi-causal thesis
about beliefs (and knowledge-claims) as such. The contemporary Mannheimian sociology of knowledge and belief has perpetuated, within
sociology, this constitution of members' beliefs-about-society (or about
certain of its features) as *essentially competing sociological theories*
rather than as integral parts of the societies within which they are held.
Since many of the substantive states of affairs about which members
hold and express beliefs are also addressed methodically by professional
sociological inquiry, this competitive attitude toward "commonsense
beliefs about society" has easily been sustained. Lay sociological beliefs
are investigated for their possible *truth-value,* rather than as empirical
features of a society to be analyzed, along with other beliefs, in terms of
their socially organized properties. Occasionally, some lay belief about a
society or social phenomenon will be considered "correct" or "true" if it
is found to accord with the professional's sociological "findings" concerning the matter, but for the most part lay social beliefs have fared
badly with sociologists, and this has tended to buttress the view that lay
beliefs are fit only for debunking. Given such an attitude, the preference
has been to inspect the social conditions which could be claimed to
engender the false beliefs. In this way, two birds are killed with one
stone: members' beliefs are to be investigated for their social determinants, which in turn deprives them of consideration in terms of the
reasoning which may inform them, a consideration of which they
would be worthy only if they were true. Furthermore, sociologists have

sometimes sought to rationalize their concerns with the "sociohistorical determinants" of members' (predominately "false") beliefs in terms of the general Mannheimian thesis; this has tended to backfire in the sense that, under such a general thesis, sociologists' *own* knowledge-claims become similarly suspect as transient, partial, and/or value-laden articulations of a particular vantage point within the social order. From here, the debate about the possibly ideological basis of *sociological* knowledge-claims ensues. Since much sociology consists in the formulation of explanatory statements about the social world which have the logical status of normative appraisal and contestable argumentation[7] rather than strict causal modeling and prediction, the charge of ideological perspectivism in the guise of disinterested scientific inquiry has gained a foothold within the discipline itself.

The abandonment of the ironic attitude toward members' beliefs permits us now to begin the detailed investigation of these beliefs as *constituent features of organized social conduct*. We need no longer seek to scientize our appraisals of members' beliefs about substantive and moral matters. Given the ethnomethodological reorientation of our attitude to "commonsense knowledge of social structures"[8] and its insistence upon studying such ordinary knowledge as constitutive of the construction of social interaction, we are ready for an extension of the analytic perspective afforded by this reorientation to the area of "ordinary beliefs" in all their variety. In what follows, some preliminary attempts will be made to map out the ground now available for analytic inspection and documentation.

Members' Beliefs Treated As Phenomena: 1. *Beliefs as Presuppositions in Speech Exchanges.*

It is a commonplace in the study of the pragmatics of natural languages that we employ as resources for the production and comprehension of our utterances not only our knowledge of the lexicon and our syntactical capability but also our knowledge of and beliefs about the world. Ethnomethodologists have similarly been concerned for some time with the analysis of members' "tacit resources" or "background understandings" and with the description of a "machinery" for the production of orderly communicative interaction which specifies the role of such tacit resources.[9] A point of convergence between both approaches may be located in the analytic use and elaboration of the notion of *presupposition*.[10] It can be argued that members display and assign beliefs to each other in virtue of the occasioned production and understanding of utterances analyzable for what they presuppose. Along with explicit avowals, ascriptions, etc., which we shall examine further on, presupposition-analyses made by members as an integral feature of much communicative interaction form a routine but unnoticed basis for the observability of beliefs. Of course, presupposition-analyses may reveal (or justify the ascription of) knowledge, intention, and other, "subjective" aspects; our interest here is restricted to belief.

We must first address ourselves to the broad issue of the relationship between presuppositions and communication generally. Fillmore has proposed that speech communication situations consist in, among other elements, the *exchange of "illocutionary actions"* (the phrase belongs to J. L. Austin, who used it to characterize activities performed in and through the use of language[11]) and the *reciprocal monitoring of utterance-presuppositions:*

> In every conversation, we constantly make use of both the implicit, or presuppositional, and the explicit, or illocutionary, levels of communication. We know, for example, that our utterances can be judged as inappropriate or incorrect not only on the grounds that some state of affairs has been wrongly described, or that one has acted in bad faith in promising something or warning someone, but also on the grounds of presupposition-failure. We also know that by counting on the addressee's knowing the presuppositions of sentences, and by using sentences deliberately under conditions of presupposition-failure, we can sometimes communicate certain special messsages or attitudes or achieve certain secondary communication goals—as would be the case if somebody were to ask me *When did you stop beating your wife?*[12]

Although Fillmore proposes here that the illocutionary level is explicit, there are many cases where the identification of an illocutionary action in conversation itself depends upon the hearer's performing the relevant presupposition-analysis. This is especially noticeable in the case of those illocutionary actions (e.g., answering a question, complaining, offering, rejecting offers, etc.) that are not typically prefaced with an explicit performative formula or what Searle terms a·"function-indicating device"[13] such as "I promise. . . " or "I warn you that. . . ." In these cases, the illocutionary level may also be thought of as implicit, and for some of them an adequate identification for practical purposes may turn upon an adequate analysis of what the associated utterance presupposes. The elementary procedure of reasoning in conversation in this respect appears to be: analyse an utterance (or turn-at-talk) into an appropriate action if you can. For example, while we can arguably discern an explicit offer in the following first utterance, we need to perform a presupposition-analysis on the second utterance in order to hear it as a sequentially tied next-action.[14] viz., a rejection of that offer:

1. A: Would you like a lift home?
2. B: My car's just outside, thanks.

Or, again, in the following exchange *both* the offer and the rejection appear to be identifiable as such at the level of contextual presupposition:[15]

1. A: Dr. K. asked us to call to take you to hospital.
2. B: I'm all right as I am.

The second utterance here may be thought of as something like an explicit, unsolicited personal-state disclosure, but it implicitly operates to reject the offer (order?) of a lift to the hospital, which is itself identifiable as an offer (or order) at the level of presupposition only. Fillmore does not consider presuppositions in their variety, restricting himself to dealing with *semantic* presupposition. However, it is clear that features of a context of speaking (e.g., the categories of the interlocutors, the occasion, and so on) can facilitate a hearer's analysis of what is presupposed by what is said which extends beyond presupposition-determinations predicated purely on the content of the utterance in question. A major constraint upon these extra-semantic presupposition-analyses seems to be discourse-organizational: analyze a return-utterance as an appropriate second part of an adjacency pair, if you have just produced or heard a first part, wherever possible (e.g., as an answer to a question just asked; as an acceptance/rejection of an offer/invitation just made; as a return-insult to an insult, etc).[16]

Presuppositions, then, are resources for both speakers and hearers in ordinary conversations and other speech communication situations. They can be employed to render intelligible both an utterance and the activity it accomplishes in the interaction. We can begin our examination of the mundane observability of beliefs by considering some recent work on the analysis of various verbs in terms of semantic presupposition, bearing in mind that there are further dimensions of presupposition relevant to the display and ascription of belief which will be discussed further on.

Fillmore's own analysis of some verbs of judging[17] illustrates that the selection of any one of them by a speaker in the construction of a declarative utterance may commit him to certain beliefs (or, in cases of deception, may seem to commit him) where hearers become entitled to assign such beliefs to the speaker. Thus, if I assert, "I accused Harry of writing the letter," my use of "accused" commits me to the belief that writing the letter was in some way a wrongful act, as well as to the belief (not necessarily still held at the time of my utterance) that Harry committed that act. In contradistinction, if I say: "I criticized Harry for writing the letter," my belief-presupposition about the wrongfulness of the act is sustained, but in this case I am presupposing (or at one time presupposed) that Harry did *in fact* write the letter. In a similar vein, Austin provides a treatment of the verb "blame" which illustrates how its use may carry different presuppositions:

> Sometimes when I blame X for doing A, say for breaking the vase, it is a question simply or mainly of my disapproval of A, breaking the vase, which unquestionably X did: but sometimes it is, rather, a question simply or mainly of how far I believe X responsible for A, which unquestionably was bad. Hence if someone says he blames me for something, I may answer by giving a *justification,* so that he will cease to disapprove of what I did, or else by giving him an *excuse,* so that he will cease to hold me, at least entirely and in every way, responsible for doing it.[18]

My analysis of the belief-presupposition of someone's ascription of blame to me can inform (conventionally) the sort of illocutionary act I produce in response to it. If what I say, when someone has told me that he blames me for action A, is hearable as a justification, then I (or my utterance) can be found to presuppose the belief that action A was not unquestionably bad, whereas if my response is hearable as an excuse, then I (or my utterance) can be found to presuppose the belief that action A was unquestionably bad. Here again it is clear that the analysis of presuppositions by interlocutors can be consequential for the organization of their activities; to borrow again from Sacks, a presupposition-analysis can be *sequentially implicative* in social interaction. I shall return to this point later.

Searle's analysis of the concept of "promise" contains references to aspects of its use which could be thought of as conventionally assignable presuppositions of its ordinary employment. (Searle himself is interested in characterizing the *necessary and sufficient conditions* for the performance of the illocutionary act of promising, from which he seeks to extract some *constitutive rules* for promising. I think that there are serious difficulties with this program.[19]) Among the aspects isolated by Searle, we can locate some belief-presuppositions for the analysis of any one of which members may hold each other responsible in their interactional affairs. Paraphrasing Searle,[20] we can note that, in making a *sincere* promise, the speaker commits himself to the (assignable) beliefs that (i) the hearer would prefer his performing the future act in question to his not performing it (which distinguishes what he is doing from making a threat);[21] (ii) the hearer does not think that the speaker will do the action in question in the normal course of events;[22] (iii) the hearer will place him under an obligation to perform the action; and (iv) the hearer will believe that *these* beliefs (i—iii) are appropriately assignable to the speaker by means of the hearer's recognition of the intentions signalled in the promising utterance.[23] Fillmore has indicated that Searle's analysis (and, by derivation, this paraphrase for our present purposes) would be unable to handle sincere promises in which the speaker promises that someone *else* will perform an action or series of actions (e.g., "I promise you that your husband will be well looked after in hospital.")[24] Our belief-presuppositions must therefore be appropriately complicated to include such a common feature of promising; this could be done by expanding the formulations to make reference to the *alternative* possibility of predicating the future action in question of a person, persons or collectivity(-ies). Thus, for example, belief-presupposition (i) above would have to be rewritten as: (i) the speaker commits himself to the belief that the hearer would prefer (a) *his* performing the future act in question to his not doing it *and/or* (b) *the agent's* performing the future act in question to his not doing it. And so on through the series.

The final example of semantic presuppositions to be considered here is the work of Kiparsky and Kiparsky, who have analyzed a class of verbs which they call "factives."[25] They include in this class such verbs as "know," "understand," "regret," "forget," and "ignore". A speaker's use of one of these verbs in a declarative or assertion conventionally commits him to claiming the *truth* of the object-complement of the verb, and, in reports about others (e.g., "Mary regretted that Dave did not believe her story"), can commit him to ascribing to the subject of the factive (here, "Mary") a belief in the truth of the object-complement (here, "that Dave did not believe her story"). Verbs like "feign" and "pretend," on the other hand, could be termed "counterfactives" in that their declarative use commits the speaker to the (assignable) presupposition that their object-complements are false. This class of verbs is interactionally interesting, in that their conventional belief-presuppositions do not remain constant under negation of the assertion in which they are used. In this, they are unlike factives, all of which "sustain" their belief-presuppositions in declaratives under negation. Thus, one can say of someone: "He's pretending to be ill" with the belief-presupposition that the person is *not* ill (the falsity of the object-complement), but one cannot negate the assertion and sustain that belief-presupposition. This stands in contrast to factives: take "realize," the truth of whose object-complement is presupposed in *both* affirmative and negative assertions. ("He realized that he was ill" and "He did not realize that he was ill" both presuppose that he was, in fact, ill.) This negation-test for presupposition also holds for a verb of judging, such as "criticize": "John didn't criticize Harry for insulting him" presupposes Harry's responsibility for the insult just as much as in the affirmative version of the utterance. In the case of "pretend," then, the negation-test[26] breaks down, since "He's *not* pretending to be ill" does not entitle a hearer to assign to the speaker any belief at all about illness. The person in question could actually *be* ill, or illness may simply have nothing to do with his situation.[27] In such cases, a speaker using a negative form of utterance containing a counterfactive and its object-complement may tag on a clarifying remark; failure to do so, where the context does not provide for a determinate sense, can generate interactional difficulties or misunderstandings. For example: A man sees his wife moaning and holding her head and challenges her with, "You're just pretending to be sick!" She retorts, "I'm not pretending to be sick at all," following which he leaves, goes to the drugstore, and brings back some aspirin, saying, "I've got something for that headache of yours." His wife could then intelligibly respond by claiming she had no headache at all but was merely worrying about the housework to be faced after the party that evening or some such problem having nothing to do with being sick as such. There is no single linguistic convention to which to appeal here to settle the question of what the wife's return-utterance ("I'm not pretending to be sick at all") could have been heard to presuppose.

We must now turn to consider some cases in which belief-presuppositions are assignable but in which such assignations are mundanely entitled not by the conventional semantics of lexical items in themselves, but by trading upon wider cultural and contextual resources. In these latter cases, a belief-presupposition is assignable to the speaker on pragmatic rather than narrowly semahtic grounds.

In the following brief exchange, the location of a referent for (the disambiguation of) a pronomial usage seems to hinge upon the hearer's assigning a relevant belief-presupposition to the second speaker:

1. A: Phil just borrowed $50 off Joe!
2. B: Yeah? I didn't know he was so generous
3. C: Yeah Joe's O.K.

In hearing the pronoun "he" in B.'s utterance (line 2) as a transformation of "Joe" rather than "Phil," we (and speaker C) may follow a search-procedure such as: Try to locate the substantive for a pronoun in the just-prior utterance to which it can be heard as tied. This will yield two disambiguation candidates ("Phil" and "Joe") between which some decision has to be assembled if the utterance is to be understood. It seems that we (and speaker C) tacitly employ as a resource here our belief that borrowing is not ordinarily a generous act, whereas what it presupposes, namely lending, may be so characterized. Since by that presupposition analysis it is Joe who has lent Phil the fifty dollars, and lending may more readily be thought of as generous than borrowing, then it must be Joe who is being called generous. Speaker C's comment may have depended for its appropriateness on having made these determinations. Note that we can see clearly here how a presupposition-analysis can have sequential implications in discourse. A strong example of this can be found in the ensuing sequence:[28]

1. A: Who got arrested at the busing
       demonstration?
2. B: Gregor
3. A: Typical... a black guy

Where conventionally available *alternative* beliefs about something are not explicitly discriminated within an utterance or its context, the hearer may find it difficult to determine the relevant belief-presupposition to assign to the speaker and may consequently have difficulty in knowing how to design his subsequent utterance. In this exchange, A's utterance in line 3 could have been informed by either racist or antiracist beliefs, where "typical" might have intended something like "typical of the cops to pick out a black guy," or "typical of a black guy to do something that gets him arrested." This sort of ambiguity at the level of assignable presupposition is known to designers of computer programs aimed at either machine translation or the production of natural speech. Conventional beliefs do indeed, on occasion, inform the capacity to disambiguate, and sometimes it is difficult to determine which of a set of equivalently disambiguating belief-presuppositions may be operative. Winograd provides us with a telling case in which belief-presuppositions may be crucial resources for disambiguation. He proposes that our disambiguation of "they" in the following utterances is clearly contingent upon the beliefs we can conventionally assign to the categorial identities: "The city councilmen refused the demonstrators a permit because they feared violence" and "The city councilmen refused the demonstrators a permit because they advocated revolution."[29] Given a set of fairly conventional beliefs about the category-appropriate conduct/beliefs of "councilmen" and "demonstrators" in our culture,[30] we may be more likely to hear the pronoun "they" in the first utterance as a transformation of "the city councilmen," while in the second utterance, we may more readily hear "they" as a transformation of "the demonstrators." D.G. Williams has pointed out[31] that the reasoning procedure for such potentially ambiguous expressions seems to be: *Where the context of the expression cannot resolve some ambiguity, choose whichever hearing makes better sense in terms of your beliefs, and/or the beliefs assignable to the user of the expression.*

Grasping the beliefs hearably presupposed by the utterances produced by an interlocutor is consequential for the organization of interpersonal communication; so far, we have focussed upon cases in which presupposition-analysis has been a situated condition for adequate, practical comprehension, but there are also cases in which arguments can get started in virtue of a presupposition determination. Where a speaker is formulating a contrast of some kind, it is often done *enthymematically*[2]—the tacit premiss or presupposition being the basis for the contrast. For instance, in uttering the expression, "She may be a student, but she sure·dresses smart," the contrast operates on the basis of the presupposition that students do not normally dress smartly, and a hearer can find the contrast by assigning such a belief-presupposition to the speaker. Of course, such contrasts often lead to arguments or contradictions when the presupposed property of (the class of) persons or objects is not believed by the hearer to be.properly ascribable; e.g.,

1. A: My landlady's a redhead, though I must
        say she's pretty even-tempered
2. B: Hey! My girlfriend's a redhead; they're
        not all uptight, ya know!

Where someone makes an explicit presupposition determination of the just-prior utterance, its articulation is conventionally questioning or argumentative. Such articulations of a prior speaker's assignable presuppositions are usually geared to *disputing* them or *defeating* them (unless merely clarification-seeking). In this way, presuppositions are usable as a *hearer's argumentative device.* When invoked as such, they are typically adjacently-placed utterances in discourse. The presuppositions so articulated may be either semantic or pragmatic: e.g.,

1. A: He wants to appoint her in Mike's place
2. B.   That presupposes he's got some power in
   the matter

Speaker B's presupposition-determination is semantic, predicated upon the conventional use of "appoint" by speaker A. ("Appoint" is an illocutionary verb whose use in declaratives carries the semantic presupposition that the subject of the verb is endowed with some power, authority, or rights relative to the object.) A pragmatic presupposition-determination occurs in the following:

1. A: We'll get to Buffalo while it's still twilight
2. B: You're presupposing that we'll be able to
   leave at sun-up!

Here, there is no semantic convention at issue; the presupposition rests upon purely contingent and local knowledge and/or belief. Clearly, members may feel that a pragmatic presupposition-determination is more arguable than a semantic one. Belief-presuppositions, then, may be either semantic (relative to the choice of words in the language) or pragmatic (relative to conventional or local knowledge or belief about persons, objects or events). The former may be thought of as *sense-constitutive* presuppositions for a range of uses, while the latter are not (except in the limited sense that we may, as noted, identify an illocutionary act by assigning a pragmatic presupposition to the speaker). Stalnaker has argued that—

> In general, any semantic presupposition of a proposition expressed in a given context will be a pragmatic presupposition of the people in that context, but the converse clearly does not hold. [33]

Thus, to have used "appoint" appropriately in his declarative, the speaker who uttered the expression "he wants to appoint her in Mike's place" may be thought to have *made* the presupposition in question (namely, that "he" has the power to make appointments). However, the belief that lending money can be generous, which may be thought of as pragmatically presupposed by speaker B in our earlier example about Phil's borrowing fifty dollars, cannot be semantically paired with uses of the verb "lend."

A speaker's actual presuppositions are ordinarily believed by him to be true except for cases of deliberate deception, joking, and so on. However, some occasions are more informative for hearers than others as to the speaker's beliefs about the truth-value of what his utterances presuppose. We routinely analyze speakers' utterances for what they presuppose in order to glean contingent information, to learn about their subjective states, attitudes, and dispositions. We can also discover instances of imitation, improved or reduced competence in some area of knowledge, ideological or religious conversion, and even insanity by discerning a *disjunction* between what is seeable as presupposed by what a member says and the state of knowledge and belief normally assignable to him or claimed by him on prior occasions. Presuppositions are immensely general and wholly mundane, yet are powerful resources for participants in a communication community.

We have seen that the sort of beliefs which figure in presuppositions can be both *propositional* (factual) beliefs (e.g., beliefs *that* something is the case) and *moral* or *normative* beliefs (e.g., beliefs *in* something). The belief-presuppositions semantically associated with the expression "I accused him of doing it" consist in both types, as noted earlier: the propositional belief-presupposition would be that he did it, while the moral belief-presupposition would be a belief in the wrongfulness of the action in question.

It has been claimed, then, that much of our ordinary, practical understanding of each other's talk requires the assignation of beliefs to speakers and the presupposition of beliefs in the construction of our own assertions and other illocutionary activities. Little has been said so far about nominal categories and category-phrases, so we must turn now to consider this class of linguistic devices.

Although various presuppositions tied to the conventional, declarative-forming use of certain verbs may be thought of as *constitutive* of their intelligibility and appropriateness, in the case of nominal categories and category-phrases, the situation is more complex. Our contemporary uses of various nominal categories in declaratives are no longer tied to the belief-presuppositions that once conventionally informed their employment, and yet their sense in most respects remains constant. Take the ascription of the category of "melancholia" to someone; although once tied up with the bile theory of the temperaments, its use no longer carries such belief-commitments, just as speaking of "information" does not bind us to a belief in the Aristotelian doctrine of form and materia from which the concept was compounded.[34] But does our use of a category-phrase like "mental illness" in ascriptions commit us to a belief in the dominant biogenic nosology of madness? Not at all, since where we employ this category-phrase in serious ascriptions we may warrantably intend only the observable conduct of a person in various situations for which there are no available excusing, justifying, or entitling grounds, [35] although we may keep open the possibility of expanding its associable commitments in the light of our acceptance of biogenic claims in psycho-pathology. Such "revisability" or "presupposition-openness" is available only for a certain subclass of nominal categories; in Putnam's analysis, this subclass is that of "natural-kind" concepts such as energy, light, water, gold, etc. [36] It makes no sense to suppose that such concepts as *mistake* or *stepmother* are amenable to revision by empirical experience.

There is room for misunderstanding here: Gellner, for example, consistently confuses concepts with theories in his discussion of the use of the concept of witch (and of witchcraft).[37] He argues that someone who does not believe in witchcraft and denies that witches exist is at the same time also "recommending the abolition of a whole genre of speech, witch-language."[38] This simply cannot follow, any more than it can follow that to use the concept of melancholy is to commit oneself to a theory of the humors. It would be quite absurd to wish to abolish *all* discourse about witches (which I take it would be entailed by the abolition of "witch-language") simply because one did not believe in witches. There is a world of difference between denying that something could have *xyz* properties and denying that any talk at all about that thing could make sense. Among many others, anthropologists and historians need to speak sensibly about witches and witchcraft, even though they may in no way ascribe mystical powers to them nor presuppose any supernatural beliefs. Gellner has further proposed that "the fact that there are standard cases for the application of the term such as 'miracle' in a given society in no way proves that such terms have a *legitimate* use . . . in no way proves that the terms are justified.[39] But if a concept or term has *no* legitimate use in a society for communicating something *intelligible* (which is by no means the same as communicating something that is *true*), then there can be no such concept for that society, since what a concept amounts to is decidable only with reference to examples of legitimate uses. What could "justified" mean in the above quotation? A concept in itself is neither justified nor unjustified; it can be used in propositions, theories, etc., which alone can intelligibly be assessed as justified or otherwise. Gellner is confusing the truth or falsity of a proposition about something (miracle, witch) with the grammar (proper uses) of the concept of that thing (miracle, witch). To entertain discussions about the truth of some proposition containing such categories, we must first understand them—which presupposes that they have some standard uses in our cultural discourse. To say, for example, that miracles never could have occurred in the way in which the Bible depicts them is not to deny that the category of "miracle" makes sense to us—we have, after all, just used the category to make a countertheological claim. And there are nontheological uses of the category quite independent of religious beliefs (as in: "it was a terrible crash; his escape was a miracle").

We can see, then, that although beliefs do operate as presuppositions in much of our ordinary understanding, we have to be careful when, as hearers, we seek to identify a belief-commitment informing a particular use of a nominal category or category-phrase. We can go wrong when we try to treat belief-commitments of certain sorts as *invariantly* presupposed by the user of such a category, or when we treat certain categories as if they somehow *embodied* a specific belief-commitment.

What we have argued so far goes some way toward the goal of formulating an "organization" for beliefs as constitutent features of ordinary reasoning and conduct.[40] In the remainder of this paper, I want to consider (schematically) some aspects of the relationship between belief-commitments and the construction of intendedly factual accounts of conduct and claims about the world.

Members' Beliefs Treated as Phenomena: 2. *Belief-Commitments and the Production of Factual Accounts.*

Our factual beliefs can sometimes prevent us from formulating an account of someone's conduct and/or claims in terms acceptable to him as an accurate account. The phenomenon is widespread. It is strikingly evident in the practice of psychotherapy and psychiatric social work in which the patient or client articulates his (psychiatrically problematic) claims in terms of *knowledge*, while the therapist characterizes them as beliefs. Between the paranoid and the psychiatrist there often arises a communication fracture due to this asymmetry in ascription; for the former, it is not a question of believing, but of knowing, whereas for the latter, those things claimed as known by the patient can only be accorded the status of belief. The following extract from a former mental patient's account of his condition illustrates this quite clearly:

> I had not *thought* I was Jesus Christ when I had burned my hand. I had *known* that I was. It had been more than a conviction or a belief, and far simpler than either of these things. It had been knowledge in the same sense that I now knew that this was my right hand.[41]

Unless he shares the delusion, the therapist cannot characterize such claims as knowledge, and yet to characterize them as beliefs hearably downgrades their status in the eyes of the patient. Such initial asymmetries have further consequences as we shall see. They also appear in the work of anthropologists. Evans-Pritchard encountered the discrepancy generated by the differential distribution of belief-commitments in the ways in which he sought to characterize Azande witchcraft; he described the Azande as holding *beliefs* about witchcraft and oracular power where the Azande claimed *knowledge* of these things.[42] We may propose, then, that the ascription of belief to someone who makes a knowledge-claim hearably downgrades that knowledge-claim and articulates an asymmetry between the ascriber and the person to whom belief is being ascribed. Belief-ascription can be a method for expressing one's reservations about the truth-value of someone's assertions.

A member's corpus of beliefs will be consequential for how he describes the world he encounters; since some of the items held as beliefs by some are held as items in a corpus of claimed knowledge by others, there arise disjunctions (in both gross and fine detail) between the corresponding sorts of accounts produced. These disjunctions have orderly features. Hanna Pitkin, discussing the work of anthropological description of alien cultural practices, suggests that—

> sometimes the anthropologist *must* diverge from the natives' account of what they are doing, in order not to deceive his readers, because of the commitment entailed in *his* act of speaking or writing. Suppose the natives engage in certain

procedures they tell him are "making rain." How
will he truthfully report what they are doing? If he
says simply "they are making rain," he is implying
that their magic really can causally produce pre-
cipitation; such is the nature of our language. If
he says "they are engaged in a magic ritual designed to make rain," he is at least strongly suggesting that their actions cannot produce rain; in
that case, he is true to knowledge, but in a significant way false to their world, their way of perceiving and acting.[43]

Even Pitkin's own discussion here is not free from assignable belief-
commitments; she accords the status of knowledge to one version rather
than the other, and in her remark that the anthropologist is "true to
knowledge," she leaves the world "knowledge" anonymous, constituting it as knowledge for whoever reads her discussion, which
presumably excludes the natives in question. She speaks also of the
possibility of "deception" were the anthropologist simply to reiterate the
natives' way of talking about their practices as a final account of those
practices. That is, she takes it that a reader of the anthropologist's account, if it reproduced the natives' way of talking, would assume that the
anthropologist actually concurred in the claimed efficacy of those practices in bringing rain and would perhaps read this as a (peculiar?)
discovery-claim about the ways in which the world does in fact work.
Whichever way the anthropologist chooses to formulate the native practices, the account cannot stand as one which would be considered fac-
tually correct by both parties—by the persons being described and by the
persons reading the description back home along with the anthropologist
himself. Even if he (or any visitor) were simply to propose that the
natives "call" such-and-such a set of procedures "making rain," this
would stand in obvious contrast to his unqualified description of such
other procedures as, say, "chopping wood." If we were told that the
natives observed had a practice which they "called" chopping wood, we
may suspect that, whatever it was that the natives were doing, it was not
succeeding in getting the wood actually chopped. For these reasons, we
can suggest that our beliefs may be, for a range of occasions of describing and reporting, generative of divergences among us. Not only do our
belief-commitments provide for the appropriateness of our selection
from the categories of "belief" and "knowledge" in characterizing the
claims of others, but they provide also for further (often unnoticed)
features of account-production.

So far, we have been looking at one aspect of belief-ascription.

Another important consideration is the way in which a belief-ascription can be heard to signal, not a reservation on the user's part about the truth-value of the other's claim or account, but the ascription of *guardedness* or uncertainty to the recipient in respect of his propositional avowal. (Often, in such instances, the verb "think" may be employed). An example of the form of belief-ascription involving the ascription of guardedness would be the following:

    1. A: I see . . . you're not sure . . . you believe
             its $40, but—
    2. B: Yeah, I think it cost around $40 . . .

An example of the form of belief-ascription which signals a reservation on the part of the ascriber as to the truth-value of the other's claim (where the latter may strongly contest the implicit downgrading of that claim) would be the following:

    1. A: He could <u>not</u> have committed suicide
    2. B (to C):   See what I mean? He still believes
              it was an accident
    3. A: I don't <u>believe</u> anything of the sort; it <u>was</u>
              an accident.

Call the first ascriptive form type (i) and the second type (ii). Type (i) belief-ascriptions do not display the cognitive orientation of the ascriber to the claim made by the recipient of the ascription, whereas type (ii) belief-ascriptions turn upon such a display. Type (i) ascriptions register the ascriber's recognition of a lack of full confidence on the part of the recipient of the ascription in his claim or account. Of course, an exception to this can be found in the conduct of arguments between theists and atheists, in which both sides of the dispute may employ the category of "belief" in characterizing the theist claim despite the possibility of the theist's having full confidence in that claim.

    Avowals of propositional (factual) beliefs in the present tense may also conventionally signal a guardedness with respect to their object-complements. (However, there need be nothing necessarily guarded about the *actions* expressing a held propositional belief: if I believe that the ice is thin beneath me, I may well skate just as warily as if I knew that it was thin.) To obtain a strong sense of this occasioned guardedness of belief-avowals, consider the following. A proposition entertained at time t which later at time t_1 turned out to be false in the eyes of the propounder, would conventionally, at time t_1, retrospectively be classified as a propositional *belief,* even though the member characterizing it as such would, at time *t*, have characterized it as a *knowledge*-claim. Thus, at time *t* he might have said: "I know that *p*," while at time *t*₁, when he had determined its falsity, he would have to say: "I believed that *p*; now I know better." Members conventionally describe any factual claim, formerly claimed in terms of knowledge, but currently held to be false, in terms of *former belief.*

At the level of the social organization of their use, we can speak of the categories "belief" and "knowledge" as forming a *disjunctive category-pair.* We shall mark this by the use of an oblique as follows: knowledge/belief. Other such pairs would include vision/hallucination; telepathy/trickery; ghost/illusion; flying-saucer/UFO; and ideology/ science. Where one part of these pairs is invoked to characterize some phenomenon seriously, *the speaker's belief-commitment may be inferred, and the structure of subsequent discourse may be managed in terms provided for by the programmatic relevance of the disjunctive category-pair relationship.* Thus, to the nonbeliever, Joan of Arc suffered hallucinations; to the believer, divine visions. To the nonbeliever, Uri Geller is a sophisticated conjurer; to the believer, a telepath and telekineticist, and so on. Beliefs, then, may provide not only for the constructional features of descriptions of conduct and claims about the world, but also for a preference in the selection of a referential category (e.g., "vision" rather than "hallucination," or the reverse). Members who make perceptual claims while acknowledging their unconventionality may prefer to select a descriptor from the nonbeliever's part of a disjunctive category-pair, if only to suggest or argue for its equivocal applicability to the phenomenon in question; e.g.:

> As a former manager with the Aero-Club of France and having served in the air force, I have not been the victim of a hallucination, and this machine was not a balloon, but a thick circular wing that hovered over one spot, then moved off at very great speed, climbing steadily as it did so.[44]

and, again,

> I hoped what I did see would add to the national interest or national information that would maybe help understand these things a little better. I do know that they exist, now that I have seen it myself. I am not saying that it was a flying saucer,

I don't know. I do know there are at least such
things now as UFO's.[45]

The same concern to acknowledge the *possible* applicability of a
nonbeliever's category to a phenomenon or situation held as real by the
account-producer arises frequently in self-reports made by psychiatric
patients. One instance, chosen only because of its rather stark exhibition
of this practice, is drawn from Binswanger's classic study of Ilse;[46] in a
letter to her physician, she wrote:

> It is not my fault that I got this way. You think it is
> delusions—religious delusions—that I think,
> speak, write like this. But this is not true; it is my
> nature, my innnermost nature, which clamors for
> an outlet in order to relax again, or rather which
> you have dragged out of me with your torturous
> tools which torment me deeply. There is nothing
> other in me than what I have shown you, there is no
> breath of falsehood and no sensationalism in it,
> that I know of.[47]

There is clearly something quite conventional involved here; members
do attend to the belief-displaying character of their descriptive categories
and to the organization of those categories into disjunctive sets. The consequences of this remain to be worked out empirically in detail.

Concluding Remarks

Ethnomethodology has had a long-standing commitment to the study
of members' methods of understanding and reasoning,[48] methods of
account-construction,[49] and the specification of a "machinery" for
describing the orderliness of situated social interaction.[50] Although the
role of commonsense knowledge has been fundamental within various
studies of an ethnomethodological kind, there has been little explicit attention to the study of ordinary beliefs as phenomena susceptible to
analysis along similar lines. This report has sought to contribute a series
of observations on the relationship between beliefs and interactional
understanding, and between beliefs and account-construction.

The alternative conceptualization of the analyst's problem recommended here intentionally consigns the *evaluation* of members' beliefs to the realms of moral appraisal and commonsense assessment—that is, to the domain of the *practical* attitude, with its attendant commitments. Sociologists no longer need to adopt a moral stance and remain within the practical attitude or to assign truth-values to lay beliefs as their only approaches to the phenomena; nor do they *have to* remain content with questionnaire or interview schedules as exclusive methodological devices in their study. The practices and methods of belief-ascription and avowal, along with other related phenomena identified here, may be treated as phenomena of technical interest.

NOTES

1. See, e.g., Bryan R. Wilson (ed.) *Rationality* (Basil Blackwell, 1974). The exceptions here are Peter Winch and Martin Hollis.
2. See, e.g., Nigel Harris, *Beliefs in Society: The Problem of Ideology* (C. A. Watts & Co., London, 1968).
3. Karl Mannheim, *Ideology and Utopia* (Routledge & Kegan Paul, London, 1966), p. 62.
4. Ibid., p. 67 et seq.
5. Ibid., p. 69. It is not possible here to document the variety of objections that have been made to this formulation of the problem of the sociology of knowledge, most of them of a logical kind. Two of the most obvious ones are: (i) there is insufficient attention paid to the distinction between knowledge and beliefs (both are often lumped together as "ideas") and the corollary distinctions in their treatment, and (ii) if we restrict our focus to knowledge only, Mannheim seems (programmatically, at least) to be committed to a logically self-defeating enterprise—to know the grounds of my knowledge is, as Hayek and others have noted, to know more than I know, which is absurd.
6. Karl Marx and Frederick Engels, *The German Ideology* (Lawrence & Wishart, London, 1965), pp. 29-78. It should be noted here that Engels postulated a more all-embracing notion of ideology than the one to be found in *The German Ideology;* in a letter to F. Mehrring (14 July 1893, *Selected Works,* Vol. 1, p. 388) he argued that "Ideology is a process accomplished by the so-called thinker consciously indeed but with a false consciousness. The real motives impelling him remain unknown to him, otherwise it would not be an ideological process at all. Hence he imagines false or apparent motives." The strangely psychoanalytical twist in the use of the notion of motive derives from Engels' mistake in attributing the ideological function or consequence of a thought to the thinker as his real motive for producing it—although this may *sometimes* be accurate, Engels claims that such a thinker *must not know anything about it,* which is a contradiction in terms. Of course, if such a formulation of ideology were sustained, then it would clearly backfire onto Marx and Engels themselves, since they may be argued to have imagined false or apparent motives in the construction of *their* thoughts about social life. There is nothing in Marx's own writings nor in his collaborative work with Engels which is consistent with this peculiar version of ideology, however.

7.   See A. R. Louch, *Explanation and Human Action* (Basil Blackwell, 1966).

8.   See Harold Garfinkel, *Studies in Ethnomethodology* Prentice-Hall, N.J., 1967), especially Chapters Two and Three.

9.   See ibid., and H. Garfinkel and H. Sacks, "On Formal Structures of Practical Actions" in J. C. McKinney and E. A. Tiryakian (eds.) *Theoretical Sociology: Perspectives and Developments* (Appleton-Century-Crofts, N. Y., 1970).

10.   See, *inter alia*, the contributions by Lakoff, Langendoen and the Kiparskys in D. D. Steinberg and L. A. Jakobovits (eds.), *Semantics: An Interdisciplinary Reader in Philosophy, Linguistics and Psychology* (Cambridge University Press, 1971), Section entitled: "Meaning, Presupposition and Reference"; the contributions of Garner, Keenan, Langendoen and Savin and Fillmore in C. J. Fillmore and D. T. Langendoen (eds.), *Studies in Linguistic Semantics* (Holt, Rinehart & Winston, N.Y., 1971); contributions of Fillmore and Stalnaker in D. Davidson and G. Harman (eds.), *Semantics of Natural Language* (D. Reidel Co., Boston, 1972) and the following specific papers: Bas C. van Fraassen, "Presupposition, Implication and Self-Reference," *Journal of Philosophy* 65, 1968; Richard Montague, "Presupposing," *Philosophical Quarterly* 19, 1969; R. Lakoff, "Some Reasons Why There Can't Be Any *Some-Any* Rule," *Language* 45, 1969; and Jerry L. Morgan, "On the Treatment of Presuppositions in Transformational Grammar" in R. I. Binnick *et al.* (eds.), *Papers from the 5th Regional Meeting of the Chicago Linguistics Society* (Chicago, 1969).

11.   J. L. Austin, *How To Do Things With Words* (Oxford University Press, London 1962).

12.   Charles J. Fillmore, "Verbs of Judging: An Exercise in Semantic Description" in C.J. Fillmore and D. T. Langendoen (eds.) *Studies in Linguistic Semantics* (op. cit), p. 277.

13.   John Searle, "What is a Speech Act?" in Max Black (ed.), *Philosophy in America* (Cornell University Press, 1965).

14.   On adjacency-pairing and sequential issues generally, see Harvey Sacks, Emmanuel Schegloff and Gail Jefferson, "A Simplest Systematics for the Organization of Turn-Taking in Conversation," *Language, 50*, No. 4, Part 1, December 1974.

15.   "Dr. K." is an anonymized use for transcription purposes; the full name was actually uttered in the extracted talk.

16.   For a detailed discussion of adjacency-pairing as the basic organizational unit for conversation, see Harvey Sacks, *Lecture 1*, Spring 1972; April 4 (SS 158X—mimeo, University of California at Irvine).

17.   C. J. Fillmore, "Verbs of Judging," op. cit.

18.   J. L. Austin, "A Plea for Excuses" in his *Philosophical Papers*, eds., J.O. Urmson and G. J. Warnock (Oxford University Press, London, 1970), p. 181n.

19.   John Searle, *op. cit.* Those philosophers and linguists who treat communicative activities as if they had a *constitutive*-rule structure like, e.g., chess games, seem to overlook the consideration that, whereas the rules of chess, such as the rule that a bishop moves diagonally along squares of its own color, may be thought of as definitive of playing chess (since if a chess-player found his partner moving his bishop in violation of that rule it would not be a case of poor play but of the opponent's not playing *chess* at all), for most ordinary communicative activities there is no definite, codified set of rules available. There are only preferential, or normative, rules for such activities in the sense that whatever rules can be formulated are always relative to a conception of "proper," "appropriate," "reasonable," etc. communicative action, whether that be complaining, insulting or even promising. If one of these rules of, for example, apologizing, were to be broken, then the action being performed may still be thought of as a case of apologizing, but a clumsy, jocular, or insincere apology in its context. If the rules were truly *constitutive*, then all of our communicative actions should be assessable in terms of correctness or incorrectness;

but how could one be said to apologize "incorrectly" or to insult "correctly"? They do not have these adverbial tolerances at all.

20.   Searle's actual formulation of his conditions goes as follows: given that a speaker (S) utters a sentence (T) in the presence of a hearer (H), then, in the utterance of (T), S sincerely (and nondefectively) promises that *p* to H if and only if:

(i)   Normal input and output conditions obtain. [E.g., both speaker and hearer understand the language, are conscious,not joking, not under duress, not playacting, not suffering from some impediment like deafness, aphasia, etc., etc. It has been argued that, until Searle can specify *all* of the contextual conditions which must obtain to fulfill this initial condition, he cannot be credited with having *specified* a set of necessary and sufficient conditions at all. I think this a potent objection.]

(ii).   S expresses that *p* in the utterance of T.

(iii)   In expressing that *p*, S predicates a future act A of S.

(iv)   H would prefer S's doing A to his not doing A, and S believes that H would prefer his doing A to his not doing A.

(v)   It is not obvious to both S and H that S will do A in the normal course of events.

(vi)   S intends to do A.

(vii)   S intends that the utterance of T will place him under an obligation to do A.

(viii)   S intends that the utterance of T will produce in H a belief that conditions (vi) and (vii) obtain by means of the recognition of the intention to produce that belief, and he intends this recognition to be achieved by means of the recognition of the sentence as one conventionally used to produce such beliefs.

(ix)   The semantical rules of the dialect spoken by S and H are such that T is correctly and sincerely uttered if (and only if) conditions (i) to (viii) obtain. ("What is a Speech Act?", op. cit.)

21.   Paraphrase of condition (iv) above, for our analytical purposes.

22.   Paraphrase of condition (v) above, for our analytical purposes.

23.   Paraphrase of condition (viii) above. I should point out that I think such a version of Searle's analysis saves it from a good deal of criticism.

24.   Charles J. Fillmore, "Subjects, Speakers and Roles" in D. Davidson and G. Harman (eds.), *Semantics of Natural Language*, (op. cit.), p. 17.

25.   Paul and Carol Kiparsky, "Fact" in D. D. Steinberg and L. A. Jakobovits (eds.), *op cit.*

26.   Bas C. van Fraassen, "Singular Terms, Truth Value Gaps, and Free Logic," *Journal of Philosophy* 63, 1966, and his "Presupposition, Implication and Self-Reference," op-. cit. In van Fraassen's terms, an assertion *p* presupposes *Q* if *Q* is necessitated by both *p* and not-*p*. D. T. Langendoen makes use of this formulation in testing for presuppositions in his "Presupposition and Assertion in the Semantic Analysis of Nouns and Verbs in English" in Steinberg and Jakobovits (eds.), op. cit., although without explicit reference to van Fraassen's formulation.

27.   See the relevant discussion in George Lakoﬀ, "Linguistics and Natural Logic" in Davidson & Harman (Eds.), *op. cit.*, pp. 576-77.

28.   I am indebted to Lena Jayyusi for drawing my attention to the implications of this extract.

29.   Terry Winograd, *Understanding Natural Language* (Edinburgh University Press, 1972), p. 33.

30.   For a detailed discussion of "category-bound activities" and their role in ordinary understandings, see Harvey Sacks, "On the Analyzability of Stories by Children" in John J. Gumperz & Dell Hymes (Eds.) *Directions in Sociolinguistics: The Ethnography of Communication* (Holt, Rinehart & Winston, 1972).

31.   D. G. Williams,   "Some Reflections on the Methodology of Conversational

Analysis", Unpublished Master's Dissertation, University of Manchester, England, May 1975.

32.   Mundane discourse is overwhelmingly enthymematic. An enthymeme is an argument, (assertion, discourse on a topic) in which the premisses are not explicitly articulated. It seems to have been one of the features of discourse to which Garfinkel was alluding in his discussion of conversation in "Studies of the Routine Grounds of Everyday Activities" in his *Studies in Ethnomethodology, op. cit.,* Chapter Two, and which informs much of the analysis of 'glossing practices' in Garfinkel and Sacks, "On Formal Structures of Practical Action" in McKinney & Tiryakian (Eds.), *Theoretical Sociology, op. cit.*

33.   Robert C. Stalnaker, "Pragmatics" in Davidson & Harman (Eds.), *op. cit.,* p. 387.

34.   See the brief discussion in Mats Furberg, *Saying and Meaning* (Basil Blackwell 1970), pp. 44-5.

35.   For a fuller discussion of some of the conventionally assignable presuppositions involved in insanity ascriptions, see J.Coulter, *Approaches to Insanity,* (Halsted, N. Y., 1974), Part Two, and "Notes on Insanity and the Moral Order" Appendix to *The Operations of Mental Health Personnel* (unpublished Ph. D. thesis, University of Manchester, England, 1975). Contrary to some of the arguments of Szasz and Scheff, many *un*committed psychiatrists and laymen routinely employ the phrase "mental illness." It is above all a practical reasoning device, and does not presuppose any biological or ontological or mentalistic commitments, except where these are made *explicit.*

36.   Hilary Putnam, "The Meaning of 'Meaning'" in *Minnesota Studies in the Philosophy of Science,* University of Minnesota Press, Minneapolis, Vol. VII (forthcoming).

37.   Ernest Gellner, *Words and Things* (Pelican, 1968), pp. 37-40.

38.   *Ibid.,* p. 39.

39.   *Ibid.,* p. 37.

40.   The formulation of such a goal is clearly derivative of Sacks' approach to the study of conversational objects.

41.   F. Peters, *The World Next Door* (Farrar, Straus & Co. Inc., N. Y., 1949), p.24 (quoted in H. Schwartz, *Mental Disorder and the Study of Subjective Experience: Some Uses of Each to Elucidate the Other.* Unpublished Ph. D. thesis, U. C. L. A., 1971, p. 263).

42.   E. E. Evans-Pritchard, *Witchcraft, Oracles and Magic Among the Azande* (Clarendon Press, Oxford, 1965).

43.   Hanna F. Pitkin, *Wittgenstein and Justice* (University of California Press, 1972), p. 258.

44.   Excerpted from a French newspaper story by Jacques and Janine Vallee, *Challenge to Science: The UFO Enigma* (with foreword by J. A. Hynek), Tandem, London, 1974, p. 185.

45.   Direct quotation reported in J. and J. Vallee, ibid., p. 194.

46.   Ludwig Binswanger, "Insanity as Life-Historical Phenomenon and as Mental Disease: The Case of Ilse" in R. May, E. Angel, and H. F. Ellenberger (eds.), *Existence: A New Dimension in Psychiatry and Psychology* (Simon & Schuster, N.Y., 1958).

47.   Ibid., p. 216

48.   H. Garfinkel, *Studies in Ethnomethodology, op. cit., p. 31 and passim.*

49.   *Ibid.,* Chapter One. See also D. Zimmerman and M. Pollner, "The Everyday World as a Phenomenon" in Jack D. Douglas (ed.), *Understanding Everyday Life: Towards the Reconstruction of Sociological Knowledge* (Aldine, 1970).

50.   H. Garfinkel and H. Sacks, "On Formal Structures of Practical Actions," op. cit. Section entitled: "Formal Structures in Accountably Rational Discourse: The 'Machinery.' "

The Radio Raiders Story

Jim Schenkein

Schenkein presents an example of practical reasoning drawn from the newspapers, an account of a robbery. His examination of the newspaper story considers the methods newspapers may routinely use to transform stories about events "in the world" into stories "in the news." The reading of the headline and the story in the newspaper can involve the reader in solving a puzzle of references, i.e., in trying to determine to whom and to what the story refers. The reader's reading of preceding days' newspapers may be necessary to enable him to solve such referential puzzles.

News stories achieve their status as reports of events in the world in some fashion. How they do so is a topic deserving of detailed exploration. It is such issues as these which Schenkein shows can transform the reading of the newspapers into a topic of study to determine how members make sense and what methods of practical reasoning are used as resources by news writers to make their reports sensible.

Although I habitually scan the headlines of street-peddled newspaper, I am seldom moved to buy one. As it happens, in the fall of 1971 I bought a copy of *The Guardian* I had seen on my way to catch a train from London to Manchester. The night before I had seen a television news report on a wonderfully embarrassing bank robbery and I wanted

187

to entertain my long-standing fascination with perfectly executed crimes while on the train:

POLICE INQUIRY INTO WHY THEY MISSED THE RADIO RAIDERS

By Our Own Reporter

An informal inquiry is to be held in London with a view to tightening police procedures after the Baker Street bank raid discovered yesterday. The review will be at divisional level only, but some senior Scotland Yard officials recognise "disturbing aspects" of the case.

Valuables estimated as worth several hundred thousand pounds were stolen from private safe deposit boxes at Lloyds bank branch —in spite of an early warning from an amateur radio enthusiast, who, from his home half a mile away in Wimpole Street, picked up the thieves' walkie-talkie conversations.

Alerted by the remark "we are sitting on three hundred grand (300,000)," Mr. Robert Rowlands, who has been a radio "ham" for many years, telephoned Marylebone Lane police station late on Saturday night. But police did not call in Post Office engineers to trace the source of the transmission until after midday on Sunday, more than 12 hours later. Five minutes after detector vans arrived at Marylebone, the transmissions ceased.

At 3:30 p.m. on Sunday, police and security guards visited the branch in one of hundreds of checks on banks in the London area. They reported "premises checked and found secure." They did not open the time-locked vault.

When branch staff—including the manager, Mr. Guy Dark, who had been on holiday, returned to work yesterday, they found that the door of the vault had been pierced with a 15-inch hole by a thermic lance.

The thieves had tunnelled 40 feet under the vault from the basement of an empty shop two doors away. They did not touch the bank safe,

Judge wants labour corps for criminals, page 7; Crime and technology, page 11; Text of the robbers' radio talk, back page

but forced a quarter of the boxes containing jewellery, cash, documents, and other valuables deposited by clients from the affluent neighbouring areas of St. John's Wood and Baker Street.

Worried depositors gathered outside the branch as news of the robbery spread. Mr. John Bull, a Baker Street ward member of

Westminster City Council, said he had some 30 antiques on deposit, many of them uninsured. "They're what I've put aside for later life, as investments," he said. "I can't bear to think how much I've lost if they've been stolen."

Mr. Rowlands, aged 32, a doctor's son described later by a relative as "an absolute fanatic" for radio and television communications, was then under police guard four streets away. But he is understood to feel that he was regarded by police as "a nut case" when he reported the transmissions shortly after 11 p.m. on Saturday.

He had been turning his receiver dial at random before going to sleep when, on 27.15 megacycles, he heard conversation between a man named Bob, who was acting as a lookout, and another who appeared to be complaining about fumes from cutting equipment.

Police suggested that Mr. Rowlands should tape the conversations, which ceased on Sunday morning. Mr. Rowlands recorded a conversation late on Saturday night which appeared to be a lookout demanding eight hours' sleep. A woman's voice told him work would restart at "about half eight to nine o'clock."

Mr. Rowlands is understood to have made further calls to the police during the night and when the conversation was resumed on Sunday morning.

The Post Office said yesterday that if it had been notified before midday on Sunday it could have been "certain" of tracing the transmission. It ruled out a suggestion that high buildings in Baker Street might have confused its equipment.

Police at the bank yesterday found the walkie-talkies in the basement, with a thermic lance, gelignite, oxyacetylene equipment, spades and other tools. Earth from the three-foot wide tunnel had been transferred to the basement and the tunnel neatly shored up.

Bank staff will not know the extent of losses until clients have disclosed their deposits. A spokesman said an unofficial estimate that the robbery might run into a million pounds was "unlikely to be true."

Officers at Marylebone Lane and St. John's Wood, centres of the police investigation, declined to confirm or deny the time at which the first "ham" report had been logged. This will be a central issue for the police inquiry which will ask why such a long time lag occurred before local police took the call seriously, and why the vault was not opened on Sunday afternoon.

Mr. Rowlands said last night in an interview on ITN's "News at Ten": "I just happened to tune in to the frequency. Anyone could have picked it up."

Asked why the police were "so slow off the mark," Mr. Rowlands said: "I think they did not understand the problems, because this was the first time this had happened. They did not grasp the situation. I told them I thought the signals were coming from about half a mile away."

Asked what clues could have told the police the location of the bank, Mr. Rowlands said: "We knew it was in a main road, there was a large amount of money—at least £300,000—and there was a road drill nearby."

Although I carefully clip and save thises and thats from newspapers, I rarely give one a serious second look once it has been processed into a suggestion box I have somehow had with me since junior high school. As it happens, in the spring of 1973 I came upon the radio raiders headline for a second time in the midst of packing for a move from Holland to California. Distanced from my original encounter with the story by a year and a half, the headline filled my eyes with the squinting of my imagination:

POLICE INQUIRY INTO WHY THEY
MISSED THE RADIO RAIDERS

I considered the sorts of things the "radio raiders" might be, and the kinds of "missing" the police might have experienced in relation to them: were the police inquiring after their longing for an old radio show? why were they late for a rendezvous with their own radio-dispatched vice squad? or why did their marksmen fail to hit the revolutionaries besieging the radio station? With a glance through the story beneath the headline, my long-standing fascination with perfectly executed crimes was again aroused and I could resume my packing with the headline deciphered.

Here were two encounters with the same headline, but each involved me in a sharply different relationship to the story beneath it. The first time, the radio raiders story had been in the news a couple of days and when I saw the headline on the street I understood it at a glance; I bought the paper precisely because I wanted to dwell on the story I knew would be under the radio raiders headline. The second time, the robbery had been out of the news for a year and a half, and when I saw the headline among my things I was baffled by it; I had to consult the story to figure it out.

The headline is, of course, considerably more than a short statement of the contents of the story it foreruns. Whatever circumstances this headline can be construed to encode, it is announcing at least a second report about some state of affairs already "in the news"—I have come to think of that story as the radio raiders story. The headline invokes that ongoing story in announcing some latest development, namely, the "police inquiry into why" they missed whatever it is they missed.

The headline is constructed as a referential puzzle. Unless certain crucial details are in hand,[1] a reader would be unable to know who, in particular, these radio raiders were, and what, in particular, they had done, so that the police, in a particular way, had missed them and were now going to investigate all of those particulars. But while the events to which the headline refers are circumstances "in the world," solving the referential puzzle requires no field trip there; rather more conveniently, the puzzle can be adequately solved by attention to "the news"—recalling an earlier report, inspecting the text of this report, watching for the radio raiders story in some other organ of the news, and so on.

One of the ways the referential puzzle presented by this headline transforms events "in the world" into stories "in the news" is by its sharp focus on the kind of relationship a reader has with "the news." The reader who is baffled by the abbreviated announcement of the headline is alerted that his relationship with "the news" is something less than intimate. As long as the headline is currently in the news of the day, a baffled reader is alerted that his involvement in "the news" (i.e., the news of the radio raiders story, or of front-page stories generally) lags behind the pace of its emerging developments; when the headline is no longer current, a baffled reader is alerted that his involvement in the radio raiders story deteriorated more rapidly than the newsclipping. In or out of the news of the day, a reader who understands the headline at a glance enjoys a certain intimacy with "the news" (i.e., the news of the radio raiders story, or of front-page stories generally).

Neither the baffled nor the wise reader is any "closer" to the action "in the world" of course—it is just that the wise reader is more familiar with "the news" than the other reader. In observing that this headline presents a reader with a referential puzzle[2] that focuses on his relationship to "the news" we have begun to consider how events "in the world" come to be experienced as stories "in the news."

Other observations will naturally lead elsewhere. Inspect the headline again:

POLICE INQUIRY INTO WHY THEY
MISSED THE RADIO RAIDERS

and notice this time that it involves us in the bank robbery as a mistake of the police rather than, for example, a success of the robbers. This observation suggests inquiring after the selective moral perspectives with which a headline can serve up its story. An official anticriminal morality in the version proclaimed by this headline is plainly but one of the available versions. With that version, however, the headline displays its own proper place in a world suffering certain moral assaults and protective failures. As it transforms various states of affairs into "the news" we are provided a moral universe in which the attitude of the headline occupies just the right position. The negotiation of public morals surely deserves greater attention than my mention of it here offers; but for now, let us simply collect up that topic as another analytic direction which a closer look at this newspaper clipping can inspire and provide phenomenal detail for.

Now consider the byline of the radio raiders story:

By Our Own Reporter

It is not without its curiosities when a second glance is paid it. Notice that it presents the newspaper account as some kind of exclusive package offered to the readers of *The Guardian* —a package put together just for them without mechanically reproducing the story of some other news agency or wire service. But while the story may be a declared triumph of the newspaper, it apparently takes a different kind of triumph for the reporter, whoever that might be, to earn public exposure with a name in the byline. It is, perhaps, not a byline at all, but a byline-like item that declares the local origins of the account printed beneath it while giving credit to no one but the publisher of the newspaper.

Unlike the headline above it, "By Our Own Reporter" does not strike us as glossing some events "in the world," nor does it present to us a version of some events "in the news." Who the reporter may be is very well "in the world" of course, and reporters getting their stories might very well be "in the news" as well. But for the radio raiders story, "By Our Own Reporter" renders us witnesses-in-passing to some private declaration of the newspaper. The referential puzzle we might formulate to describe an obvious feature of the byline-like item (e.g., what reporter is it referring to?) would not bring into focus our relationship with "the news," but rather, our relationship to "the newspaper" as an enterprise whose practical activities generate "the news" on our behalf.

These observations suggest inquiring after the practices and concerns which organize the reportage of "the news" within a format willing and able to mark such things as the relative exclusivity of the presented account, the local origins of the text, the career status of an unnamed reporter, and other presumed details of the labors therefore involved in producing "the news" for us to read. Apparently, newspaper coverage is not limited to reporting on events "in the world," nor do all the components of a newspaper account serve to elaborate stories "in the news"—events for the newspaper itself can be granted their place in print. Further study could well detail other ways in which the routine reporting of "the news" provides space for displaying the practical achievements of the newspaper.

As a final introductory sketch, let us inspect the lead paragraph of the radio raiders story:

> An informal inquiry is to be held in London with a view to tightening police procedures after the Baker Street bank raid discovered yesterday. The review will be at divisional level only, but some senior Scotland Yard officers recognise "disturbing aspects" about police handling of the case.

Here the text of the story is initiated with a declaration that locates this account somewhere within an unfinished story, one that began with the "Baker Street bank raid discovered yesterday" and will develop at least through the results of the police inquiry "to be held in London." Yet the interim report offered readers now can already disclose officially recognized misgivings about police performance on the case; the present account will presumably fill its column inches with details of the "disturbing aspects" which the policy inquiry will report officially sometime in the future. The represented news is marked for its position in a temporal order not only to identify the story as the current news it ought to be, but, as we can see, temporal marking can be mobilized to accent the special services a newspaper performs on our behalf (e.g., follow-ups, retrospectives, news analyses, anticipatory investigations, and other temporally linked items). This story is not constructed merely as "the news" it ought to be, and it is more than a follow-up on the account of yesterday's robbery: today's account will offer the reader the results of a reporter's investigation into the "disturbing aspects" initiating the official inquiry whose findings are days or years away.

These observations suggest inquiring after the negotiation of temporal structures by news reporting. Through the artful design of such things as a story's beginning, middle, and projected end, an account of "the news" can position itself in a temporally ordered stream of events. The matter-of-fact chronologies constructed by an account can themselves be used as somehow independent and objective indices for the pace of the world vis-a-vis the pace of the newspaper. With one temporal order, the products of the newspaper enterprise can emerge well ahead of an official police inquiry; another set of temporal parameters for this story sometime later can render the newspaper research full of the caution and sobriety that a decidedly hasty conclusion from a speedy policy inquiry sadly lacks. Doubtlessly, the negotiation of temporal structures through the reporting of "the news" is another fruitful direction for further analysis of documents such as the radio raiders story.

Any of the lines of inquiry sketched out thus far might have captured our analytic energies. Each is a satisfying starting place methodologically since each is rooted in observations that seriously treat the newspaper clipping as a socially organized corpus of pehnomena all through its course. The experiential, moral, practical, and temporal features brought into view by these introductory observations are classically interesting topics; an analysis that sought to rigorously describe the unfolding transaction of such things in the details of this utterly routine newspaper account could generate findings of interest to students of both classical topics and mundane phenomena. I have sketched these possibilities for analytic direction to involve us from the start with the organizational integrity of the newspaper clipping, and to offer an immediate appreciation of the sorts of analytic issues closer scrutiny of such documents can enliven.

Let me now develop some observations on the story told to us in this clipping. The story indeed confirms the appropriateness of the inquiry proclaimed in the headline: police failed to apprehend these bank robbers, we are told,

> In spite of an early warning from an amateur radio
> enthusiast. . .

To make matters worse for police, a security guard and police inspection of the bank Sunday afternoon uncovered no trace of the crime:

> They reported "premises checked and found
> secure."

And as if that was not enough,

> The Post Office said yesterday that if it had been
> notified before midday on Sunday it could have
> been "certain" of tracing the transmissions.

On top, of that, the ham radio operator had developed a list of clues
from his eavesdropping that could have been exploited to narrow down
the source of the transmissions:

> ". . .I told them I thought the signals were coming
> from about half a mile away. . . We knew it was in
> a main road, there was a large amount of-
> money—at least £300,000—and there was a road
> drill nearby."

The newspaper account also implies that missing the radio raiders under
these circumstances plunges police into an unhappy responsibility for the
misfortune depositors in the bank will have suffered:

> Worried depositors gathered outside the branch
> as news of the robbery spread. Mr. John
> Bull. . .said he had some 30 antiques on deposit,
> many of them uninsured. "They're what I've put
> aside for later life, as investments," he said. "I
> can't bear to think how much I've lost if they've
> been stolen."

And at the center of the story is the ham radio operator who intercepted
the walkie-talkie communications of the bank robbers. Consider the
following description of him:

> Mr. Rowlands, aged 32, a doctor's son described
> later by a relative as "an absolute fanatic" for
> radio and television communications. . .

We would think it unlikely that the newspaper description of this central character has its origins in a reporter's dream about the man's name or age, in a guess about his reputation in the family, or in a wish about his father's profession. We can, in fact, rely on the factual status of description not merely because we can formulate certain conventions of newspaper journalism or laws of libel which we abstractly believe govern the printing of such a description; we can rely on the factual status of the description because it is prominently displayed in its telling. The descriptor "an absolute fanatic" is delivered as an exact quotation to show that its source lies in a relative's fancy about the man. Marking this descriptor as somebody's fancy renders that fancy a kind of fact (e.g., that somebody said he was "an absolute fanatic") On the other hand, the descriptors "Mr. Rowlands, aged 32, a doctor's son" are delivered without noting the sources of those bits of information, as though name, age, and father's profession are immune from fanciful versions and stand, as presented, as objective facts about the man.

But now imagine a somewhat different distribution of fact and fancy for this description of the ham radio operator:

> Mr. Rowlands, aged 32, an absolute fanatic for radio and television communications, was described later by a relative as "a doctor's son". . . .

In this imaginary variation, report of the man's reputation is delivered as fact instead of a relative's fancy, and his filial relationship to a doctor is reported as but one person's formulation instead of incontrovertible factual information about him. To some of us, the differences between the actual newspaper description and this imaginary variation can only betray someone's analytic fancy—the differences mark the imaginary description as necessarily imaginary because it proposes an arrangement of fact and fancy foreign to the world we know. To others, the differences simply dramatize alternative reporting possibilities—both arrangements of fact and fancy deliver reports for possible circumstances in some world.

No matter how we argue the relationship between the actual and the imaginary arrangement of fact and fancy, we have no trouble in understanding either of them. Each gives us a glimpse into some world (either "real" or "imaginary") where one sort of item is treated as generally available fact and another as appropriate only as somebody's fancy. Alternative arrangements of fact and fancy do seem to resonate from within alternative existential systems.

For example, when the newspaper account reports that a relative described Mr. Rowlands as "an absolute fanatic" we seem to place that relative, whoever that may be in other respects, in an existential system organized around a different arrangement of fact and fancy than the system inhabited by Mr. Rowlands. There is surely some sympathy for the harmless eccentricities of others in "an absolute fanatic," and it is surely less ugly than "frustrated spy" or some other possibilities; yet we tend to suppose that this relative is outside the ham radio operations of Mr. Rowlands since mention would properly be made of their joint fanaticism should that be the case. Moreover, there is a striking difference between Mr. Rowlands's characterization of his activities and this relative's description of him; the newspaper account tells us that—

> Mr. Rowlands said last night in an interview on ITN's "News at Ten" [a television broadcast]: "I just happened to tune into the frequency. Anyone could have picked it up."

We find ourselves knowing that only certain sorts of anybodies would be in a position to intercept the walkie-talkie conversations of bank robbers by happenstance. Indeed, from the biographical glimpses selected to tell the newspaper story, Mr. Rowlands is exhibited as inhabiting an existential system liable to appear fanatical from the outside. Although he says that anyone could have done it, the way he had done it is not without its peculiarities:

> He had been turning his receiver dial at random before going to sleep when, on 27.15 megacycles, he heard conversation . . .

Here we are peeking at a man who finds himself listening to the world through this radio receiver at random in preparation for sleep. The relative's description of him as "an absolute fanatic" reverberates as a prominently appropriate outsider's characterization in this picture of how Mr. Rowlands actually made his discovery.

By contrast, the newspaper distances itself from describing Mr. Rowlands as either "anybody" or "absolute fanatic" and uses instead the phrase "amateur radio enthusiast." When compared to the versions reported as proffered by the man himself or his relative, this version employed by the newspaper comes off as dispassionate factual description. While the newspaper's description may indeed be selected to exhibit its objectivity in reporting equivocal circumstances, *each* version is finely poised to exhibit an attitude deeply appropriate to the existential system through which it necessarily resounds. The newspaper version is appropriately preoccupied with a display of *impartiality,* the relative's version declares an appropriate *familiarity* with Mr. Rowlands's activities, and Mr. Rowlands's own characterization that his deed could have been done by anybody is full of the *modesty* that any hero really ought to have the good taste to exemplify during his public glorification.

When Mr. Rowlands contacted the public agency specifically responsible for official response to his discovery, the negotiation of an interaction between substantially discrete existential systems gives rise to yet another description for the man; we are told that

> he was regarded by police as a "nut case" when he reported the transmissions after 11 p.m. on Saturday.

Care is taken to mark the descriptor "nut case" as no simple fact about the man but rather as somebody's fancy about him again. In this instance, however, the source of the descriptor earns considerable preliminary attention:

> But he is understood to feel that he was regarded by police as a "nut case" when he reported the transmissions after 11 p.m. on Saturday.

Reporting that it is the "nut case" himself who has determined that the police regarded him that way provides *both* Mr. Rowlands and police an understandable and arguable position within alternative existential systems now converging. Obviously, the police did not receive Mr. Rowlands information as a factual disclosure, and consequently they were not filled with a sense of urgency in their official response to his report:

> Police suggested that Mr. Rowlands should tape the conversations, which ceased on Sunday morning.

The police emerge as embedded in an existential system professionally alert to reports from fanatics and other nut cases late on Saturday night, but nonetheless having policies and engaging procedures with which to process such reports into possible legitimacy. Mr. Rowlands, on the other hand, knew that his information was authentic, and in order to achieve an assembly of fact and fancy through which he and police officials could participate in a common "reality," he undertook additional work that evening, presumably in lieu of going to sleep:

> Mr. Rowlands recorded a conversation late on Saturday night which appeared to be a lookout demanding eight hours' sleep. A woman's voice told him work would restart at "about half eight to nine o'clock."
> Mr. Rowlands is understood to have made further calls to the police during the night and when the conversations were resumed on Sunday morning.

Mr. Rowlands emerges as embedded in an existential system wise to its own appearances to others, but nonetheless having policies and engaging procedures with which to persist in authenticating itself.

In delivering to us "the news" of the radio raiders story, the newspaper account somehow manages, among other things, to give us glimpses of alternative existential systems interacting in the aftermath of the robbery. We are provided these glimpses through a series of alternative descriptions for the story's central character, Mr. Rowlands. Each description represents another view of Mr. Rowlands, each generates a comparison between itself and the other descriptions as they accumulate through the text, and each can be compared to the reader's own emerging vision of Mr. Rowlands. Together they comprise a universe of discourse with densely interacting spokesmen for alternative existential systems. The spokesmen are neatly arranged, the newspaper's own characterization appearing first, Mr. Rowland's own version of himself coming last, and in between a systematically ordered presentation of three progressively vulgar colloquial versions.

The first, *an amateur radio enthusiast,* is the most benign of them all. While all succeeding descriptions are presented with quotations marks to identify a source outside the editorial policies of the newsroom, this first description of Mr. Rowlands's relevant avocation, as the newspaper's own, appears without quotation marks. It serves as an intial dispassionate characterization against which all subsequent characterizations can be compared. As the alternative descriptions successively appear, this first one emerges as quite proper, formal, and unprejudiced by slang, blood, or bureaucracy. It is, in the end, if not right from the beginning, a model for civilized reference to the fateful sport of Mr. Rowlands.

The second description, *a radio "ham" for many years,* dips into the vernacular for a more informal reference to Mr. Rowlands's hobby. This second characterization, moreover, embellishes the prior one by adding substantial experience to the enthusiasm Mr. Rowlands holds for his communications activities. That he is no newcomer to the conversations coming through his radio receivers somehow suggests that he can be no newcomer to the public responsibilities established citizen band radio operators are famous for. In moving to a quotable colloquial ("ham") we are shown the ready availability of a popular description for Mr. Rowlands. It may not be entirely illiterate in fact, but it is considerably more common on the tongue than the prior, unquoted construction. If the originatlity of *amateur radio enthusiast* makes it a candidate for literature, then perhaps it is the utter conventionality of "ham" that makes this second description a credible report of what "we" must call it—even though neither a particular nor a general speaker is formulated for us to concretely commune with. This popular ham description, while apparently vulgar in some places, is not so rude as to insinuate eccentricities about the man's way of life. Although it only quotes some ghost, "ham" seems to be included in the newspaper account as some kind of lesson of good taste for the common tongue. Alas, not one of the subsequent quotations from actual humans employs this tactful option; once it is no longer literature, so it seems, there is simply no stopping the steady vulgar march.

The third description, *described by a relative as "an absolute fanatic" for radio and television communications,* represents a departure from the civilities of the prior two descriptions. It is not as civil as *"ham" radio* nor as civilized as *amateur radio enthusiast;* but it is familiar, revealing, and it comes from living lips. This third description reports another conventional colloquialism for describing Mr. Rowlands, but "an absolute fanatic" merely invokes the revelation without specifying the details of Mr. Rowlands's involvement with his equipment. One of the things captured for us by "our own reporter" is a conventional betrayal of Mr. Rowlands's peculiarities of hobby and habit by an unnamed relative. Familiarity, among other things, seems to permit a conventional disclosure of intimacies which neither a phantom tactful stranger or a literate newswriter is allowed.

In the fourth description, *"a nut case,"* Mr. Rowlands's enthusiasms receive an ever more unbecoming characterization. Of course, the punch of the story depends upon the suspicions aroused about police handling of Mr. Rowlands; in linking police to this least generous description of the man—even if the link consists, as we have seen, of what the man himself thinks police thought of him—the official police response is tainted with a crude and tactless error of judgment.

The fifth description, *"anyone could have picked it up,"* delivers Mr.

Rowlands's own version of his activities. This last characterization
asserts the normality of his involvement in the radio raiders story by
promoting the dumb luck of his discovery. That "anyone" might have
intercepted the walkie-talkie communiques of the bank robbers is a possibility closed off by the fact that someone in particular has already done
so and transmission has by now ceased; yet the sheer possibility of other
citizen interceptors can be summoned here as Mr. Rowlands plugs himself into an ordinary way of life.

A substantial chunk of the column inches taken up by this account of
the radio raiders story is devoted to the systematically arranged appearance of alternative descriptions for Mr. Rowlands' involvement in the
affair. As it happens, two of those descriptions are from Mr. Rowlands
himself; and in fact, other quotes from him stand as the most frequently
used source of acknowledged information in this version of the radio
raiders story. Although other central characters are surely possible for
the radio raiders story, we somehow find that in the version told as "the
news" of the robbery, Mr. Rowlands is the central figure out of whose
utterances "the news" is assembled. It may seem only natural to pre-
occupy "the news" of the radio raiders story with Mr. Rowlands: he
intercepted the criminal conversations, notified police, and through considerable persistence transformed a silent bit of routine civic duty into a
frontpage story drawn largely from his version of the radio raiders story.
But to some of us, the radio raiders story of interest is the version which
some cops in hot water are telling to division headquarters: what and
how and why they did what they did, and why they did not do something
else instead would be the details of *that* radio raiders story. It would
make perfectly wonderful "news"—if only the police would make themselves available for comment. To others of us, the radio raiders story can
only be told by the radio raiders: what and how and why they did what
they did, and what they now plan to do with their riches would be the
details of *this* radio raiders story. It would make perfectly wonderful
"news"—if only the radio raiders were available for interview. Notwithstanding our other interests, for example in cops and robbers, Mr. Rowlands's version of the radio raiders story is the one which makes it into
"the news"—not because if is especially newsworthy, but because it was
told to "our own reporter" by a willing informant in time for the morning edition.

Although my early encounters with this newspaper clipping were
excited by my long-standing fascination with perfectly executed crimes,
closer scrutiny of the clipping can, of course, enliven other curiosities.
Indeed, a newspaper clipping can be inspected for how it confronts a
reader with a relationship to "the news"; or, how it transforms events

"in the world" into stories "in the news"; or, how it assembles orders of fact and fancy to authenticate "the news"; or, how it portrays a variety of existential systems converging to make "the news"; or, how the practical circumstances of a reporter's work have an impact on those versions of stories presented as "the news" of things. Close scrutiny of ordinary documents can sustain and enrich an interest in these and other phenomenal domains.

NOTES

1. Just which details of the story I would need in order to understand the headline at a glance is a great mystery to me. I do not know how what we call "memory" brings either current or old "news" into understanding, and I am not all too wise about how "understanding" works either—especially since it is clear enough that what would pass for understanding in one circumstance might fail in another. It does seem to make good sense to suppose that my recognition of the headline both times had something to do with my long-standing fascination with perfectly executed crimes, but for all I know, I bought the paper and saved the clipping to commemorate journeys here and there—the first time, I saw the headline while on my way to catch a cross-country train, and the second time I was packing for an intercontinental move. Even if questions of memory, understanding, recognition, and fascination are left unanswered, we can pick away at questions of referentiality. To put it another way: we can consider features of the referential puzzle presented by this headline without pausing to build, invoke, acknowledge, or pledge ourselves to any particular theory of mind or meaning.

2. Not all headlines, certainly, are constructed as referential puzzles. To be sure, among the other qualities the reputation of a newspaper can turn on, its policies for publishing one kind of headline or another are a convenient object for reputational attention. In his description of the activities of the *New York Times* newsroom, William L. Rivers has noted that "during slack periods, copy editors sometimes amuse themselves by telling history's most important stories in typically brief *Times* headlines: Jehova Resting/After 6-Day Task; Methuselah Dies/Judean was 969; Moses on Sinai/Gets 10-Pt. Plan" (Rivers, 1965).

REFERENCES

Rivers, William L. (1965). *The Opinion Makers.* Boston: Beacon Press.

Organizational Features of Direction Maps

George Psathas

Maps drawn to assist persons in finding a place are studied to discover what the map's features are, how these features are organized, and how this organized set of features produces the sensible quality of their being "maps" for locating a place. The readable-interpretable properties of written-drawn maps of directions, by virtue of their organization, serve to communicate directions to a place.

The map is shown to contain and use as resources members' methods for maintaining orientation, discovering and following a route, and getting to a destination—methods which are practical, understandable, and usable by members using practical reasoning. These methods are, in themselves, methods of practical reasoning.

Just as spoken materials can be examined to discover the methods of practical reasoning which their users depend upon to make what they say understandable, so written materials can be studied with the same purpose. Writings of authors of various kinds, whether professionally trained and skilled or ordinary laypersons engaged in such ordinary activities as writing letters, diaries, notes, reports, essays, and the like can, on close examination, be found to contain methods of practical reasoning.

It is this orientation which guides the present study of maps. The maps to be examined are those drawn by laypersons in order to provide directions to a particular place for another person who is presumed not to be knowledgeable about either the location of the place or of routes to get there.

Giving directions or giving instructions to be followed by another person can be accomplished in a number of ways, such as describing verbally a route or routes to be taken, drawing a map in the other's presence and providing "filling in" directional details verbally, drawing a map consisting of lines and names of streets and landmarks, drawing a map and including a written set of directions, and so forth. Maps can be "drawn" on paper, in the air, on a chalkboard, traced on one's hand or back or in the sand—in short, on any number of materials and with any degree of permanence intended. They can be produced for a one time-one person occasion or duplicated and distributed to a number of potential users.

The maps which will be examined in this paper were all drawn and then reproduced and sent by mail or delivered to the reader without any further explanation thought to be required by the maker. They were provided as complete in themselves, as matters which could be read independently by the reader without the presence of the maker, as self-explanatory and self-contained maps. They were accepted by those receiving them as maps providing information as to how to arrive at a given destination. I refer to these as "maps to our place," since they are made by those who know the destination well, for whom it is "home."

By contrast, the "occasioned map" is drawn in the reader-user's

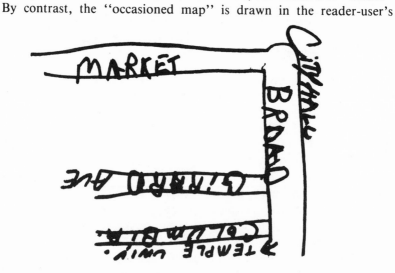

Figure 1A: Occasioned Map

presence, talked about while it is being drawn, with questioning and answering possible at the time of its drawing, drawn for just this reader-user and drawn for just this particular journey. Two examples are offered as Figures 1A and 1B. Neither can be understood without further explanation. For example, 1A was drawn for me by a person at an information booth at the Visitor's Center, Bicentennial Exhibit, March 10, 1976 in Philadelphia, Pennsylvania in response to my request to "draw a map to show me how to get from here to Temple University." Such maps lack written or sketched detail because such details are provided in and through talk and gestures at the time the map is drawn. Their study requires audio- or videotaped recordings of the occasions on which they are produced, since the visible-on-paper product is not understandable apart from the situated occasion of its production. In this paper, occasioned maps are not considered.

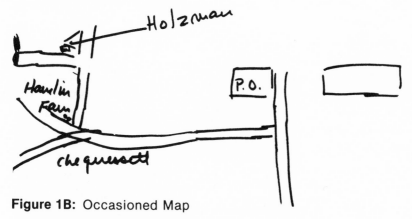

Figure 1B: Occasioned Map

The questions I am concerned with in examining the "maps to our place" are: what are the methodical and orderly features of the map which make it recognizable, readable, and interpretable as a map by the recipient-reader; how is the work of the map accomplished in the reading; and how does the map provide methods for finding the destination?

It is the map as a recognizable, readable, and understandable direction map as read by the reader which is being considered. I am not considering the use of the map on an actual journey. The map, when accepted and read, is accepted by the reader as a "potentially usable" map, as a map whose features provide for an actual use.

It is intended by its maker as a map for anyone who understands what we know-in-common and take-for-granted, readable and recognizable by such persons, and potentially usable by such persons whenever they may undertake an actual journey. But its status as a "map" does not depend on whether it is ever used by anyone, whether if it is used it "helps", "assists," "orients," and the rest, whether a user "likes" it, actually "follows" it, manages to "use" it, or whether, even if used, the user successfully locates the destination "following" the map. All such matters are not what makes it acceptable to both the maker and the reader as a map, since it can be read without ever being used. The reader does not need to undertake a journey yet is able to read it as a map. It is therefore just this matter which is being considered here, namely, how the map is recognizable, readable, interpretable, understandable *as a map,* what it "tells" the reader, and how in the "telling" conveys that this is just what it announces itself as being.

A Map with a Purpose

The map is read as purposeful. In the reading, the reader finds its purpose. The map is not read as a cartographer's map, a geographer's map, a drawn-to-scale, objective, descriptive, all-inclusive, map of the areas shown. It is not read nor taken to be a "general purpose map," a map to be given to persons interested in learning more about the area; it is not about streets and highways though it may contain these; it is not *about* "this city" though it is *of* "this city."

It is a map to be read as "showing a way to a particular place." It is a map for finding the place, for locating the place as a destination, as a place to which one can "go" and, having undertaken to go, can "arrive," and, having undertaken to "arrive" can discern, distinguish, and differentiate "the place" from among other places. It is a map for "finding," "locating," "getting to" a place, a destination for which the map provides a route.

It contains, necessarily, the place, the destination, to which the reader is directed as the place to be found. The place is marked, or named by a name to be used for this collection of reader-users. Its name, whether it be the street number, a phrase such as "our house," an arrow, an X, a description ("second house on the left"), or a combination of these (26 Oakridge Road), is the name which will suffice for this use. It is a name which allows for its being discerned, selected, and noted in relation to, and in contrast to, its surroundings. This name may be placed in the map in just that area where the place it names is reported to be and also repeated in a heading or title for the map. The title can provide the expanded locational features of the place, i.e., the street name, the town's name, the state's name, the country's name, etc., thereby setting the area shown in the map in the larger context in which it is located (e.g., Figure B, "Sable, 4 Plymouth Rd., Lexington"; Figure F, "Selwin, 6 Kingswood Road, Newton (Auburndale) Mass. 02166").

The Map's Space

The map's space is about this space and this space only. The map's space is bounded by the surface on which it is drawn. No matter what the size of the surface, the entire map can be drawn, and is drawn, within this area. It is this area, the surface of the material on which it is drawn, that furnishes the maker with the "edges" of the map, the "scale" which ·can be used within the boundaries provided. This applies to any continuations of the map on additional pages or to insets and enlarged areas drawn in a section or area on the same map.

The map begins and ends at its edges. The "real world" within which its depicted places are depicted as existing is not claimed to end at these edges. There are connections to, continuations of, and extensions onto other roads, areas, and places from the roads, areas, and places shown; but these other roads, areas, and places are not shown.

The map is offered as a selection out of, lifting up from, rather than a drawing on to any other geographical-physical version of the area represented. It is not a map to be read as an overlay by superimposing it onto the surface of a "real" map, i.e., a cartographer's map, since as a *map-in-itself* it contains its own scale, its own way of showing relations between places, its own code and legend.

It is related to other maps, to other versions of the same area, but it is not a corrected version of those other maps. It is not a map designed to clarify, explain, or remedy the faults of other maps. It is a map in and of itself. It can be read by itself, without references to other maps, without of necessity requiring its reader to refer to other maps. But since it is a map for a purpose, to be used to "get to" a particular place, the streets, pathways, and their connections are shown in their relevance for that project. It is only in this sense that the streets and the area shown are now readable as being *about* the area shown. The map can be studied in order to understand it on *its* own terms, to understand how *its* streets connect, where they are in relation to each other, how *they* are to be located and followed in order to get to the destination. Such information about the "map's world" is information in relation to the project of the map, i.e., how to get to the destination.

Getting On the Map

The map is offered and read as connected to the world in just this way: the connection is present but is not shown, for it cannot be shown; it is already there, already connected since this is a map *of* places in the world, *of* places already existing, actual, real, known-in-common places, places which can be found, which have been found, and which will be found again. In this sense, since its connections are understood, known-in-common and taken-for-granted, they need not be shown.

The connections shown are those to be noted, to anticipate finding and to remember having found. These streets, in just these ways in just these connections, are offered as adequate to the task of orienting the reader, enabling him to find the routes, enabling him to find the place by following the routes.

Where streets end they end for the purpose of the map. Whether the actual street continues or not is not relevant. To follow the street, beyond where it is shown to end, is to be "off the map," it is to be off the space and off the routes shown by the map. To be "on the map," to be oriented to and in the space of the map, is to be in those places and on those streets shown.

These are the places the map is about—and to ask of the map, where any other streets are, or where they "actually" end, is to be asking about matters the map is not concerned with. The questions to be asked of the map's beginnings or edges concern whether places where one can enter the map are shown, whether the map's streets are streets that are located *in* a named area, lead *to* or *from* a named area so that such matters as finding just this street in just this area can be solved. For example, the streets on the map's edges may be shown as leading *to* a named area (Figure A—"to Waltham, Boston," "South, to Newton, Needham," "North to Waltham, Lexington, Burlington, etc.," "West to Leominster, Harvard," "West to Weston, Wayland") and thus also leading *from* those same named areas *to* the area of the map. The named areas provide for the map's street being just this street in just this area. The area that the map shows is in itself not necessarily a named area—its "name" derives from showing where it is in relation to those named areas to and from which its streets lead. So whether it has a name or not does not matter when the streets shown are shown as leading to (or from) named areas. Whatever "name" it has is thus indexically tied to other areas.

Examples of such solutions are demonstrated in (Figure D) where at one end of a line labeled 195 is the name "Tolland" and at the other end "Storrs" or (Figure C) "Rt. 2 West" when "◄——Lincoln" is at one end and "——►Acton" is at the other, or (Figure B) where Mass. Ave. is shown "——►Arlington" at one end and "Lexington Center" at the other. Thus, the relevant part of the street is that section of it located between two such named areas.

Being "on the map" is not a matter of being between any two named areas because there are a large number of places "between." The map provides specific solutions by naming landmarks which are the "significant" places "between." Thus in Figure A, to be on Route 128 from Newton and heading North is not adequate but to be on Route 128, heading North and just having passed Route 20 (a landmark) is to be "on the map." The map instructs the reader as to just what places and points are to be found along the route in just what sequence and location. Thus, in Figure E, one can follow along Cambridge Street and look for Sanders Theater on the left and Fire Station on the right and then Ambassador Hotel on the left and IBM on the right. This sequence of places and their positions (on the right or left) provide not only an orientation concerning how one could tell if one was "on the map" but also whether one is "on the way," on the *right* way. (This will be discussed further in the section on directionality.)

Getting to the Destination

There are multiple starting points available on the map. The starting point is not the location used to organize the map—the *destination* is. There is thus provided for the reader the sense that wherever the map is entered, routes are discoverable which will lead to the destination. The roads or pathways are depicted as "already in progress," paths available to be taken. These are not just any paths; these are the ones which will do because they will and do lead to the destination. These are the ones to be sought for, to be found, to be followed.

That there are other paths which may intersect, cross over, under, parallel, merge, or whatever is not noted in each and every case where these happen in the world. The absence of such notation is not what is meant by "the map is not drawn to scale." The ones noted are noted as the ones to *take* and these set the ones *not* noted into the background, as furnishing the context from which those noted are selected. Those not

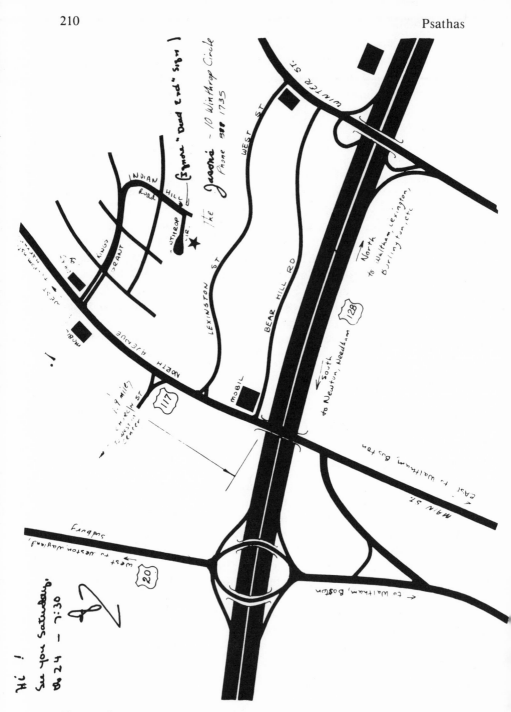

Figure A

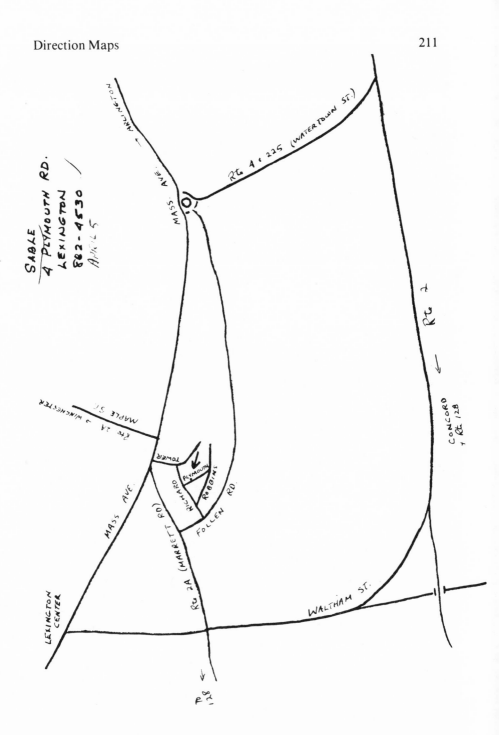

Figure B

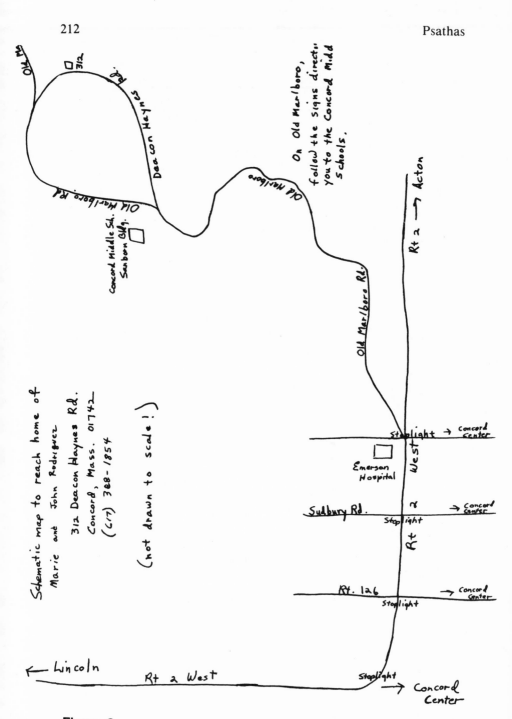

Figure C

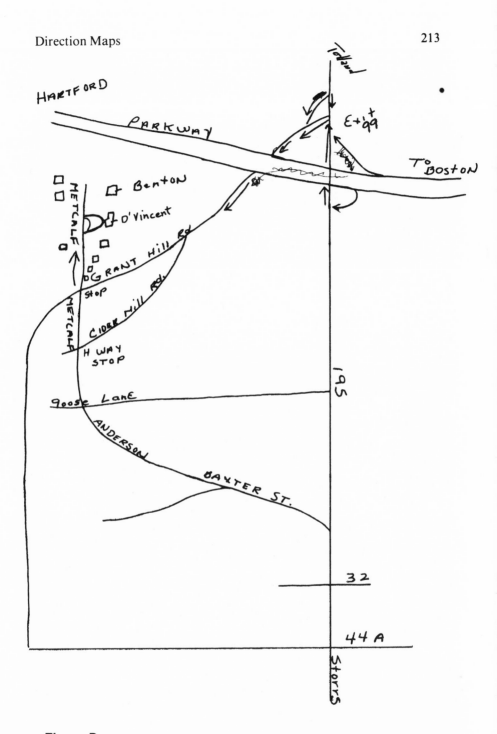

Figure D

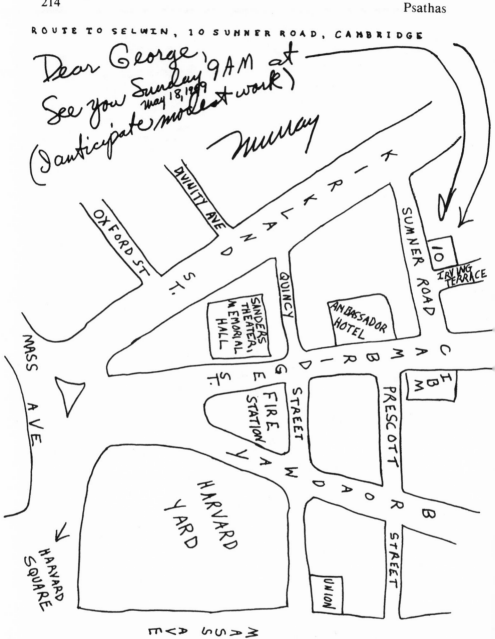

Figure E

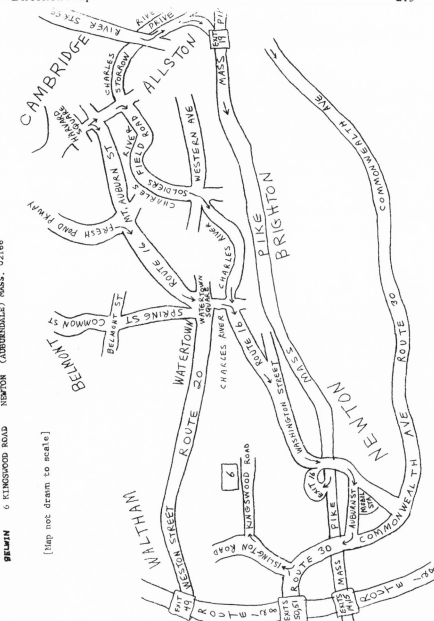

[Map not drawn to scale]

BELWIN   6 KINGSWOOD ROAD   NEWTON (AUBURNDALE) MASS. 02166

Figure F

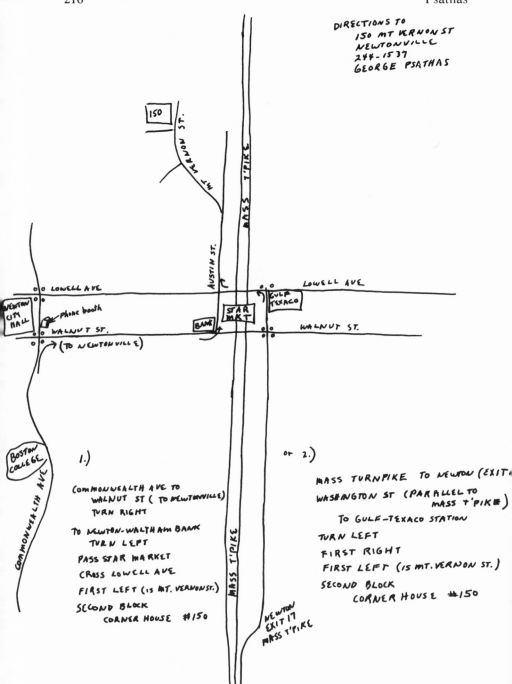

Figure G

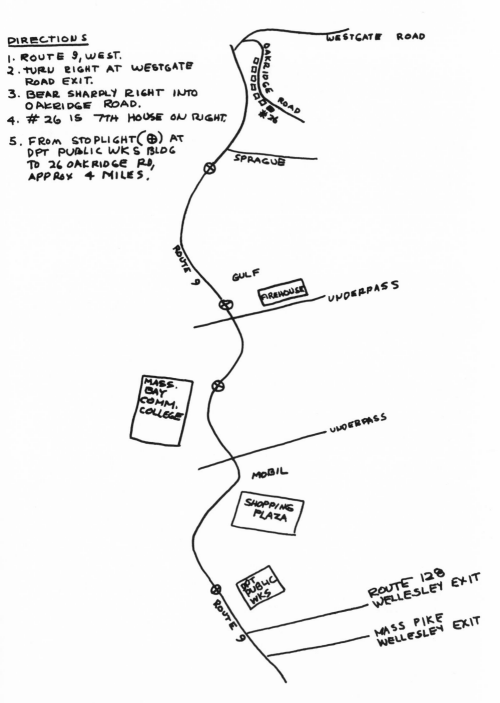

DIRECTIONS

1. ROUTE 9, WEST.
2. TURN RIGHT AT WESTGATE ROAD EXIT.
3. BEAR SHARPLY RIGHT INTO OAKRIDGE ROAD.
4. # 26 IS 7TH HOUSE ON RIGHT.
5. FROM STOPLIGHT (⊕) AT DPT PUBLIC WKS BLDG TO 26 OAKRIDGE RD, APPROX 4 MILES.

WESTGATE ROAD

OAKRIDGE ROAD
26

SPRAGUE

ROUTE 9

GULF

FIREHOUSE ── UNDERPASS

MASS. BAY COMM. COLLEGE

── UNDERPASS

MOBIL

SHOPPING PLAZA

DPT PUBLIC WKS

ROUTE 128 WELLESLEY EXIT

MASS PIKE WELLESLEY EXIT

ROUTE 9

Figure H

noted on the map are those which one need not know about. They are, if known, to be considered unnecessary or dispensable. They are, as noticeably absent, reminders that the map is not about *all* paths and routes but about just *these* paths and routes, just these places at just this time and for just this purpose.

The Map as a Motivated Project

That there are a large number of places, streets, and landmarks in the world, in the world referred to in the space of the map, is not at issue. That "fact" is known, as is the "fact" that there are numerous possible representations, numerous routes to the destination, and numerous starting points over the time span of the lives of those persons who may read the map. The "facts" motivate just this *one* drawing, this *one* representation, this *one* for these readers at this time. The selection, simplification, reduction, distortion, and/or magnification of the world as shown in the map is not the issue. That such things are being done is taken without question. The warning that "this is not to scale" (see Figure C for one such expressed warning) does not even come close to saying what the map is not. As a warning it is inadequate—the warning is written much more plainly. *The warning consists in the map itself,* for the map warns that the world is more complex than anyone can show or tell and that this way of presenting the world is one answer to that complexity. As such, it will, it must, it necessarily has to be simplification and a distortion, which stands in a relation of inexact correspondence to the places and objects in the world. But it is a solution offered by the maker of the map who is able to show a way to the destination, who is able to make intelligible-readable a way to get to the destination. It is expected of the maker that he will be able to and will select, and that this selection will be relevant to the purpose. The maker is not to hand over just any map, not the map already available as in the street or highway map, without some note or amendment, for it is just that selection capability which the maker offers himself as qualified to do. It is his knowledge of *a way,* a way to the destination and of methods to present such ways that the maker offers the reader through the map. Thus, it is not a solution to hand over an existing street map and say "find it,"though that would be a way for *the reader* to solve the problem of finding it. The solution the maker provides is a solution to the question of "can you draw a map to the destination?" By offering the map drawn, he offers his own competence as one who can achieve the task, achieve the simplification and selection which will make this map adequate to the purpose for which it is drawn. The "map to our place" especially does this, for it is a map to the place which the maker knows, it is the place to which he returns regularly. It is, of all the places in the world, the one which he is expected to know best. If anyone can get there he can. If anyone has ever found it, he has, and if anyone in the world should know how to get there, he does.

Yet this very competence, as a routinized, regular set of practices done without studied attention on each occasion of an actual journey home, can create a problem for the maker of the map. As a competent member able to locate his own home, the explication of the procedures followed in the process of locating is a task not regularly undertaken. The actual journey home may follow familiar routes which are the shorter, easier, less crowded by roads rather than main roads. Now, called upon to provide a map for one who will make this one journey for the first time, the selection of roads, and pathways will be focused on those more readily locatable: the main roads, the well-traveled roads rather than the byroads. The choice of a "best route" or "the easiest way" is oriented to presumed common knowledge—what anyone might reasonably know or might most easily be able to find in the course of an actual journey— rather than to that route which the maker "knows" with familiarity, knows so well that its features cannot be named with known-in-common names since it is their "gestalt configuration" which orients him on his own particular journeys. That configuration must be decomposed by the maker in order to produce the map.

Directions

As a map about getting to a particular place, how is it done that directions to the place are provided by the map? Here we will note that one solution is found in a variation of the map to our place, that which provides, along with the map, a set of written instructions or directions which can be read and related to the map. Examples of these maps are included here—Figures C and H. Such maps provide the reader-users with instructions which may fill in or elaborate the details of the map, which are to be read along with it. Such written instructions provide such matters as a "best way" to read the map, an elaboration of how to actually follow the map, or details which are not drawn on the map because of their complexity but can be more easily provided in a written elaboration. One thing such instructions do, and do specifically, is describe *a* route, a route which can be located on the map, and as such, provide the directions to be followed by the reader of the map.

In maps *without* written instructions, the sequences of steps to be taken to arrive at the destination are unformulated for the reader. The destination is named and/or marked. At the edges of the map, streets which may be entered from particular named areas and other streets are named. The reader is able to construct a route *to* the destination by starting *from* the destination and tracing outward or backward to any of the roads shown at the edges of the map. Or a route may be traced from one of the edges to the destination by noting one's progress in getting closer and closer to it. This method of tracing is not unlike the tracing of a path through a maze when the general direction and location of the destination is known but the exact routes to take are to be determined. The tracing of a route reveals, in an unfolding manner, the route's progress toward the destination. The route can be retraced or restarted if it seems to lead away from rather than toward the destination. Approaching the destination is not in itself an adequate criterion for the selection of that route, for in the course of the tracing it is possible to see alternative routes to the destination. Such alternatives can emerge as (alternative) routes to be taken at particular points along a route. The reader can then reexamine the map, restart his route and select from among the alternatives which appeared in the course of the initial tracing.

Figure F provides an interesting example of alternative routes starting from the same general area on the right hand edge of the map—Cambridge-Allston-Brighton—each designated by an arrow. The arrows do not flow as direct, connected lines but are short and unconnected. Once on the streets designated as beginning places (Common St. in Belmont; Fresh Pond Pkway in Cambridge; Mt. Auburn St. or Soldiers Field Road in Cambridge; Commonwealth Ave, in Brighton) the reader can follow the streets, turn onto other streets, and come closer and closer to the destination and arrive at places where the several routes converge (e.g., points of convergence are Commonwealth Ave. and Auburn St.; Route 30 and Islington Road). Prior to these places other points of convergence are Watertown Square; Route 16 and Soldiers Field Road; and Exit 16 off the Mass Pike and Washington Street. The alternative routes converge as the destination is approached. The reader can reexamine these routes and select among them or recombine them in a manner unique to his own particular journey. This particular map notes the various routes and their convergences with directional arrows. Figures A-E lack arrows but provide alternative routes regardless.

Figure C provides an example of another method of showing a route—namely, a single route is selected, it is the route to get onto, and it is the route which can be gotten onto in any number of ways. Once gotten onto, it is the only route to take because the reader is provided no alternative connecting pathways to the road (Old Marlboro Rd.) leading to the destination (Deacon Haynes Rd.). The alternatives indicated are only alternative ways of getting onto Rt. 2—as shown, these are the intersection of 126, the intersection of Sudbury Rd., and an unnamed road marked at its intersection with Rt. 2 by a "stoplight" and its proximity to "Emerson Hospital"; but Old Marlboro Rd. is not shown as connecting with any other road. Thus, the intersection of Rt. 2 and Old Marlboro Rd. is the critical point, the starting point in this sense, of the final stage of a journey which cannot be completed without locating this and just this intersection. (Missing this particular intersection would be to be "lost" in any actual journey.)

The maps with written instructions offer the reader a description of a route or routes, a selection among routes, or a selection which does not allow much choice. The written instructions elaborate a route, offer it as *the* route to take and provide an accompaniment to the map drawn. The reader is not advised to seek alternate routes. The one or two offered are those which clearly "will do." The instructions are not in themselves different from the matters discernable in the drawings—though they may contain elaborations and details not easily providable in drawings. H, "bear sharply right"; Figure G, "Washington Street (parallel to Mass T'pike)"; Figure C, "follow the signs directing you to the Concord Middle Schools.")

The Map as a Detailed Set of Instructions

Various observable-reportable features can be discerned which make the map readable as a set of instructions concerning how to get to the destination and how to find it.

Places and streets are noted in relation to each other. A street can be followed, moved along, taken, and as such it moves the reader to a next place, along its own route, along the route it traces in relation to other places. There are along its way a number of things that can be noted.

    a. Streets have names though their names may change (Figure D). Metcalf "becomes" Anderson at about Goose Lane.

b. A street itself *"moves."* It is shown as going *from* and *to* places. It is a route, depicted as a line or double parallel lines, with directionality. Its directionality is in relation to named places, e.g., names of streets as in intersections; parts of town as in proper names (e.g., Figure F, Newton, Brighton, Allston, Cambridge); or cities and towns (e.g., Figure D, Storrs, Hartford, Boston). Such places as named at the points where the street "ends" offer the names of places "to" which the street goes and also the places "from"which the street comes. The street is itself moving toward or from such places. It will "take" one to the next place.

c. Streets are locatable as *between, across from, before* and *after, over* and *under* (e.g., Figure B, Tower is *after* Rte. 2A/Maple St. and *before* Rte. 2A/Marrett Rd. when coming on Mass. Ave. from Arlington; Figure D, Baxter St. is *between* Goose Lane and 195; Figure F, Washington Street crosses *over* the Mass Pike in Newton).

d. *Places* are locatable *along* streets, and *at* intersections of streets (e.g., Figure C, Emerson Hospital is *at* the intersection of Rt. 2 West and Old Marlboro Rd.; Figure E, Sanders Theater, the Fire Station, the Ambassador Hotel, and IBM are *along* Cambridge St., and The Union is *at* Mass Ave and Quincy Street; Figure A, there is a Mobil *at* Bear Hill Rd. and North Avenue).

e. Places are locatable *along* streets and in relation to each other in such ways as *before, after, next to* and *across from, on the right* or *on the left* (e.g., Figure A, The Dairy Joy is *on the left* and *before* the Mobil when coming from Leominster, Harvard on North Avenue; Figure E, the Fire Station is *across from* Sanders Theater).

f. The destination is locatable by tracing the streets shown which "take" one to it, along just those streets, passing just those places shown. Orientation can be seen to mean having just such a relation to those places passed and those yet to be passed.

g. Any point along the way can be located as "between" any set of points along the way. The relationships of before, after, next to, in front of, etc. can be used to characterize any point along the way which is, in relation to the destination, not there yet but on the way to. "Being lost" along the way is not possible in reading the map since any point along the way appears with these features.

h. There are points which can be read to be "beyond" an important point, "off course," or "past" a critical landmark or street. There are places to which roads are described as leading but those places are themselves "off the map." The map warns of the possibility of such occurrences in actual journeys.

i. Places can be noted as "next" and "after" such that their succession provides the sense of being on the route to the destination, proceeding along the route, and that one is still on the right route, i.e., that which will lead to the destination.

j. Distances are not provided in standard measurements such as feet or miles but in such ways as blocks, sequences of intersections, or in a succession of landmarks. To have gone the distance "shown" is to have passed particular streets, particular landmarks, in particular sequences, namely, in the sequences shown. Not to have passed them yet is not to have gone "far enough." The length or distance of the "far enough" is provided in just that "measurable" way and no other measure is needed. (Thus, in Figure F it is possible to show the distance—length of line—between Islington Road and 6 Kingswood Road as of a length (measured in inches) equivalent to the distance between Harvard Square and Fresh Pond Pkway at Mt. Auburn St., whereas the actual measurement in miles may be something of the magnitude of three blocks in the first case and over one mile in the latter. The reader has no clues provided as to the relative differences in these lengths in the real world. Thus, makers of maps may warn "not to scale" as a way of referring to just this matter. However, just those landmarks and just those sequences of streets and intersections provide the solution to the matter of distance.) In Figure F, the distance along Mt. Auburn St. which is to be "counted" or "noted" is that distance which is marked by reaching Fresh Pond Pkway, joining Route 16, and then reaching Watertown Square, etc. The map provides the measure of distances in and through the use of these notable features. It is this selection of features (features to be "looked for" in any actual journey), which is offered as a wholly adequate solution to the problem of distance.

k. There is no possibility of "being lost" while reading the map. The areas, streets and landmarks noted are offered as wholly adequate to the purpose of the map. The solution to finding the destination is accomplished in the map. There are no places noted which are unconnected or unconnectable by reading—i.e., by tracing the lines shown as streets—and there is thus no knowledge available to the reader as to what those other possibilities might be. They remain unfulfilled possibilities and, as unfulfilled, indeterminate. Their unavailability makes the possibility of "being lost" while reading the map impossible.

Conclusion

It is remarkable that a number of lines on paper can be interpreted by members as being about a world, a world known in common and capable of being found in and through the lines on the paper. How these lines come to be so readable-interpretable brings us to the question of how sense is achieved. Sense-making is an active process engaged in by those able to read the lines and words shown here as "maps." As members able to achieve such readings they are not necessarily engaged in reflecting on the how-it-is-that-they-are-doing-it.

The map, as a direction map is, through our analysis, revealed to be a member's method for providing the reader (and potential user) with a display of a world known in common. It contains and incorporates, and essentially so, those methods required for its construction and interpretation as a map.

It is read by members as a map in and through which one can discover routes to a destination. The map's world contains the place to be found. it shows that world in an accountable, rational, readable, and understandable way.

The map is read as a solution for a practical problem, namely, how to get to the place named. Each of its features can be examined in relation to this problem—its streets and landmarks are thereby related one to another in and through their relation to this task. They are presented and organized in ways which offer the materials for making or finding a route to the place, i.e. for those readers able to use those methods of practical reasoning which the maps themselves contain and draw upon as resources.

For example, the presence of sequential particulars whereby items are noted on the map as being before, after, next to, across from, at, along, over, under, etc. enable the reader to discover those sequences which are notable, relevant, and potentially usable. A route becomes that set of sequential particulars and relational features which can be marked as satisfactory for the matter at hand. The reader can consider this set as a discovery, a discovery whose possibility is provided by the "map itself," as though little or no work on the reader's part were needed—as though the maker of the map "did it." That the discovery is not all that certain, however, is evidenced by makers adding verbal lists of what to find first and next, etc., until the place itself is found. The list stands as a reminder that the reading involves sense-making work. What such work consists in is to discover the methods of practical reasoning which members must and do use to make and read the map. These methods have their ordered properties discernable in and through the careful examination of the maps.

Acknowledgments:

I wish to thank Jeff Coulter, Richard Frankel, Don Wetmore, Fran Waksler, Nancy Goldner, Mark Kucera, and Lee Perlman for their helpful comments. I am also grateful to those persons who have allowed me to use their maps for purposes of this paper and to students in my ethnomethodology seminar who undertook to collect maps. Names of persons and street numbers of residences have been changed.

REFERENCES

Psathas, George and Kozloff, Martin (1976). The structure of directions. *Semiotica* 17:111-130.
Schegloff, Emanuel (1972). Notes on a conversational practice: formulating place. In *Studies in Social Interaction,* D. Sudnow, (ed.) pp. 75-119. Free Press, New York.

Explicative Transactions: Making and Managing Meaning In Traffic Court

Melvin Pollner

Pollner develops an important formulation in describing how transactions may provide their participants information sufficient to enable their full participation in the activities of the setting. Municipal traffic courts are used as an example of a setting in which some participants, e.g., defendants, arrive in the setting without prior experience or understanding of how to behave. The behavior of other participants, e.g., the judge, provides ways whereby defendants are able to constitute the sense and meaning of their own and other's behavior. Being able to witness the proceedings also serves to inform one of possible actions, precedents, and the like which may be applied to one's own case. The sense of particular rulings and the bases on which such decisions are made are explicated in the course of their being accomplished and witnessed. The methodic character of the proceedings can thus provide

This chapter is a revision and synthesis of drafts written between 1970 and 1973 which were circulated under titles which usually included the term "self-explicating settings." I am much indebted to Aaron V. Cicourel, Robert M. Emerson, and David Goode for pointed critique and commentary.

those participating in it with its sense as well as an assurance of the unexceptional treatment of their own case. Settings, following Pollner's approach, can be examined for those ways in which they provide the participants with explications of their sensible and methodical features.

There is a variety of transaction in which what one does next will be seen as defining the import or significance of what another did before. These are interactional moments in which a subsequent response is seen as capable of endowing preceding actions with meaning by acknowledging, honoring, or deferring to them. Such moments occur perforce when normative orders are yet to be established or when an established order becomes uncertain or threatened. It is at such times that what is done about, with, or in response to particular behaviors is laden with precedential and exemplary potential: the consequences or effects of behaviors threaten to become their meaning. Any parent whose child persists in getting out of bed at ten in the evening to speak to dinner guests has intimate knowledge of the explicative moment: to allow the encounter to proceed is to risk establishing cuteness and charm as sanctioned methods for staying up late. Or consider the scene described by Sartre (1966, p. 97):

> But then suppose he takes her hand. This act of her companion risks changing the situation by calling for an immediate decision. To leave the hand there is to consent in herself to flirt, to engage herself. To withdraw it is to break the troubled and unstable harmony which gives the hour its charm.

The explicative force of the moment is intensified when onlookers are present; indeed, it is the presence of onlookers which allows a transaction to have exemplary or definitional power.

> But Yaacov could not disattend to Chai for very long. Not only had Chai first intruded into territory Yaacov considered his own, but Chai was also peering over Yaacov's shoulder and thus intruding into his personal space. Furthermore, Chai was standing and so attracted the attention of other workers in the room.
> ... Yaacov could not maintain his definition of Chai as a non-person without increasing the risk of other workers interpreting his lack of reaction

as acquiescence that the location in question was public territory. (Handelman and Kapferer 1972, pp. 486–487)

As the above suggests, even inaction may acquire explicatory significance, particularly when an audience is present. Participants may find it impossible to do "nothing" or to adopt a "neutral" stance, for even such responses furnish preceding behaviors with a particular significance (Haley 1959): the absence of a remark can render the preceding action unremarkable (i.e., acceptable). In effect, such situations are often bereft of a behavioral sanctuary in which one can nonconsequentially while away the while until the critical moment has passed.

Explicative transactions have special sociological and interactional import. They are moments in which meaning is deobjectivated (Berger and Luckman 1966), that is, in which the relation between human praxis and its product is vivid from both participatory and analytic points of view. On such occasions the constitutive power of the response comes to the foreground. Merleau-Ponty (1964 p. xiii) speaks of the "retrospective illusion" in which we take the "objects constituted by our perceiving consciousness as pre-existent causes of perception." In these special liminal (Turner 1974) moments, the veil of the illusion is briefly lifted and the *en*active (not merely the *re*active) capacity (Weik 1969, pp. 63–71) of actions is momentarily visible.[1]

I should like to consider a setting in which the frequency of such explicative transactions is particularly high—a municipal court. The frequency is maximized by a simple structural feature, to wit, defendants may and typically do observe arraignments prior to appearing before the judge themselves. This means that transactions may be monitored and analyzed for timely, successful, propitious, or otherwise usable actions established by the judge's response to the actions of preceding defendants. Such potential or actual monitoring transforms encapsulated episodes into explicative transactions and endows them with their exemplary and definitional power. Thus while the judge may feel that s/he is simply reacting to the features of the cases at hand, the structure of the interaction may induce an appreciation that s/he is enacting them, that is, constituting the situated meaning of the particulars to which s/he responds. The recognition that s/he is *making* meaning may in turn lead to manipulations which attempt to *manage* meaning, that is, to control responses so as to achieve or preserve particular meanings.

The aspects of the explicative process as it occurs in court comprise the foci of this report. Specifically, following a brief description of data collection procedures I shall consider some of the ways in which the transaction between judge and defendant functions to explicate situated meanings. I shall then consider the ways in which explicative transactions are monitored, analyzed, and used by onlooking defendants as grounds of inference and action. The judge occasionally attends to the fact that explicative transactions are "appropriated" by defendants. Illustrations of the consequent attempts to manage and control the explicative process constitute the final descriptive section. In the conclusion we shall consider the import of our analysis for an understanding of meaning-making and meaning-management processes in general.

Data Collection

The data were gathered as part of a study of members' ordinary (i.e., nonscientific) practices for discerning, demonstrating, and establishing "truth." Traffic courts seemed to be extremely rich settings in this regard, since they promised numerous instances of conflicting accounts and equally many occasions in which the "truth" or "what really happened on the highway" would become problematic (Pollner 1974). The operations of four municipal courts (and a total of seven different judges) were observed for a period of anywhere from several days to three months. The courts varied in character and context. Big City Court was probably the largest traffic court in the United States and was capable of and often successful in arraigning over 250 defendants in traffic cases in a single three-hour morning session. Small City Courts I and II served smaller municipalities: most traffic cases were typically batched together at the beginning of a session, but others were also interspersed throughout the day's agenda of misdemeanors, trials, prehearings, and so forth. Resort City Court reserved several court sessions a week for traffic arraignments. One of the sessions was held in a courtroom adjacent to the student living area (Student Court) of a university and the overwhelming proportion of defendants came from the student population.

In three of the four courts it was possible to secure audiotape recordings of entire sessions, either through direct use of my own recorder or through use of the tape recording regularly made by the court itself. In one court, the bench had become rather controversial owing to unorthodox methods of sentencing and he denied permission to make tape recordings of sessions. Whenever possible I would attempt to speak to the judges immediately following the traffic session. Given my interest in the problem of "truth" and the structure of "mundane reasoning," the preceding session usually provided me with a schedule of "What did you think when he said X?'' and "Why did you lower the fine for Defendant Y?'' type questions. Geared as they were to interests somewhat different from those which will be developed in this paper, the data collection procedures do not afford as deep a documentation or instantiation of the claims and arguments to be developed in the following pages as one would like. It would have been extremely useful, for example, to have sought more precise understanding of judges' management work by replaying the audiotape of the session for them and eliciting comments on each case in accord with the triangulation procedure recommended by Cicourel (1973). Similarly, asking defendants what they made of the ongoing session as it unfolded would have furnished useful information on the cognitive processing and appropriation of explicated meanings. While these omissions preclude a highly textured analysis, the existing materials are sufficient to outline some basic structures. (See Carlen 1976 for a superb analysis of meaning-management in magistrate's court.)

Visibility Arrangements and Explicative Transactions

While the judge may know in varying degrees of clarity what an arraignment ought to consist of, and while he may be able to specify in advance how he will react to, say, various actions on the part of defendants, matters are not so well known from the latter's point of view. Consider, for example, that while the gross legal features of an arraignment may be specified at the outset of a session, the initial instructions do not and cannot contain specifications of how the judge will react to every move, utterance, gesture, etc. To do so would entail a discourse as long as the list of possible actions one's imagination could provide (see Garfinkel 1967 on essential incompleteness).

To a certain extent, then, defendants must act in an interactional field in which the methods by which they are being assessed and evaluated, while perhaps known anecdotally in advance, are given concrete substance only after their actions are completed. There are, however, certain features of traffic sessions which may function to mitigate this uncertainty. Prominent among them is the fact that almost invariably defendants can witness arraignments prior to their own. Both the rapidity and public quality of traffic court arraignments assure most defendants—bar perhaps the first of any session—of at least some opportunity to observe in earlier cases specific court procedures, the judge's response to particular defendant behaviors, etc.

Observational opportunities for yet-to-be-arraigned defendants differed substantially from court to court. In Big City Court, the great amount of background noise from both court personnel working about the bench and mumbling spectators in the large room could prevent a defendant seated in the audience from hearing the dialogue between judge and defendant. In fact, often only the judge could be heard, since his voice was amplified somewhat by a public address system. However, since defendants were lined up before the judge a row at a time, the defendant may have an opportunity to hear several arraignments prior to his own. In Student Court, on the other hand, a defendant can hear every arraignment prior to his own. The room is small, hardly larger than a good-sized living room, and carefully monitored for appropriate demeanor, which minimizes background noise. Courts vary between these two extremes but in each court a defendant (but for the very first) can hear at least a few of the preceding arraignments.

By virtue of occurring in a public context, each transaction between judge and defendant is endowed with a capacity to preserve, alter, or even constitute the phenomenological and practical features of both preceding and subsequent transactions. One way in which any current case could exert this effect was by establishing the local significance of particular actions and utterances. Thus, for example, what could stand as an "adequate plea" was constituted and explicated as defendants entered pleas and were responded to by the judge. In Student Court, an adequate plea was constituted as nothing less than the legally specified utterance of "guilty" or "not guilty." Any other response was treated as a legally incomprehensible and therefore unacceptable formulation.

> J: How do you plead?
> D: Technically guilty.
> J: Well, how do you plead without "technically" or "not technically?"
> D: Guilty your honor. . .

—   —   —

> J: How do you plead?
> D: Guilty with an explanation.
> J: We have to have a clear-cut plea.
> D: Guilty. . .

—   —   —

> J: How do you plead?
> D: Well I guess guilty.
> J: Well, is it guilty?
> D: Yes, guilty. . .

In other courts, there was often considerable latitude in the definition of an adequate plea to the point where a judge might actually advise the defendant.[2]

*J: Mister Moonly yer charged with violating one six sixty four, driving slower than normal traffic. I take it thetchu heard'n understood my statement concerning yer legal rights?

D: I understand my rights yessir.

J: And having that in mind are you ready fer yer plea sir. (pause)

D: Ahah,—guilty in part sir. With extenuating circumstances.

J: 'Djuh like go t'the board en show me what happened? Or, ken you // tell me-

D: I don't think it's // necessary to draw it ez uh,

J: Alrightchu tell me.

DEFENDANT GIVES EXPLANATION

J: Well, I don't know,—car in fron' of yuh I, don't know thetchud' be guilty, why don't yuh plead not guilty en set it down fer trial.

D: Well it's a matter of uh, (pause)

D: Of,

J: ⌈Of econo//mics?

D: ⌊-time en inconvenience sir. ((clears throat)) (pause)

J: Fine'll be eight dollars. Dju wanna take care of it now sir?

D: And, ken I write a check fer a fine sir?

( ): Mm hm/

J: Yes.

D: Thankyou.

In one of the Small City courts, the proceedings could assume a loose, almost folksy quality as the following excerpt suggests:

J: Alright. Yuh gunnuh have a lawyer in this case,

D: Well I'm not sure if I'm really guilty or not.

D: ⸢-of that-
J: ⟦Well
D: (-one eight.)
J: D'you wanna jus' talk about the case then
D: Yes.

Similarly, the adequacy, permissibility, and success of an "excuse"
was explicated over the course of a session. As might be expected, there
was substantial variation from court to court as to what would be honored as an excuse. Particulars which would be honored as grounds for
lenient treatment were made visible as the series of defendants offered
explanations and the judge responded to them. Consider, for example,
the fate of ostensibly similar explanations of an "unsafe lane change" as
it is made visible and constituted by judges in two different courts.

SMALL CITY COURT I

*D: Uh, I received this tick about- forty five-minnits ago, and
     uh::,— that's on the new bridge there — (you) remember,
     an' it's merging traffic (coming uh there), and uh,— Uz:: I
     was- — I w's drivin tuh Los Angelees, this way. And uh::,
     the <u>traffic</u> begin kind jammin up there's-there's two
     lanes coming on the merging traffic. I was on the, left
     hand lane. The tra- en, the traffic begin kinda jammin up,
     en so, uh, I s- put on my signal, muh left hand signal, en
     speeded up en changed lanes. Now the <u>of</u>ficer who gave
     me the ticket said that I'd cut somebody <u>off</u>, in the- lane
     thet I'd changed to. But I wasn't <u>aware</u> of that, and
     I'd-looked in my rear view mirror, in fact I turned my head
     to the side also. And uh, — I was suhprized when, uh
     later I, noticed a red light in the rear view mirror.·So uh
     — So not thet I feel I don't feel I hadda ticket comin.
          (pause)
D: So —
J: Well akchully, you don't drive that very often (as that on
     this charge),
D: ⸢No.
J: ⟦(What)—
D: I live in San Maria,
J: Wuh- what's yer business.
D: Uh::m a <u>bu</u>siness representative fer the (located in) in
     San Maria.

J: Well that's a bad section there uh, ((clears throat)) I think unner the circumstances we're gonna dismiss this. Insufficient evidence. Alright, that'll be all.

BIG CITY COURT

J: Martin, how do you plead?
D: No contest your honor.
J: What happened?
D: Well, uh, I was going down Moonrise Blvd. to deliver some ice to a cafeteria, along about 3 o'clock (   ). And uh, and almost between the middle of the two lights, the light behind me and the light in front of me, and the traffic was stopped and the extreme left lane was open, clean, nothing was coming, traffic was stopped, so I give this signal to turn out of that lane to that lane, and a cop was coming down and he hails me and he turned right around at the other light, he comes right behind me, and he says there's a Buick behind me and I almost hit him, but there was no car, otherwise it would have been between me and him because the traffic was stopped.
J: 15 or 3.
B: Would you go through the door, see the cashier.

As these episodes suggest, the developing session may act as its own socialization agent. Explicated features become available as a set of instructions and resources for further action and inference. Practical exigencies such as vagueness of plea or missequencing furnish the occasion for the application of the remedy and in its application observers are (potentially) informed of the setting's enforced criteria. Similarly, even the routine, nonexceptional flow of events explicates the situated meaning of events as routine and nonexceptional. By virtue of the non-exceptional, unremarked accomplishing of arraignments, the setting makes observable its exploitable possibilities and its "silently tolerated inexactitudes," to borrow Reichenbach's phrase (1938, p. 7). In this way, every transaction in the ongoing activity may become fraught with instructional possibilities.

The transactions in a particular case may affect the experience and structure of preceding and subsequent cases in yet other ways. For example, courts varied markedly in the nature, extensiveness, and spirit of the arraignment format. In some courts the procedure might be relatively brief and informal, whereas others employed a more legalistic format phrased in stentorian tones.

Under certain circumstances the immediate import of the formal format may be ambiguous to defendants. In commonsense terms, traffic violations are among the most trivial of violations and yet the seriousness of the questions suggests the seriousness of the offense. Thus, for example, in one instance where a defendant was arraigned in isolation in the judge's chambers (the defendant had traveled a substantial distance only to arrive after the session had ended), the question "Are you going to be represented by a lawyer?" was answered with an apprehensive "no." The response indicated to me and, as later conversation revealed, to the judge that the defendant had momentarily lost a sense of security regarding the ostensible triviality of the violation and gained an appreciation of its potential consequentiality. Like first defendants in a traffic session, the isolated individual could not distinguish those features of the format which are generic features of an arraignment. It was difficult to discern the particular from the perfunctory, the rare from the routine. The lawyer question was momentarily ambiguous as to whether it was the product of a mechanically applied procedure or based on the judge's perception of the seriousness of the case. The question might be mere formality or it might be saying, "Are you going to be represented by a lawyer—because it looks like you might need one."

For defendants appearing later in a traffic session, that which is generic to the arraignment and that which is case-specific are explicated by the repetitive application of the format. The question regarding the lawyer is seen and revealed as having all along amounted to "Are you going to be represented by a lawyer? I have asked everyone else that and so I ask you." In this sense, the developing course of the session elaborates its own features and, as in the current example, renders observable the method of its own production.

I have attempted to indicate the ways in which the session cannot help but explicate its constituent features in and over the course of its development. Each feature—an utterance, a movement, or whatever—receives its situated sense by virtue of its consequences, and each feature is doomed to have its consequences. That fate is clearer if we relinquish a lay notion of consequences in order that we may adopt an analytic notion which embraces the consequence "nothing happened" as one of its distinctive modes. Under the revised version of consequences, actions that might be accorded residual or negative status are transformed into a positive phenomenon. And with this positivization there emerges an ability to see the sense in which any feature of the setting is assured of being elaborated by its consequences in some way, even if its consequences consist, from a member's point of view, of "nothing at all."

The Appropriation of Explicated Meanings

The preceding examples are best regarded as analytic or, as the anthropologists might say, etic examples of the explication of meaning (Pike 1954). While an outside observer may acknowledge that meaning is situationally constituted, whether or not defendants in the setting actually orient to, analyze, and use the explicated meanings and structures remains problematic. To this extent I have treated only the "implicit" or "virtual" explication of meanings. Such meanings assume emic, explicit, or actual form only as they can be shown to have been appropriated by defendants. In this section I want to explore this process of appropriation and furnish indications that defendants analyze and use preceding transactions as grounds for subsequent action and inference.

It is difficult to assess and to exhibit the extent to which the significances established in the session are in fact appropriated and used by defendants. In part, this has to do with our lack of information about how defendants monitored the ongoing interaction. But this difficulty also derives from the fact that a good deal of what could be gleaned by defendants could lead to acts of omission, deliberate attempts to mask the acquisition of such knowledge, or to silent acts of compliance. For example, appropriation of the locally honored features of an adequate excuse could mean simply that defendants refrained from giving what they now found to be a situationally impoverished explanation.[4]

While these problems are insurmountable given the data, there are nevertheless several indications that defendants monitored and analyzed the ongoing setting and formulated locally established sequences and significances that were employed explicitly and implicitly as the grounds of further action in the setting. There are, for example, direct references to preceding cases, as when, for example, the second of two consecutive defendants arraigned on charges of failing to appear in court prefaces his explanation with, "I know you're going to do to me what you did to him." Somewhat more subtle instances occur when defendants abstract the explicated order and actually use it as the basis for some current action.[5] For example, defendants might display and use their analysis of established sequences by answering questions before they are asked:

J: Mr. Ricks, also charged here two three one two three. Owner allowing open container in car. Understand that charge?

D: Yes sir.

J: All right. You gonna have a lawyer in this case?
D: Well, no sir I'm not and I'll plead guilty on it.

Or they might request that established sequences be observed:

J: Joseph . . . uh . . . Halsworth? Yes sir?
D: I'm waiting for the question.
J: How do you plead?
D: Not guilty, your honor.

Perhaps one of the most subtle and therefore one of the most difficult to detect appropriations are those in which defendants analyze preceding arraignments for a paradigm for the construction of a "successful" excuse. Quite literally, such an analysis could have cash value and one might expect careful and close monitoring of preceding cases. At the same time, however, the products of such monitoring work would be difficult to detect since they would be masked in actual usage: a defendant would presumably advance his explanation as though it reflected reality and not the pragmatics of the immediate context. Nevertheless there are occasional instances in which defendants appear to scavenge successful predecessors for usable parts. In the following excerpt a number of defendants with several parking violations apiece are arraigned in a "batch."

*J: And uh, Rolman? Anything you wish to say.
D1:   Yessir, uh, I let my roommates borrow my car quite often and I was only aware that I had—three, this was my third violation.
D1:   Now, / / uh, what-
 J: Well you shouldn't-
D1:   ⸤⸤What-
 J: ⸤⸤You shouldn't let somebody borrow it if they're gonna run these up (   ) pay for 'em,
D1:   Well I- uh-I, I-apparently he paid for 'em but he never told me about them. So I was unaware of them.
 J: Well, I'll make this one five dollars.
      (pause)
 J: And u, Mr. (   )?
D2:   Yeah I also uh, didn't receive all the tickets the car received. This is my third ticket (but) uh, one of the other tickets that been charged to me uh, uh one of my friends had the car, and he paid for it and everything.

> J: I'll cut it- I'll treat you like the (last gentleman), five dollars. Mr. Kearney?
> D3: Uh my excuse was- is similar to the other, (I guess), (in the matter of fines),
> J: Except you have more tickets than anybody (in line). (   ) (   ). Ever been in jail for anything else before?[6]

Similarly, in a session in which the judge often rebuked defendants who attempted to explain away violations by reference to various pressing matters (e.g., parking illegally in order to get to a job on time) or who attempted to evade what the judge felt was the defendant's personal responsibility, one could find instances of accounts permeated by an unusual number of mea culpas.

> J: You're charged with Section 22450, failing to stop for a stop sign. Did you hear and understand your rights?
> D: Yes sir.
> J: Do you want to see an attorney?
> D: No.
> J: How do you plead?
> D: Guilty.
> J: Do you want to be heard and sentenced now?
> D: I would only like to point out that first of all, I am guilty...
> J: But you do want me to hear what you have to say and sentence you now?
> D: Yes. I would like to point out the time, traffic conditions, and speed. This is my home neighborhood, and I was going home, you know. I didn't come to a full stop, which is, of course, illegal. The only other vehicle in the area, it was a block away, and it happened to be this highway patrolman. But I did come to a crawling stop.
> J: You do have to come to a complete stop.

We have furnished a number of examples which suggest that defendants monitor and analyze preceding transactions and use them as the grounds and guides for further action and inference.[7] In effect, a language game is being played and prospective players have the opportunity to observe the game and learn at least some of its subtleties prior to having to speak.[8] That transactions function to constitute and reveal the situational meaning of setting features and that the transactions are mon-

itored and analyzed for such meaning establishes the context of judges'
activities. At times judges explicitly attend to the explicative character of
their work and, when they do, it is often with an eye to the control and
management of explicated meaning.

Management of Meaning

The presence of onlooking defendants assures that each case is informed by and itself informs the order of affairs in which it is considered. The transcendant implications of the current case—its capacity to
inform and be informed by the ongoing order in which it is embedded—
as they are encountered by the judge shall be termed the *horizon* of the
current case. The horizon, in other words, consists in the current case's
perceived capacity to alter or preserve the already established features of
the order in which it appears and to furnish the actionable precedents in
the development of what remains to be done. Moreover, the horizon consists of those "implications" attended to from within the order to which
they refer and at the time of their appearance. Put another way, the horizon consists of potentially realizable features of a now-to-be-developed
case when those features are considered in terms of their implications for
the developing order. We shall consider the judge's work in managing
cases whose horizonal features threaten or in some way jeopardize per-
ceivedly established or yet-to-be established features of the session.

The explicative character of judge-defendant transactions and the importance of case management is common lore among judges. "The Traffic Court Procedure and Administration" handbook (Economos 1961,
p. 75), for example, advises judges to handle the first case with special
care "in order that it may serve as an example for all subsequent cases."
To cite an extreme but revealing instance of just this sort of concern: One
judge took some pain to review pending cases prior to the beginning of a
session, selecting certain serious violations such as speeding in excess of
85 or 90 miles an hour. He would then begin the session with one or two
cases, which seemed likely candidates for a jail sentence or a substantial
fine, and intersperse other serious offenses over the course of the session.
In this manner, the judge felt that it was possible to display the fact that
highly discriminative activity was taking place, or, in the words of the
judge, that "the good men were being separated from the bad." The
judge also noted the dysfunctional effects of giving reduced fines and
dismissals at the outset of a session. In sessions where time or circumstances did not permit the a priori ordering of cases (or simply as a sup-

plement to that procedure), the judge imposed standard bail schedule fines (at least) to most cases at the beginning of a session. The disposition of early cases, the judge felt, furnished yet-to-be-arraigned defendants with a baseline with which to gauge the extent to which he had discriminated among explanations. Insofar as defendants were led to believe that everyone received, say, a five dollar reduction, the judge felt that he was denied a valuable resource for revealing to defendants that their case had received special and individual treatment.

In some instances the judge found that his attempt to establish an aura of seriousness by selecting serious cases to appear at the beginning of a session could force him into positions and policies he would rather not have adopted. Thus, for example, the judge somewhat regretted his sentence in the following "first" case, though he felt the sentence imperative precisely because it was the first case.

    *J: Yer charged with section // two three four nine, of the vehicle code, excessive speed. Didju hear en un//derstand yer rights?

Baby: (   )!

Baby: ((crying))

    D: Mm hm?

    J: Do you wanna see an attorney.

    D:°   No? (I did it.)

    J: How do you plead.

    D:°   Guilty,

    J: D'you wanna be heard an' sentenced now?

    D: Yes sir.

Baby: (   )! (   )!

    J: And uh what've you to say (   ).

    D:°   Nothing much,

    J: Are-

    D:°   (We were) driving a car, 'n we were out driving it, 'n, the speed creeped up, 'n that's what happen'.

    J: This speed, most everybody goes to jail, I'm concerned becuz I see that you have a baby, are these yer parents with you?

    D:°   No, my grandmother, and, granduncle.

    J: How old is the baby.

    D:°   He's fifteen months.

        (pause)

    J: We'll make it uh simply uh jail until uh eight uh'clock

tomorrow morning. So you'll simply spend one night in
jail, en then you'll be free tuh- go back down. We won't
impose an additional fine. You should expect that if yer
gonna drive at these speeds, why you'll be spending
considerably more time in (institutes).

D: ° Mh hm.

J: Alright,

No other judge attempted to order or select cases prior to the beginning of a session in order to achieve a particular effect. Typically, the
order in which defendants appeared before the judge was tied to clerical
preprocessing procedures. In some cases a vast domain of organizational
activity would have to be rearranged in order for the judge to see the tickets prior to the beginning of a session. In most courts, then, the order in
which defendants appeared before the judge was from his, the judge's,
perspective a given feature of the setting. Indeed, even the previously
mentioned judge suspended his concern with the a priori manipulation of
the session when rotated to a court with a fairly elaborate preprocessing
procedure. Because of the practicalities which prohibited an a priori ordering and because of the general disinterest in engaging in such ordering
procedures even if they dould be done, judges "lived within" the session.

The notion of "living within" an order is intended to highlight the fact
that the judges' management work could rarely be planned in advance,
but had to be continually accomplished throughout the actual course of
any given session. Such work thus occurred in real time, in public, with
the consequences of any decision unavoidably feeding back into the session and furnishing the conditions and context of subsequent decisions.
To live within the session meant that whatever the session and any of its
constituent features came to was made to happen in and over the course
of its development. To live within the session meant that the developing
session furnished the resources and constraining circumstances of its own
construction.

To live within an order stands in contrast to a situation where one can
manipulate and alter the texture of events from an Archimedean vantage
point, in one's own time, in isolation and with full control over disclosure of decisions. Making and editing a videotape of a traffic session in
such a way that it displayed intended and idealized features, relations,
and meanings associated with justice, consistency, economy, and so
forth would approximate management from outside an ongoing order.
The production of those relations and meanings "live," without benefit
of altering the temporal ordering or deleting undesirable or jeopardizing

segments, and, as the occasion arose, for control, comprises management from within (see Wieder's brilliant analysis 1974).

That judges lived within the order committed them to a course of ad hoc (Garfinkel 1967), i.e., on the moment and aprincipled, work, through which the relations which potentially obtained among cases were managed.[9] The nature of the work is best illustrated by concrete examples. Each of the following episodes illustrates the judge's judgmental work in preserving an established or envisioned relation among cases.

In Small City II a defendant asked the judge for additional time to pay the fine which had just been imposed. The judge, who was sensitized to court costs incurred by the paperwork of a great number of similar requests, was generally reluctant to give any extensions, particularly in public. Though the judge felt that this woman's request had some merit, a concession in public would have meant that he might be besieged by similar requests in the future. After stating that he did not give time, he had the woman sit until the end of the session, at which time she was granted an extension.

In Small City II, a judge, rather than dismiss a case in public, would request that a defendant whose case the judge felt warranted a dismissal be seated so that he—the judge—could "think about it." Near the end of the session, he recalled the defendant and dismissed the case.

In Small City I, a young man was the defendant in the first traffic arraignment of the morning. His case was dismissed because of "lack of evidence." The judge felt compelled to dismiss several subsequent cases which he implied would not have been dismissed had the first defendant not been so young. Subsequent defendants were considerably older and by appearance more substantial members of the community.

In Resort City, an elderly black woman told a

charming story about how she had to violate a minor traffic law in order not to run over some ducklings. The explanation was barely audible to the judge and could not be heard by the vast majority of the audience. The judge imposed a "token fine" of one dollar. The judge later told me that he had wanted to dismiss the case and would have, had the defendant spoken loud enough for the audience to hear. Since she had spoken so softly, the judge feared that the dismissal would be associated with the fact that she was black, i.e., with favored treatment, particularly since she was the only black to appear in the session and very few, if any, dismissals had been granted that day.

In Student Court, a defendant explained that he had to make a "rolling stop" through a stop sign because if he stopped short his children would hit the dashboard with their heads. Afterward the judge told me that he had wanted to reduce the man's fine substantially because his appearance and general demeanor indicated a "poor soul" type. The man's excuse, however, did not warrant as great a reduction as the judge was prepared to give, particularly given the judge's general propensity to highlight defendants' responsibility (e.g., "Why were you going so fast in the first place? could have been the beginning of a harsher response). Consequently, the judge felt compelled to search the story for some feature that might be seen by the audience as the critical feature which discriminated it from similar stories previously offered. This led to the judge's loud formulation, "You say your children were in the car and if you stopped short they'd hit their head or something."

In Small City II, the judge, in delivering his opening remarks, stated that "if you plead guilty don't go and add 'but I want to tell you why I'm not guilty.' " The judge felt it was incumbent upon him to castigate defendants who attempted to offer explanations so as not to negate what he stated initially. He felt it was particularly important to do so at the beginning of a session in order to avoid having everyone come up with an explanation and thus increase the length of the session. Later in the session, however, explanations were permitted, although the ways in which they were permitted were often masked so as to preserve the integrity of the initial instruction. For example, one defendant stated that he was guilty but he would like to explain, to which the judge responded, "Explain what?", which led to the giving of the explanation.

Several features of the management work warrant mention.

1. The substantive dimensions about which the horizon organizes itself consisted of the judge's practical interests. A judge attending to the ostensible "consistency" of his actions would see jeopardizing prospects in a case and jeopardizable features of a developed session which a judge not attending to such matters would not, even though the two judges might confront "identical objective circumstances." The practical interest constituted the session's and each of its particular case's portentious character as scenic circumstances. Thus while current case and developed session mutually elaborated one another's features, they did so under the auspices of a practical concern. The impending horizon of a current case consisted in the case's potentially realizable futures that could jeopardize some practically significant established or to-to-established feature of the session such as "justice," consistency, running time, cost, and so forth.

2. Though the practical and policy interests of the judge could be articulated prior to the adjudication of any case, the in-detail specification of what would be required to appear "consistent" in one's judgements, "to get the session over with quickly," or to "avoid having everyone give a story" could not. The appreciation of the detailed work necessary to preserve a session's appearance as one, for example, in which cases were decided on universally applicable grounds awaited the case in which that work would have to be done. To display "racial equality" as a court policy required consideration of the thus-far developed session in light of the particulars of the current case and vice versa. Insofar as there were no a priori guarantees as to what sort of work would be necessary to make observable the policy under whose purview they were examined. were no a priori guarantees as to what a case or a session would come to there were no guarantees as to what sort of work would be necessary to make observable the policy under whose purview they were examined.

Similarly, while the judge could formulate a strategy to give cases their decided character, what that would require in detail would await the development of a concrete case which had to be searched for some feature which could be reformulated as the grounds for a reduction of fine.

3. A case assumed its horizon by reference to what had already transpired and the yet-to-come. At the same time, the relevant features of transpired and yet-to-come cases were actualized by the horizon of a present case. The present case was considered in terms of its capacity to jeopardize or preserve features of already adjudicated cases and its capacity to furnish undesirable precedents. But the to-be-preserved features and the to-be-avoided precedents did not remain invariant from case to case. Rather, over the course of each case's development, that which was to be preserved and that which was to be avoided were rendered observable. Thus, for example, the presence of a black defendant in a hitherto exclusively white traffic session rendered salient race as a feature of previous cases. For the judge, the appearance of the black defendant held forth the possibility that the disposition of earlier cases would be reinterpreted in light of the disposition of the current case. Though each case was informed by a history and a future, it was a history and a future of its own making.

Concluding Discussion

We have described explicative transactions as liminal moments in which the meaning, import, or significance of what one has done before is established by what another does next. They stand in contrast to transactions in which an initial doing is so unequivocal and well-defined that it retains its meaning regardless of what others do with, about, or in response to it. An archetypal instance of the latter form might be a question-answer sequence (see Schegloff 1968 for detailed analysis) in which the identity of the utterance as "question" is retained over and in the face of subsequent silence or ostensible failures to "answer." These responses do not succeed in transforming the "question" into a "silence-elicitor" by virtue of the fact that a silence is produced subsequent to its utterance. Rather, the utterance's unequivocal and well-defined status as a "question" serves as the grounds for noting officially the subsequent silence and more generally the absence of an "answer." The "question" establishes the cognitive dimensions for reviewing and formulating features of the next speaker's production. Relatedly, in nonexplicative moments next speakers are more apt to feel they are reacting to an established form rather than constituting or enacting a new one. At a phenomenological level, then, it may be useful to retain the distinction between explicative and nonexplicative transaction. I should like to propose, however, that on an analytic level it may be useful to regard the explicative component as present to some extent in all transactions, even in those involving what from an interactant's point of view are well-established sequences. In order to make my point in some detail and depth I would like to highlight briefly some of the less often mentioned aspects of G. H. Mead's work on meaning.

Mead viewed himself as a social behaviorist (1934). And he did so for a reason. For Mead, meaning, at least in its primordial expression and organization, was not an entity nor did it dwell in the mind or psyche of the actor. Rather, meaning was a shorthand way of referring to a behavioral process or transaction in which the actor participated. Meaning consisted of and was constituted through the transactions or, more generally, the relations between organism and environment. Thus, for example, by virtue of its physiochemical endowment, the organism responds to and thereby organizes its environment in a particular fashion.[10]

> Organic processes or responses in a sense constitute the objects to which they are responses; that is to say, any given biological organism is in a way responsible for the existence (in the sense of the meanings they have for it) of the objects to which it physiologically and chemically responds. There would, for example, be no food—no edible objects—if there were no organisms which could digest it. (Mead 1934, p. 77)

A more dynamic relation occurs as organisms behave toward one another, i.e., when the behaviors of one organism serve as the stimulus for the other. It is in such elementary, preconscious interactions (or, one might say, *interreactions*) that meaning appears in incipient form. Perhaps it is more faithful to the impulse of Mead's thought to say that such interactions constitute and comprise meaning. As organisms adjusted to the beginnings ("gestures") of the other organisms' behaviors as preludes to subsequent activities, those gestures are implicitly constituted as signs indicating the subsequent activity. In effect, to select one of Mead's frequently employed illustrations, the dog's retreat from the baring of teeth by the other dog implicitly constitutes the baring of teeth as an indication of a subsequent attack: the "retreat" simultaneously discovers and creates the possibility of "threat." Mead puts the matter more generally when he writes:

> Meaning is a content of an object which is dependent upon the relation of an organism or group of organisms to it. It is not essentially or primarily a psychical content (a content of mind or consciousness), for it need not be conscious at all, and is not in fact until significant symbols are evolved in the process of human social experience. Only when it becomes identified with such symbols does meaning become conscious. The meaning of a gesture on the part of one organism is the adjustive response of another organism to it, as indicating the resultant of the social act it initiates, the adjustive response of the second organism being itself directed toward or related to the completion of that act. In other words, meaning involves a reference of the gesture of one organism to the resultant of the social act it indicates or initiates, as adjustively responded to in this reference by another organism; and the adjustive response of the other organism is the meaning of the gesture. (Mead 1934, pp. 80–81).

As one can see, Mead never does settle down to a consistent use of the term *meaning*. Partly, I think, this has to do with his using the term to refer to both the fundamental meaning process and the substantive precipitants of the process. When meaning is conceived as product there is a sense in which it is permissible to ask about the "actors' meanings" even though it implies mentalism. Of course, in Mead's account there is a point at which actors reflexively appropriate the process in which they are involved and are subsequently able, for example, to anticipate the response of others. When, however, the focus is on the original behavioral process of meaning (i.e., the process in which substantive meaning is originated), rather than say that actors "hold" or even "impute" meaning, it might be more faithful to the behavioral thrust of Mead's work to say that actors "do" or "participate in" meaning or, to use Weick's term, to say that they "enact" an environment. Under the auspices of the Meadian perspective, substantive meanings are a gloss (Garfinkel and Sacks 1970) for transactions or relations through which those substantive meanings are achieved.

Social meanings are continuously created and recreated through the situated praxis which presupposes, preserves, and uses those meanings. Thus, "table" is a gloss for the cognitive, practical, and interactional work through which "table" is enacted. Such activities include placing plates and silverware on top of the "table," telling children to keep toys off of it, worrying about its stability and strength: these and other activities comprise the continuously applied repertoire of actions which carve out and enact a "table." On the behavioral level, the probability that such activities will continue, to use a Weberian (or is it Skinnerian?) turn of phrase, is what a table comes to. From this point of view, the table is created and sustained by virtue of what is done to, with, or about it.[11]

If we honor this retrospective and relational view of meaning, then it is possible to view the integrity, well-definedness, unequivocally, this-is-what-it-is-and-no-other quality of certain acts and utterances as (partly) a course of subsequent activity through which these properties are enacted. Such properties are themselves explicated through a course of cognitive, pragmatic, interactional and embodied activity which presuppose and assert the integrity of a meaning in the face of ostensible threats or denials. To find and note the subsequent "silence," to wait for the "answer," to recognize evasion and ambiguity—to cognitively and interactionally organize subsequent inference and action with regard to the preceding utterance's status as a question—are precisely the responses through which the property [utterance is clearly a question] are explicated. In effect, objectivation may be viewed as a situated practice through which meanings are preserved or, more accurately, postserved.

It is now possible to indicate a remedy to a certain asymmetry which informed our analysis. We have emphasized the ways in which the judge's response explicates the situated meaning of defendant's actions, but we have said nothing about the ways in which the defendant's responses explicate the meaning of the judge's actions. Of course, it is possible to argue that the judge has the "last word" on situated meanings in the court, that defendants know this is the case and try to learn from his responses, and, consequently, that there is a kind of natural asymmetry in the courtroom which is reflected in our analysis. But I think there is much in such an argument that could be viewed as problematic. It is possible, for example, to view the status of "judge" and more specifically his presumptive right to have the "last word" as the explicated achievement of defendants' responses. What does such explicative work look like?

Conceived as an explicated accomplishment, "having the last word" is constituted by the defendant's activities, such as proffering some revised version of a plea in response to the judge's statement, "We have to have a clear-cut plea.'' It is constituted by activities such as attempting to follow whatever instructions the judge may furnish. It is constituted by activities such as accepting the judge's verdict. That the judge has the last word is continuously explicated, in short, by the whole range of deferential and acquiescent activities that simultaneously presuppose and produce the authoritative character of the utterances to which they respond.

NOTES

1. Numerous refinements and distinctions suggest themselves. For example, explicative transactions may vary in the extent to which different parties find the transaction to constitute meaning. Thus, for example, cultural strangers may find the meaning of their behaviors by observing the reactions to them though such meaning may be self-evident to the natives. Explicative transactions may vary in the "well-definedness" of aspects of the transaction, that is, in the extent to which the meaning of the initial segment retains its perceived meaning invariant to the subsequent response. In some instances perceived meaning is so well-established (for at least one party) that subsequent responses are assessed in terms of that meaning, whereas in other situations, the initial segment is indefinite and indeterminate. Luft (described in Watzlawick 1967, p. 49) has constructed a radical setting for explicative transactions by having two strangers sit across from one another and instructing them "not to talk or communicate in any way."

2. Excerpts preceded by an asterisk were transcribed by Gail Jefferson. The notational system is fully presented in Appendix I and includes the following elements (Schegloff 1972, p. 119):

    // indicates point at which following line interrupts
    [indicates simultaneous utterances when bridging two lines
    () indicates something said but not transcribable.
    (word) indicates what was probably said, but not clear.

3. Schutz's analysis (1964, p. 35) of the situation of the observer observing another who disattends or is unaware of the observer captures aspects of the plight of prospective defendants. Given the inability to interact and validate his interpretation of the others' motives, the observer may (or must) resort to three indirect procedures. The observer "may remember from his own past experience a course of action similar to the one observed and recall its motive." Second, the observer may be able to derive a typification of the observed individual's typical motives from his general stock of knowledge. As Schutz notes, the observer in lecture halls, courts, and churches would be able to deduce the typical "because" and "in-order-to" motives of participants "from that segment of his stock of knowledge which referred to typical teachers, judges, and priests." Third, in the absence of particular or typified knowledge about the individual, the observer may have to rely upon inference from "effect to cause." That is, in observing an accomplished act and its results, the observer "assumes that this particular accomplished act and these results were, indeed, the 'in-order-to' motive of the actor."

In the immediate context, we are focusing on the defendants' use of the latter procedure as a means of gleaning the local language game. It should be noted that the defendant incorporates elements of both the "We-relation" and a direct observation relation: s/he observes and ultimately s/he interacts with the observed. Of course, one does not rest easy with the characterization of judge-defendant interaction as a We-relation given the enormous power skew in the relation.

4. The appropriation of explicated meaning is not a simple function of the structure of the explicative transaction. The "same sequence" may give rise to different meanings depending upon the knowledge, practical interests, and perspective of the observer. For example, observers may differ in the ways in which they "punctuate" a sequence of events (Bateson and Jackson 1964, cited in Watzlawick et al. 1967, p. 55). As Bateson and Jackson note, "The rat who said 'I have got my experimenter trained. Each time I press the lever he gives me food.' was declining to accept the punctuation of the sequence which the experimenter was seeking to impose." In addition, appropriations are likely to be affected by the nature of the background knowledge available to the observer. For example, if the observer imposes a typified version of a language game upon the game actually enforced in the court, transactions may yield an assessment of the judge in terms such as "easy," "harsh," etc. Such characterizations are a product of the use of extrinsic versions of the quality of an "excuse" against which the judge's response is gauged. Presumably, if observers suspended use of extrinsically derived typifications, then features attributed to the psyche or personality of the judge would be transformed into situationally objective properties of the case, i.e., instead of a "hard judge" one sees a "weak excuse." In sum, we may note that just as there may be variation in the punctuation of a sequence, there is also variation in the ways in which the significance is apportioned between components of the sequence. There are, of course, many other factors affecting the appropriation of meaning, many of which are described by Schutz (1964), particularly in his discussion of the problematics confronting the observer. Neisser's critique (1976) of James J. Gibson's work provides a very provocative and useful complement to Schutz's discussion.

5. Many of the sessions observed begin with a recital of the defendant's rights qua defendant and as often as not with a description of how an arraignment will proceed. The procedural directives are sometimes rendered with a fairly high degree of precision in that they might include, for example, a specification of the sequential flow of the arraignment, the questions the defendant is entitled to ask and so on. It is possible, therefore, that the session is self-explicating not in the fashion we have attempted to display, but rather simply because instructions are specifically furnished and the activities are carried out under their jurisdiction. I should like to suggest that rather than view the instructions as governing the subsequent activities, the subsequent activities served to explicate the situated sense of the instructions.

The arraignments explicated the initial instructions in that it was only in the here and now of an actual arraignment that the status of the instructions was made observable. For example, even though the judge might have specifically precluded the possibility of giving explanations by saying, "I don't want to hear any explanations," his response to a defendant who nevertheless offered an explanation could serve to explicate the instructions as "mere talk" or as "rules which will prevail." Similarly, while the judge may have instructed defendants to enter a plea before they offered an explanation, the sense of the instructions could be radically altered when a defendant begins with an explanation and is allowed to continue by virtue of the judge's patient silence. In effect, these and other "tests" served to explicate the sense of the instructions. The "tests" necessarily received a response which would pass on the permissibility of the testing action.

6. A major methodological problem which haunts these exhibits of appropriative activity is the inability to distinguish between sequences in which defendants' circumstances are actually similar from those in which defendants are striving to contruct similar

accounts. The best that can be said for our evidence is that it indicates the form which appropriative activity might assume.

7. It also warrants mention that there are numerous instances of defendants who fail to appropriate presumptively established significances and sequences. There are "runs" of defendants in which the same "error" reappears, as when, for example, consecutive defendants enter a plea improperly. There are also "runs" of defendants who have had the opportunity to monitor preceding cases and who nevertheless formulate excuses and justifications which seem to reiterate and preserve the unsuccessful features of unsuccessful predecessors.

In the overwhelming proportion of arraignments, defendants are not held responsible for failing to appropriate presumptively explicated features. In effect, the sanctionably episodic, discrete, or self-contained character of an arraignment is explicated as defendants become confused or repeat others' "mistakes" and have their confusion clarified and errors remedied without the judge's reference to what should or could have been gleamed from preceding transactions.

8. Don Sutherland provided me with an illustration which suggests that the explicative process is operative on both sides of the bench.

> Justice is sometimes served in mysterious ways. U.S. Supreme Court Justice Harry Blackmun told a commencement day audience at Hamline University last week that when he took his place on that exalted bench, he was amazed to find that each Justice had a box of cough drops in a drawer in front of him. "I don't know why," said Blackmun, "because we don't say much." In Blackmun's box was a single cough drop. "It tasted like it had been there since 1902. Then I didn't know what to do with the empty box. I glanced around and saw another Justice throw his empty box on the floor. I thought it was strange, but it was picked up immediately and the Justice was brought a fresh, full box. I tried the same thing, and it worked." (Time Magazine, June 7, 1971, p. 30)

9. Bateson's (Ruesch and Bateson 1951) distinction between selective and progressional integration amplifies the distinction I am trying to draw between living outside and living within the ongoing order and the type of decisional work characteristic of each context. Selective integration refers to choices among articulated alternatives in a comparatively static and closed field. Progressional integration, by contrast, occurs in more dynamic and indefinite contexts. Bateson illustrates progressional integration in extemporaneous dance:

> The dancer's choice is influenced to a much greater extent by the ongoing characteristics of his sequence of action, and even, perhaps, by the ongoing dancing of a partner. This second type of decision we shall call decision by progressional integration, and we shall amplify the example by saying that the phenomenon is not confined to activities involving rapid physical movement, though the movement of the dancers is a convenient model to characterize the state of any person whose actions involve relatively rapid complex movement in "psychological space." It seems that this type of progressional integration is especially characteristic for action sequences in which the component acts are imperfectly

> differentiated and categorized, and in which speed of decision
> is important. (p. 184)

10.   Goffman (1971) comes close to aphorizing this part of the Meadian insight when he writes:

> ...what makes a precipice a precipice is the physical limits of
> sure-footedness and the tendency for organisms to splatter
> when they fall from heights; and what makes a precipice
> merely a precipice is the adaptive competency of animals and
> men in dealing with paths and footings. (p. 251)

A delightful and intriguing exhibit of the psychophysiological constitution of objects and *umwelts* is found in Jacob von Uexkull's "A Stroll Through the World of Animals and Men" (1951).

11.   Mead's thought invites an interesting revision of the Durkheimian exhortation (1938) to "consider social facts as things." Durkheim was animated by the need to overcome the commonsense thinking which led to easy and loose theorizing about social process. Treated as things, social facts would be recognized as objective processes requiring close and persistent empirical examination. From a Meadian point of view, the commonsense perspective also poses a problem in that the primordial process character of meaning is often masked by the objectivated meanings it produces. Thus, as good members we are much more apt to see ourselves as reacting to meanings than as enacting them. To overcome the retrospective illusion of commonsense requires a conception of meanings not as thing but as process. Were Mead forced to repent Durkheim's rule, he might write "consider social facts as *-ings.*" If social facts are to be treated as things, then socially organized meanings are to be treated as "-ings."

To attend to the -ing of things involves a radical modification of the attitude of everyday life, for it requires attending to the processes of constitution in lieu of the product thus constituted. In attending to the -ing of things one focuses on the course of activity—the form of life—which presupposes, preserves, and thereby produces the particular "thing." The analysis of -ing often requires an archaeological perspective, for there are often many levels —physiological, experiential, praxiological, and cognitive—through which social objects are created and sustained. The levels often become convoluted and reflexive, with the effect that seeming threats to particular objects and orders often turn out to be celebrations and rejuvenations of them.

REFERENCES

Bateson, Gregory, and Jackson, Don D. (1964). Some varieties of pathogenic organization. In *Disorders of Communication*, ed. David McK. Rioch and Edwin A. Weinstein, pp. 270-290. Baltimore: Williams and Wilkins.

Berger, Peter L., and Luckmann, Thomas (1966). *The Social Construction of Reality*. Garden City: Doubleday.

Carlen, Pat (1976). *Magistrate's Justice*. London: Martin Robertson.

Cicourel, Aaron V. (1973). *Cognitive Sociology*. London: Macmillan.

Durkheim, Emile (1950). *The Rules of Sociological Method*. Translated by Sarah A. Solovay and John H. Mueller. Glencoe: The Free Press of Glencoe.

Economos, James P. (1961). *Traffic Court Procedure and Administration*. Chicago: American Bar Association.

Garfinkel, Harold (1967). *Studies in Ethnomethodology*. Englewood Cliffs, New Jersey: Prentice-Hall.

Garfinkel, Harold, and Sacks, Harvey (1970). On formal structures of practical actions. In *Theoretical Sociology: Perspectives and Development,* ed. John C. McKinney and Edward A. Tiryakian. New York: Appleton-Century-Crofts.

Goffman, Erving (1971). *Relations in Public*. New York: Basic Books.

Haley, Jay (1959). An interactional description of schizophrenia. *Psychiatry* 4:321-332.

Handelman, Don, and Kapferer, Bruce (1972). Forms of joking activity: a comparative approach. *American Anthropologist* 74:484-517.

Luft, Joseph (1962). On non-verbal interaction. Paper presented at the Western Psychological Association Convention, San Francisco.

Mead, George Herbert (1934). *Mind, Self and Society: From the Standpoint of a Social Behaviorist*. Edited by Charles W. Morris. Chicago: The University of Chicago Press.

Merleau-Ponty, Maurice (1964). *Signs*. Translated by Richard C. McCleary. Evanston: Northwestern University Press.

Neisser, Ulric (1976). *Cognition and Reality*. San Francisco: W.H. Freeman.

Pike, Kenneth L. (1954). *Language in Relation to a Unified Theory of the Structure of Human Behavior, Part I*. Glendale, California: Summer Institute of Linguistics.

Pollner, Melvin (1970). On the Foundations of Mundane Reasoning. Unpublished doctoral dissertation, Department of Sociology, University of California at Santa Barbara.

———(1974). Mundane reasoning. *Philosophy of the Social Sciences* 4:35-54.

Reichenbach, Hans (1938). *Experience and Prediction*. Chicago: University of Chicago Press.

Ruesch, Jurgen, and Bateson, Gregory (1951). *Communication: The Social Matrix of Psychiatry*. New York: W.W. Norton.

Sartre, Jean-Paul (1966). *Being and Nothingness*. Translated by Hazel E. Barnes. New York: Washington Square Press.

Schegloff, Emanuel A. (1968). Sequencing in conversational openings. *American Anthropologist* 70:1075-1095.

———(1972). Notes on a conversational practice: formulating place. In *Studies in Social Interaction,* ed. David Sudnow. New York: The Free Press.

Schutz, Alfred (1964). *Collected Papers II: Studies in Social Theory*. The Hague: Martinus Nijhoff.

———(1967). *The Phenomenology of the Social World.* Translated by George Walsh and Frederick Lehnert. Evanston: Northwestern University Press.

Turner, Victor (1974). *The Ritual Process.* Harmondsworth, England: Pelican Books.

Uexkull, Jacob von (1957). A stroll through the world of animals and men. In *Instinctive Behavior,* ed. Claire H. Schiller, pp. 5-80. New York: International Universities Press.

Watzlawick, Paul, Beavin, Janet Helmick, and Jackson, Don D. (1967). *Pragmatics of Human Communications.* New York: W.W. Norton.

Weick, Karl E. (1969). *The Social Psychology of Organizing.* Reading, Massachusetts: Addison-Wesley.

Wieder, D. Lawrence (1974). Telling the code. In *Ethnomethodology,* Roy Turner, ed. Harmondsworth, pp. 144-172. Harmondsworth, England: Penguin.

Sequencing and Shared Attentiveness to Court Proceedings

J. Maxwell Atkinson

In a study conducted in England and without awareness of Pollner's work on courtrooms, Atkinson approaches the matter of how shared attentiveness is produced in the coroner's court. His work remarkably complements and supplements Pollner's study. By using the framework developed by Sacks and conversational analysts he is able to show that multi-party settings also can be studied to determine how turn-taking is organized. If we were to use Pollner's concept of explicative transactions we would say that Atkinson has analyzed, in greater detail, how utterances and sequences of activities in the courtroom provide for and produce the self-same organization to which the actors in the setting address their statements. That is, the sequences of utterances and activities, as performed by the coroner's officer and the coroner, provide for those in the courtroom those matters which are noticeable as informative and implicative of their next actions.

Atkinson offers us in this detailed analysis a further insight into how self-explication occurs in "formal settings" such as these where several persons not heretofore instructed or knowledgeable as to the proceedings can gain, in the utterances and activities of particular participants, sufficient and adequate "knowledge" as to how to proceed, what

*to do next, what to expect, etc. The extension of such analyses to other
multi-party settings, particularly those characterized by ritual,
ceremony, and formality, suggests further directions for the conversational or, more properly perhaps, interactional analysts' work as pursued from an ethnomethodological perspective.*

Studying Court Proceedings

A common characteristic of several sociological studies of courtroom
interaction (e.g., Emerson 1969, Carlen 1974, 1975, 1976a, 1976b) is the
way in which the ready recognizability (to members) of differences between the organization of talk in court hearings and various other settings has been used as a largely unexplicated analytic resource[1]. As I have
elaborated in more detail elsewhere (Atkinson 1976), one manifestation
of this is the practice of contrasting certain noticeable features of courtroom interaction with others selected from a variety of naturally occurring situations of every day life. By holding examples of these latter to be
the "norm," what goes on in court can then be displayed as
"abnormal," or as "clear violations of appropriate rules of behavior"
(Emerson 1969, p. 202). Alternatively, rather than concentrating on
noticed *differences* between interaction in courts and elsewhere, the emphasis may be placed on *similarities* between the organization of activities in courts and other multi-party settings (e.g., games, dramas,
rituals, etc.). And this focus also tends to lead to variously critical conclusions about court hearings so that, once they have been depicted as being "like" games, theatrical performances, or whatever, ironic critiques
can be constructed simply by noting that they should not be like that
and/or that they are "in fact" something else: "The court is not a
theatre. It is an institutional setting charged with the maintenance and
reproduction of existing forms of structural dominance" (Carlen 1976a,
p. 38).

Two of the most obviously noticeable features of interaction in courts,
which have recurrently attracted the attention of sociological observers,
are (1) the way in which unspoken activities (such as standing up and sitting down) appear to be closely coordinated with spoken activities, and
(2) the fact that speaking rights seem to be subjected to special restric-
tions which do not hold across all social settings. But, while such
phenomena have provided important contrastive materials for the
elaboration of complaints about court procedures and a variety of claims
about the (mostly undesirable) effects they are supposed to have on some

participants, little attention has been given to questions like whether and how their organization might provide for the resolution or partial resolution of situated problems of the settings in which they are found. That unspoken activities, such as sitting down and standing up, seem to be somehow or other tied in with specific sequences in court hearings has presumably been regarded as being too obvious to deserve serious consideration as a topic for analysis in its own right. Accordingly, both that "somehow or other" and the obvious recognizability (to members) of similarities and differences between the way such activities are organized in courts, as compared with other settings, have been taken for granted and used as resources in the production of metaphorical and ironic accounts of court proceedings.[2]

The approach adopted in the present paper, however, differs from those referred to above in that it seeks to remain indifferent to ironic and critical concerns, and to view the noticeability of continuities and disjunctions between courtroom and other practices as a problematic and central topic for analysis. To this end, it reports on some preliminary analyses derived from the early stages of a program of research which conceives of court hearings first and foremost as one type of multi-party speech-exchange system.[3] Such a focus has been prompted not just by a critical reaction to previous sociological work on courtroom interaction, but also by a more general interest in the possibility of adapting or extending conversational analysis to come to terms with two sorts of interactional problem evident in a variety of settings, of which courts are one example, which have not been extensively dealt with in the existing literature on the organization of conversations.[4] The first involves the question of how a mutual orientation or shared attentiveness to a single sequence of utterance turns can be accomplished and sustained by more than a few co-present parties to a setting. And the second general problem centers on the possible organizational significances of turns comprised of *unspoken* unit types, and the extent to which these might be incorporated into an analysis of sequencing. Some brief preliminary remarks about each of these may help to locate and clarify some of the analytic issues which may be involved.

Speech-Exchange Systems and Group Size

Most of the advances in conversational analysis have been derived from studies of data on talk between fairly small numbers of partici-pants. But this by no means implies that such work is not or cannot be related to situations where more than a few people are present. Thus, Sacks, Schegloff, and Jefferson (1974) were quite explicit in stating that, while they had sought to elaborate a model of the turn-taking system for *conversations,* their results had potential implications for the "com-parative investigation of the speech-exchange systems available to members of a single society, conceived of in terms of differential turn-taking systems" (p. 729). More specifically, they noted the following:

> The use of a turn-taking system to preserve one party talking at a time while speaker change recurs, for interactions in which talk is organiza-tionally involved, is not at all unique to conversa-tion. It is massively present for ceremonies, debates, meetings, press conferences, seminars, therapy sessions, interviews, trials, et cetera. All of these differ from conversation (and from each other) on a range of other turn taking parameters and in the organization by which they achieve the set of parameter values whose presence they organize. (p. 279)

In developing this theme, they suggested that speech-exchange systems mght be ordered along a kind of linear array according to the extent to which the ordering of turns is "pre-allocated". Whereas in conversations next-turn allocation is generally accomplished on a turn by turn basis, with one turn being allocated at a time, situations like those listed in the above quotation share the common feature that turn allocation is, in various ways and to different extents, done in advance. In court hear-ings, for example, many of the rules of evidence and procedure are con-cerned with the pre-allocation of turns, specifying (among other things) which categories of persons may do what sorts of things at which points in the proceedings.[5] More generally, it would seem to be the case that courts and other settings where turn pre-allocation is an organization feature are very often also ones where quite large numbers of people may be present, and some of the earlier findings of conversation analysis suggest that it may be no coincidence that specialized turn-taking procedures tend to be found or initiated when groups get above a certain size.

Thus, a crucially important property of the turn-taking system for conversations is the way in which the requirement that parties must be able to recognize possible turn endings, who may speak next, and what may be appropriately done at any next turn, provides a built-in constraint on conversationalists to monitor and pay close attention to the ongoing talk if they are to be able to exhibit their continuing understanding of what is going on. This pressure toward attentiveness would appear to be particularly strong in situations where only two parties are present, in that there is no doubt under such circumstances as to whose turn it will be next to deliver a sequentially relevant next utterance. But, where numbers increase, a change takes place in the form of an increasing strain on the capacity of the turn-taking system to preserve a shared orientation of all those present to the same sequence of single utterance turns. The larger the groups, the less easy is it for a present speaker to monitor closely the displays of attentiveness of all his listeners and at the same time, the less will be the likelihood that everyone present will be. able to take a turn to talk at all. Indeed, when some parties remain silent for an extended period of time, it may become ambiguous as to whether or not they are still parties to the same conversation. Under such circumstances, some of those present may, can, and often do, properly start up a concurrent conversation among themselves, the force of "properly" here being to indicate that the second (or third, or , , ,nth) conversation may receive recognition as a *separate conversation* by the failure of the active parties to the original one to invoke the "one speaker at a time" constraint with reference   to the recently started concurrent talk. In that this constraint no longer holds for all those present, but does so for members of different subgroups within the setting, everyone may then be said to be orienting to there now being two or more conversations taking place, where previously there was one.

Viewed in these terms, then, court hearings can be seen as one example of a situation where members face a rather general interactional problem of how a shared orientation to a single sequence of utterance turns can be sustained in the light of the probability that, if left unmodified, the turn-taking system for conversations provides for (and perhaps even exerts a pressure toward) the emergence of more than one concurrent conversation. And, more specifically, there is the problem of how transitions are accomplished from a situation in which *several* conversations are taking place to one where those involved in them have transferred their attention to the shared monitoring of a single sequence of utterances. An instance of such a transition at the start of a court hearing is examined below. Before proceeding to the analysis, however, a brief comment on the problem of analyzing unspoken activities is necessary.

Unspoken Activity Turns[6]

As was noted above, uncertain unspoken activities—such as sitting down and standing up—are particularly noticeable features of court proceedings, at least in the English legal system and others derived from it. And, as will be noted in one of the transcribed versions of the data to be considered below, descriptors of several such activities have been included along with the written representations of the utterance turns. That this has been done, however, is not intended to indicate that the selection and inclusion of activity descriptors for the purposes of analysis is a straightforward or unproblematic matter. For it raises a whole series of very complicated issues relating to, among other things, the inevitable availability of alternative descriptions of some activity in the world, the indefinite extendability of any one description and, perhaps most important of all, the problem of how some unspoken activity may be warrantably said to be oriented to by members. In other words, the present study has proceeded *as if* there were no such problems, rather than under the auspices of some claim to the effect that they had been adequately resolved *prior to* the empirical investigation.

This raises the further question of why it might be deemed worthwhile to include unspoken activities at all, given the vast range of issues associated with the organization of spoken ones still awaiting exploration, and the sorts of analytic advantages associated with a more or less exclusive concentration on talk. The preliminary references to the noticeability of certain unspoken activities in courts would, however, seem to suggest that they are oriented to somehow or other as organized phenomena by participants and observers, whatever the details of some particular description of them may be. More specifically, they would appear to be *sequentially ordered* with the talk in a way which seems to relate closely to what is already known about the sequencing of spoken activities.[7] And this would seem to apply much more generally in a wide variety of social settings, as can be exemplified by considering the way in which an unspoken activity can constitute one or both parts of an adjacency pair (on adjacency pair sequences see especially Schegloff and

Sacks, 1973). Thus, a wave can be a perfectly proper first or second part of a greeting pair, and a nod or shake of the head can similarly serve as a second pair part of a question-answer sequence. Many sports and games, furthermore, are characterized by sequences of unspoken activity turns so that, for example, one stroke by a tennis player has clear and limited sequential implications for his opponent's next turn, and so on, until one player fails to deliver a proper turn. And, as will be discussed in greater detail below, some utterances can be designed to elicit an unspoken activity as a next turn, and may constitute a type of sequence which is particularly suitable for doing certain sorts of interactional work. More generally, given the extensively documented importance of spoken-spoken adjacency pair sequences in the structural organization of talk, a potentially promising line of further research might be started by looking to as wide as possible a range of naturally occurring social settings for instances of these other adjacency pair types (i.e., where the first and second pair parts are respectively unspoken-spoken, unspoken-unspoken, or spoken-unspoken), as a prelude to considering their possible significance for the sequential organization of interaction.[8]

In summary, then, the suggestion so far has been that there are reasonable grounds for supposing that the approach to the study of sequential organization developed by conversational analysts, as well as some of their findings, might be applicable also to activities other than spoken ones. This kind of proposed extension does, of course, raise a number of interesting and diffiult problems such as the ones hinted at above, but it seems unlikely that either those or the question of how such work should be done will be resolved abstractly and without reference to specific and relevant sources of data.

Opening the Hearing: Preliminary Remarks

The data to be considered in the remainder of this paper are taken from the first few moments of a coroner's inquest, which was one of a number which were originally observed during the course of an earlier study of how official categorizations of suicide are decided (Atkinson, 1968, 1971, 1977)[9]. The main focus of that work was on the ways in which evidence about suicide and related phenomena were assembled and presented, and the data transcribed in the Appendix were therefore collected with different questions in mind from the present ones. One consequence of this was that the transcription conventions used were fairly minimal and include, for example, no representations of intonation differences, breaks in words, etc. Consistent with these omissions, then, such events are not addressed in the present analysis.

A further general point about the data is that there are literally innumerable ways in which the proceedings could have been transcribed, and it is partly to illustrate this point, and partly to show how interesting issues can emerge during the very process of producing transcripts, that three versions of the same sequence are included, Thus, the first (I) includes a record only of the audible utterances and their speakers, the second (II) incorporates an inaudible utterance as well as the length and location of pauses, and the third (III) introduces activity descriptors referring to unspoken activities which occurred during the pauses. A comparison of them quickly reveals that a good deal must have taken place during the time when the words from lines 1-3 in Version I were spoken. Indeed, it is probably hardly necessary for any competent reader to go much beyond the first version in order to be able to fill in much of the detail included in Version III, and to hazard reasonable guesses about a good deal more. It is obvious, for example, that something must have occurred *between* the first two sentences in that, if it had not, it is extremely difficult to envisage a situation where the three sentences could have followed on from each other in a continuous stream, and hence to make much sense of them as a "single utterance" spoken by one party to the same recipient. "Be upstanding in court. . .,"[10] however, can readily be heard as projecting a next action which is to be an unspoken one and, in the absence of repeats by the speaker or repair initiations by another, readers of it who did not witness the original scene will presumably have little difficulty in locating a possible activity descriptor for what happened immediately after its completion.

The first proposed reading to be considered analytically below, then, is that "Be upstanding in Court for Her Majesty's Coroner" can be heard as marking the beginning of the hearing as a whole, more particularly, as marking the start of a *transition* from a situation where several concurrent conversations were taking place to one where everyone present starts to monitor the same sequence of activities. Hopefully, such a reading will be seen as utterly obvious and uncontroversial, for the almost unequivocal way in which the utterance can be heard to mark the start of the hearing is precisely what gave it an analytic attraction. Thus, the problem becomes one of trying to provide for that recognizable definiteness by specifying some of the procedures usable by members (both participants in the setting and readers of the transcript) for recognizing it more or less unambigiously as the first utterance of the inquest.

A general point which can be made immediately is that the utterance in question is hearable in this way *only with reference to its serial placement* in relation to what preceded and what followed. Even the inferential work involved in identifying the first sentence as being separated from the second in Version I is prompted by the puzzle that would otherwise be posed by reading the second sentence as following on straight after the first. But, in addition to filling in some of that detail, the start of Version III refers also to what was taking place prior to the utterance "Be upstanding in Court. . .," and what appears there would seem to be fairly typical of the kind of state of affairs found in many multi-party settings where nothing has yet been done to obtain the shared orientation of everyone present to a single sequence of utterance turns. We have, in short, *more than one* conversation going on at a time in a situation where those present presumably know that sooner or later they will all have to pay attention together to *only one* sequence involving one speaker speaking at a time and speaker change recurrence. In starting the transition to a situation where that is possible (i.e., where the previous conversations have been replaced by a silence which can be filled by a single speaker), the utterance "Be upstanding in Court. . . ." appears remarkably successful and economical. This seems particularly so in comparison with other settings in which similar transitional sequences are found, such as before meetings, seminars, or therapy sessions (see Turner 1972). For in those situations, several or many utterances may be required before a mutual orientation to their having started is achieved, and preliminary attempts to get them under way may, and frequently do, fail. And, while such transitional sequences may involve, like the present example, a first utterance (e.g., "Is everyone ready?", "Shall we start?", etc.) which can be heard as a *candidate* transition starter, such candidacy may fail for the moment, and the possibility of delaying further the start of the session is left open—an option which is not obviously present in the case of "Be upstanding in Court. . . ." In parenthesis, then, it may be noted that the comparative study of different procedures for initiating such transitions would seem to be a potentially fruitful area for further investigation, though the present data do not of course allow for such an analysis. Awareness that there are these other methods for accomplishing shared attentiveness, however, does serve to emphasize the effectiveness of the apparently simply utterance "Be upstanding in Court. . . ." in achieving the transition to a situation where all those present (a) stop talking and (b) end up sitting in silence monitoring the ongoing activities so closely that not only can the next audible utterance (lines 13-14 in Version III) be heard, but the next inaudible one (at line 10 in III) can be noticed. The analytic task addressed below, therefore, attempts to explicate three sorts of things; (1) how it is that utterance gets to be heard as the first to which everyone present should orient; (2) how it brings about a fairly immediate silence; and (3) how what follows appears to bring about what is referred to below as the "consolidation" of attentiveness.

Recognizing a First Utterance to be Attended to by Everyone

It was suggested above that a problem members may face can be that of identifying some single utterance more or less unambiguously as one to which attention is to be paid by all those present in a setting where several conversations are taking place at once. That is, there is no guarantee that everyone there will hear just any utterance as that, let alone respond to it in their next activities. Given that all those at this inquest did apparently respond to it, thereby displaying their shared understanding of it as such a first utterance, perhaps the most remarkable achievement of it was the way in which the considerable potential for ambiguity and misunderstanding was avoided. In attempting to account for this lack of ambiguity, it will be proposed that it may have to do with the availability to members of not just one method for the recognition of "Be upstanding in Court for Her Majesty's Coroner" as the first to which everyone should attend, but several. In other words, were there only one or two features of it which would allow for its possible recognition as the first, there would be a good chance that some of those present might fail to locate them and hence fail also to identify and respond to the utterance as the first. If, however, there are several features of its design and placement which would enable it to be so recognized, then it is presumably likely that each person present will manage to notice at least one, and hence to hear it accordingly. And, by implication, those of us (both participants and analysts) who find a number of methods for identifying it as the first are likely to hear it more unambiguously as such. That is, it would sound like the first utterance of the hearing, "whichever way one looks at it."

While various groups of people within the courtroom may initially be engaged in separate conversations, there is, as was noted earlier, an expectation that something will have to happen to bring about the transition to a situation where everyone can orient to the same sequence of utterance turns, and there is also a predicted time when this might be expected to occur (i.e., the time set for the inquest). Thus, there is a prospective readiness to hear any utterance which could be interpreted as a first of the transition as being indeed the first such utterance. Into this situation is delivered an utterance which is clearly hearable as having been recipiently designed *for everyone* (rather than just for the one or two others a person might be talking to at the time). In saying that it can be heard as having been recipiently designed to be heard by everyone, I have in mind such features as the place in the courtroom from which it was spoken, the type of person who uttered it, its content, syntax, and, perhaps above all, its status as a simultaneous interruption of *all* the other utterances under way at the same time. To take the last of these first, its volume was much louder than any of the other concurrent utterances and, as such, it was readily noticeable not just as a violation of the "one speaker speaks at a time" constraint being oriented to by parties to the various separate conversations, but as loud enough to have interrupted everyone else's conversation as well. An easy way to make sense of so flagrant and multiple a violation, then, is to hear it as having been designed to be heard by everyone, a conclusion which can be similarly arrived at by (and hence receive some confirmation from) other methods of reasoning. Thus, at the same time as they hear it, those present in the courtroom will presumably also see that it is delivered by someone standing on the raised platform, and who is thereby set apart from everyone else. This can be taken as evidence that he is not a participant in one of the other conversations—which in turn makes it highly improbable that his remark could have been addressed *exclusively* to one or two particular people in the room. That it was designed to be heard by all, therefore, is again a readily available method for making sense of it.

But, while there may be this strong support for hearing the utterance as the first in the proceedings, there could be room for doubt about the rights of this particular speaker to do such a thing, given that he is presumably a stranger to most of those present. Competent members may be fairly sure that not just anyone would get up there and speak in this way, but this person could, after all, be a hoaxer, madman, anarchist, etc., or he could be an official of the Court. A preliminary conclusion that this latter is a possible correct categorization of the speaker is likely to have already been arrived at by anyone who has been monitoring his activities *before* this point in the pretransitional period. For these included showing people where to sit, carrying files about, chatting to policemen, and generally exhibiting a familiarity with the setting and its organization. Even those who did not notice these things, and were therefore unable to move directly from their observations of such category-bound activities to a categorization of the speaker as official, would be likely to have enough knowledge of such settings to be able to operate with some general viewers' maxim like: see him as an official of the court if you can (see Sacks 1972a, 1972b). One way of checking this out, though not necessarily the most reliable, would be to inspect his appearance (clothes, hair length, etc.) to see if the speaker would be possibly describable as "an official." But a probably more certain way of ruling out possible ambiguities as to the speaker's identity would be to monitor the reactions of other more readily recognizable officials (e.g., policemen), who can be assumed to be familiar with the court and its personnel, and who would presumably exhibit highly visible and dramatic signs of recognising any imposter, reactions which were absent in the present case.

Inspection of the content and syntax of the utterance can also yield further confirmation that it was indeed designed to be oriented to by all those present. As a command, for example, it can be heard as a candidate member of a class of events which are usable for closing down current activities and marking the start of a transition of this sort. This point is developed further in Section 4 below, and for the moment it will suffice to note the close similarity between utterances which are recognizable as commands and the summons part of summons-answer sequences (cf. Schegloff, 1968), and the way in which some sort of summons (whether it be the ringing of a bell, banging on a desk, blowing a whistle, etc.) is an expectably appropriate method for attrracting attention in multi-party gatherings. And, while such alternatives may seem strange or unlikely to anyone familiar with English legal procedures, it can be noted that at least some of them are to be found in other cultures. At the opening of Swedish court hearings, for example, all except the judges wait outside the court room and only enter when a bell is rung by those on the inside.[12]

The command, furthermore, is not just recognizable as an appropriately placed summons, but its content can be heard as being closely tied into its setting. As was noted earlier, that the utterance was addressed to everyone can be found from an analysis of where the speaker was standing, but such a conclusion can also be reached on the basis of what was said. The words "in court," for example, can be heard to reference everyone as recipients of the utterance and to exclude no one from attending to its sequential implications. Perhaps more important than this, however, is the way in which it is hearable as having been *occasioned by* a present action in which many of those present are currently engaged (i.e. sitting). In other words, independently of its status as an interruption (which of course is less relevant for those not currently involved in a conversation), the utterance can be heard as being a sequentially relevant next action not just to *any* possibly describable activity that a particular individual might have been engaged in, but to one which most of those present were doing. In so far as it thereby casts the activities being done by almost everyone in the court room as ones which should now be terminated, there is a sense in which the utterance can be seen to engage itself as a next turn in a sequence of activities in which most of those present have already been involved (i.e. sitting, walking, etc.). To the extent that this is so, the utterance can be heard to establish an obligation on the other party (where the other party is "everyone together") to respond accordingly at the turn's completion.

A further feature of the contents of the utterance, which would seem to be important in providing for its recognizability as the marker of the transition's beginning, is the reference to "Her Majesty's Coroner." For, as Turner (1972) has shown in more detail in relation to psychiatric therapy sessions, there are some kinds of sequences which cannot properly be said to have started at all before the arrival of some particular person or persons. And just as a therapy session requires the presence of a therapist for it to be properly describable as such a session, and hence to get under way, so an inquest without a coroner is similarly not yet an inquest. Thus, insofar as the utterance can be heard to herald the imminent arrival of the coroner (and indeed the information for those who may have been uncertain that he was not already in the courtroom), it announces that a necessary condition for the hearing to begin is about to be fulfilled.

In this section, then, an attempt has been made to show not only that "Be upstanding in Court for Her Majesty's Coroner" can be heard as the first utterance which is available to be oriented to by all those present at the inquest, but also that there are a variety of ways in which it can be heard as such. That there are several methods for reaching the same conclusion arguably minimizes the scope for potentially ambiguous interpretations of it, and thereby provides for the apparent obviousness and definiteness of the proposed reading. This is not to imply that everyone present must or does use every available method for reaching such a conclusion, but it is to suggest that the availability of several makes it unlikely that anyone could fail to locate at least enough of them to arrive at the shared reading. Similar disambiguating processes would seem to be at work in the sequence immediately following the first utterance in Version III, in that it is massively successful in bringing about an immediate and extended silence, *notwithstanding the fact that it contains no explicit instruction to be silent.* Given this source of potential ambiguity, the shared recognition of it by those present as a cue to stop talking and remain quiet for an extended period seems particularly remarkable, and suggests that there must be other procedures which provide for its unambiguous recognizability as an initiator of silence. The following section therefore involves an attempt to explicate what these might be.

Accomplishing Silence

A starting point for this part of the analysis was hinted at above in the reference to summons-answer sequences, and the way in which the first utterance seemed to "engage itself" as a turn in a sequence in which everyone in court was involved. Thus, once it has been recognized as the first turn to which everybody should orient, the onus shifts to them to display their understanding of it as such by doing something which can be seen as being sequentially relevant to that previous turn. One activity which the first utterance can readily be heard to project as an appropriate next turn is, of course, standing up. But it is not so obvious that or how it also projects a silence or, for that matter, that everyone should remain standing until a point at which they all sit down together without any further verbal prompting. That this occurs, it will be suggested below, would appear to be closely tied in with the way in which the utterance "Be upstanding in Court..."can be heard as the first part of an adjacency pair which projects as a second pair part an unspoken activity turn rather than a spoken one. Such a line of argument, however, depends for its sense on all those present having heard the first utterance in such a way as to have identified what activity was projected by it. In other words, it presupposes that they will have located the sequential implicativeness of the first utterance by the time that the turn was completed. To begin with, then, I want to suggest that a feature of its design may provide a particularly neat solution to a problem posed by the sequential placement of the utterance at a point in the proceedings where several conversations are still taking place.

In an earlier version of this analysis (Atkinson 1976), it was noted that "be upstanding" had a curiously archaic ring to it when compared with the more usual "stand up" (i.e., more usual as far as contemporary English usage is concerned). One possible significance of that which was suggested was that this relatively obscure usage might provide those present with added grounds for knowing that the speaker was not an imposter, in that an imposter would presumably select some more familiar sequence of words. On further reflection, however, such a proposal seems rather weak compared with an alternative one which can be seen to provide some sort of solution to a possible problem arising from the sequential position of the utterance. Thus, an utterance designed for all to hear which occurs at a point where several other conversations are taking place simulatneously runs a serious risk of not being clearly audible to all those present. In that the early turn constructional units of such an utterance serve as a signal for the other talk to cease, they occur *just before* the noise associated with that other talk has begun to die down, and hence stand a good chance of not being clearly heard. Under such circumstances, there would appear to be an advantage in delaying any sequentially implicative constructional units until later in the turn so that, by the time one occurs, the noise level will have fallen to a point where it is clearly hearable. Otherwise, some repeat of the first utterance, or at least of its sequentially implicative parts, would be necessary for those present to locate what next action had been projected. Viewed in these terms, then, the first turn constructional units (i.e., "Be up...") can be seen as a kind of prefatory silence initiator which delays the delivery of the crucial sequentially implicative unit (i.e., "...standing") to a point where its chances of being heard may be greater. The alternative "Stand up" contrasts markedly with the usage actually found here, in that "stand" would have been spoken at the point in the turn where the noise level was at its greatest. Insofar as it, too, might have served as an unclearly heard silence-initiating preface, those present who heard only the second part (i.e., "up") might use it to find retrospectively that what they missed might have been "shut." In short, had the first turn constructional units been "Stand up" rather than "Be upstanding," it could well have been ambiguous for those present as to whether what had just been said was "Stand up" or "Shut up," or indeed almost anything else. To the extent that the form "Be upstanding" has a built-in delay of two syllables, then, it can be seen to have clear organizational advantages at this point over what is perhaps the most obvious possible alternative ("Stand up").

More generally, it can be noted in passing that such built-in delays of sequentially implicative units at the start of turns may be a widely prevalent phenomenon in situations where preceding noise is a problem, and a possible line of further research might involve looking for further instances from similar settings. Other openings of court hearings would be one obvious source of such data and, while few of these have yet been examined in the course of the present research, it is perhaps worth mentioning how sessions of the United States Supreme Court begin:[13]

> Oyez, oyez, oyez. All persons having business before the Honorable, the Supreme Court of the United States, are admonished to draw near and give their attention, for the court is now sitting. God save the United States of America.

Thus, not only does it start with a *six*-syllable silence-initiating preface, but it also includes a much more explicit instruction for those present to be attentive than is the case with "Be upstanding in Court..." Another interesting case of an unusual inversion (like "Be upstanding"), which takes place in a setting where *both* noise *and* the sequential implicativeness of an utterance for a collective unspoken next activity turn are involved, is to be found in the orders shouted at military marching squads. For while in most situations where directions to go left or right are being given, it is usual to say things like "turn left," or "go to the right," the inverted forms "left turn," "right turn," "left wheel," "right wheel," etc. are preferred for giving military orders, with the first word (containing the crucial piece of sequentially implicative information) being typically long and drawn out compared with the short and snappily delivered second. And the sorts of organizational problems for military squads that might follow an utterance turn which delayed the directional word until the last second (as in the more usual "turn left") can readily be imagined.

Having suggested how the first utterance is designed in such a way that the reference to the next projected action (i.e., standing up) can actually be heard, I want to return now to the problem of how it might be that it also projects an extended silence. To begin with, then, it will be proposed that this may have to do with the fact that the utterance "Be upstanding in Court..." can be heard as the first part of an adjacency pair which projects as a second part an unspoken activity turn rather than a spoken one. As a preliminary to this, two general points about its status as a command may be noted. The first is that commands can, of course, be the first part of spoken activity pairs (utterance-utterance), as in such examples as "Answer the Question," "Speak to me," etc., as well as being possible first parts of spoken-unspoken activity pairs (utterance-activity). And the second point is that a range of syntactical formats other than commands (e.g., questions or statements) can serve as perfectly proper first parts of a U-A pair (e.g., "Would you mind standing up?", "I think we could do with a window opening," etc.).

The presence of one or another of these alternatives as a recognizable first part of a U-A pair may well have important consequences for the likelihood or otherwise of talk occurring after the completion of the first (spoken) turn. Thus, one feature of an utterance which can be heard as a command which has sequential implicativeness for an unspoken next action is that one possible procedure for next speaker selection, namely "present speaker selects next speaker" is *not* employed. But while this may substantially diminish the chances of the utterance being followed by talk (thereby increasing the probability of a silence), it nevertheless leaves open the possibility, at least in principle, that a next speaker will select himself. The likelihood of this occurring, however, would seem to be considerably less in cases where the first part of such a pair can be heard as a command rather than, for example, a question. Hence, the more ambiguity as to whether a spoken or unspoken activity (or some combination of the two) should follow a first turn which is hearable as a question than is the case where it is heard as a command. For even questions designed to elicit some unspoken activity as a next turn will invariably have *simultaneous* sequential implicativeness for a spoken activity (e.g., an answer to a question) as a possibly appropriate alternative or accompanying second part. Thus, a person who is expected to do an unspoken activity turn immediately after a question may reply with an answer to the question (e.g., A: "Have you a cigarette?", B: "Yes.", A: "May I have one then?"), a request for further explication of the instruction, apologies for a delayed start of the activity, refusals to do it, etc. In short, then, utterances which can be heard as questions designed to elicit an unspoken activity at the next turn leave open on their completion a considerable range of spoken options. By contrast, a first utterance hearable as a command to do an unspoken activity would seem to project a much narrower set of possible next actions, and to establish a clearer priority for an unspoken rather than a spoken activity turn to follow.[14] If this is so, then to speak immediately after such a first part could be seen as a failure (or refusal) to display an understanding of that priority, and would therefore be a particularly delicate and accountable matter.

So far, then, the suggestion has been that the effectiveness of the utterance "Be upstanding in Court..." in bringing about a silence may be at least partially provided for with reference to the way in which it involved *no* selection of a next speaker, and exerts a pressure against any next speaker's selecting himself. But, while no next speaker may be selected, the utterance does select a next actor to take the next turn, and this may further serve to diminish the chances of anyone's selecting himself to speak immediately on its completion. As noted in the previous section, this next actor can be heard by *everyone together,* in that the utterance was apparently designed to be heard by all and permitted no exemptions from its auspices. Given that it also projected as a sequentially relevant next turn an unspoken activity (i.e., standing up), any other subsequent activity which might be recognizable as a next turn, whether it be sitting down, waving at the speaker, walking out of the room, or, most significantly in the present context, *talking,* could be seen to be misplaced. Indeed, it would almost seem to be the case that a somewhat modified version of the "one speaker speaks at a time" constraint for conversational turn-taking would be violated, in that one of these various sequentially inappropriate turns would be identifiable as an improper overlap or interruption of the sequentially relevant turn which should now be taking place. The kind of pressure against anyone's selecting himself to talk involved here is arguably increased by the fact that the proper next action is projected to be done by a collective agent, namely, *everyone together.* In that such collective action involves participants in the careful monitoring of each other's activities and in exhibiting to each other that they are all engaged in "the same action," doing anything which could not be rec- ·ognizably so described is likely to be highly noticeable and to invite a good deal of inferential work from everyone else. One way in which others could make sense of such an event is to see the violator not merely as an incompetent member, but as *the only* incompetent member present in the courtroom. Alternatively, such an action (or the total absence of the sequentially relevant action) may be seen as having been motivated by rebellious aims, which is of course an important resource for anyone who wishes to disrupt the orderly flow of proceedings or register a protest.[15]

The projection of an unspoken activity turn to be done next by everyone together may not only reduce the chances of any *one* person doing some activity which would clearly be recognizable as something else (whether that something else were unspoken or spoken), but the "everyone together" requirement would also seem to exert a pressure specifically against the occurrence of verbal activity. Or rather this would seem to be so in situations like the present one, where participants have not been provided (either before the session or during the course of the first turn) with any prearranged script or instructions as to what it is that might be said together. Thus, were more than one, or all the parties present, to speak at the same time, the result would be immediately recognizable as "bedlam," "chaos," "Babel," etc. Conversely, situations where a group of participants (such as congregations at religious services, crowds at football matches, etc.) engage in spoken activities together are typically characterized by prearranged standardized responses, as well as a range of other organizational procedures designed to maximize the chances of simultaneous and coordinated delivery (e.g., music, drumbeats, handclapping, signals by cheerleaders, conductors, etc.).[16] The suggestion here, then, is that a group of co-present parties are very unlikely to be able to speak, or chant, or sing, *in unison,* without some explicit or implicit prior instructions as to verbal content (whether these be known beforehand, contained in a script, or provided in an utterance which precedes the start of the collectively done turn). To get such a group, as in the present case, to orient to doing a next turn together, without at the same time giving any details of spoken activities which could be done together, would therefore seem to be a potentially very powerful method for bringing about a collective silence.

To this point, the argument has been that the immediate silence which follows "Be upstanding in Court for Her Majesty's Coroner" can be provided for in large measure with reference to the nonimplementation of one procedure for next speaker selection ("Present speaker selects next speaker"), and the minimization of the chances of the other ("Next speaker selects himself") coming into operation. It may be noted further that the third possible option under such circumstances, namely, "present speaker continues," is not taken up either. Thus, having successfully established his right to speak, the Coroner's Officer (CO) quickly reaches a possible turn completion point, after which he shows no sign whatsoever of continuing. Insofar as everyone who heard the start of his utterance will presumably have been monitoring the turn during its course, they will also be likely to carry on monitoring for a possible continuation and, by doing so, they will be able to discover that what he actually does is to start to do what they have just started to do. That is, he too stands in silence, an activity which may provide visible confirmation for any doubters who may remain that this is indeed the sequentially relevant next turn that has just been projected. But it would also seem to be the case that, by joining with everyone else in doing this unspoken activity turn, the Coroner's Officer is also doing something which has prospective sequential implications for extending the silence and consolidating the shared attentiveness which has just begun. A brief consideration of how this might operate is presented in the following and final analytic section.

Consolidating Shared Attentiveness

The discussion so far has been concerned with the problem of how the various conversations taking place in the courtroom prior to the hearing were closed down as part of the transition to a situation where everyone present can monitor the same sequence of utterance turns. But, while what has been said may go some way toward explicating how the initial silence was accomplished, it does not provide for how it was that the silence lasted for about half a minute. Nor does it say anything about how, by the time line 10 in Version III was reached, the attentiveness of at least one of those present (i.e., the author) had become sufficiently focused for the inaudible utterance to be noticed. In this section, the suggestion will be made that what occurs during the period leading up to the second utterance which can be heard by everyone (line 13 in Version III) serves both to prevent any renewed talk from filling even such an extended silence, and to consolidate the shared attentiveness of those present to a single sequence of activities.

At the end of the previous section, it was hinted that the Coroner's Officer's action in joining everyone else standing in silence might have some prospective sequential implications. What was meant by this was that his action could be seen as indicating a shift in the turn-taking system that had just been initiated. Up to that point, the parties to it were the Coroner's Officer on the one hand, and everyone together on the other, but by "crossing sides" to join the other party, he could be seen to resign from his erstwhile position as the person with whom everyone together should take turns, thereby creating a vacancy for someone else to fill. But, as was noted earlier, his first utterance had already projected the imminent arrival of the Coroner, an event which had to occur before the inquest could properly start. A candidate other party with whom *everyone together* could now begin to take turns had, in other words, already been established as someone who was about to arrive. Thus, once their monitoring of the Coroner's Officer had yielded that he has, at least for the moment "one of them", the attention of *everyone together* could then be directed to looking for the entry of someone who might be possibly described as the Coroner—under the auspices of some such viewer's maxim as: see anyone who now enters as the Coroner if you can. Such a person does then enter and sit down behind the desk on the raised platform (line 7 in Version III), at which point there appears to emerge, in the absence of any verbal or other signal to sit down, a greater degree of potential ambiguity with respect to what should happen next than had hitherto been the case. From the transcript, it will be noted that this slot is filled with "Everyone else sits down except CO" which, among other things, can be seen as a report on the noticeability of CO's withdrawal from continuing as a member of *everyone together* as some sort of potentially significant marker. Thus, *everyone together* can now be seen to be, as it were, "on their own again" as far as doing a collective turn together is concerned and, faced with the problem of what to do next, they all sit down, while the person who had already established his identity as an official and an initiator goes on to do something else which could well turn out to ensure the orderly continuation of the proceedings.

Implicit in the above remarks is the idea that, by sitting down together immediately after the Coroner has sat down (and by the Coroner's Officer's failure to do so), those present exhibit their understanding that the sequence of activities that was started by the first utterance has now come to an end. That is, "Be upstanding in Court for Her Majesty's Coroner" may have indicated that there would be some sort of tie between the activities "Everyone stands" and "Coroner enters," but it did *not* provide any instructions as to *how long* everyone was to remain standing and could thus be heard, at least initially, to carry with it an "until further notice" clause. When no explicit "further notice" is forthcoming, then those present (except the Coroner's Officer) are left to find for themselves when they may properly sit, and there would appear to be at least three available methods for deciding this. The first is to see the Coroner's seating himself as marking the completion of his entry, and hence also a possible termination of the obligation of everyone else to coordinate their standing with his arrival. The second is, as was suggested above, to see the Coroner's Officer's withdrawal from doing the collective action together with everyone else as marking the possible termination of this particular activity. And the third perhaps most obvious thing to do is to monitor the activities of other officials (e.g., policemen), who may be presumed to be familiar with court procedures, to see when they sit down.

In the section on accomplishing silence, it was suggested that the active involvement of *everyone together* in an unspoken activity turn was important in bringing about an initial silence. From the above, it is possible to suggest further that both silence and shared attentiveness become increasingly assured by their involvement in a sequence of unspoken activities and with the interpretive problems they pose. Given that those present become active parties to a sequence of turn-taking with which few will have had direct experience, close monitoring of the unspoken activities others (especially the Coroner's Officer, Coroner, and other officials) is essential to discovering what should be done next and when it should be done. Those present presumably know that there are certain standardized court procedures, but are unlikely to know precisely what they are. But, though there may be patterns there to be found, they have to be found *in the course of* the proceedings, and such a task must presumably require close attentiveness and shared monitoring.[17] This requirement is arguably particularly constraining at the start of a hearing, because it is at that point where those who are unfamiliar with the court have the least amount of data on the proceedings to start locating a pattern or, in other words, it is then that their uncertainty about the sequences that constitute the court procedures is likely to be at its greatest. Added to this, what does occur initially is largely unspoken, and the parties doing the turns keep on changing at frequent intervals before an extended stable pattern gets under way (i.e., turns are taken by CO and All; All and C; CO and W; C and W) after line 23 in Version III. Under such circumstances the pressure on those present to engage in close monitoring must be very great indeed, one result of which may be that the chances of finding what to do and when to do it are very good indeed. In this sense, then, the sequentially structured uncertainty can be seen to contribute in an interesting and important way toward both the consolidation of attentiveness and the orderliness of the proceedings more generally.

One final point which may be made in conclusion about the way in which attentiveness is accomplished relates back to what was said at the beginning about the pressure for close monitoring being particularly strong in two-party conversations. Thus, the initiation of a series of two-party turn-taking sequences (between CO and everyone else together; everyone else and C; CO and W; C and W) may itself have powerful organizational implications for the consolidation of attentiveness in multi-party settings such as this.

Postscript

Given that this analysis has been concerned with such a small fragment of data from a particularly specialized setting, it would clearly be unwise to offer much in the way of definite conclusions at this stage. Indeed, it may well be the case that many more generalized remarks than are warranted by the data have already been made in the course of the discussion. Hopefully, however, the paper will at least have suggested a number of lines of possible inquiry which could be pursued, and some of the sorts of data that might eventually repay more detailed examination. Analytic topics of potential interest, for example, would appear to include, inter alia, the kinds of modifications to the turn-taking system for conversations which may be occasioned by alterations in group size, the sequential organization of transitions from multi-conversational settings to ones where all parties can monitor a single sequence of utterance turns, and the ways in which these kinds of sequences can be sustained once they have been initiated. It has also been suggested that unspoken activities can feature as turns in such sequences, and that they might have important implications for the organization of a range of interactional settings (e.g., occasions typically glossed as "ceremonial," "ritual," "formal," "polite," etc.).

The proposal that talk (and unspoken activities) from settings other than ones which would normally be regarded as "conversational" can and should provide a potentially interesting data source and focus for further study involves making a programmatic point which, at least as far as some conversational analysts are concerned, may be regarded as somewhat controversial.[18] For, in opposition to such recommendations, that are some who would counsel against attempting to analyze data from settings any more "exotic" than the kinds of "mundane" conversational materials on which most of the important advances were made. Thus, it can be persuasively argued that to focus on talk in settings such as "ceremonies, debates, meetings, press conferences, seminars, therapy sessions, interviews, trials, etc." (Sacks, Schegloff, and Jefferson 1974), is to run a serious risk of being distracted or misled by features of the talk which are peculiar to such settings. And a related line is that, as there is still a great deal yet to be learned about the sequential organization of conversation, it is premature to start looking elsewhere. A common implication of each of these themes, therefore, would seem to be that "mundane" conversations should continue to be the more or less exclusive data source for now and until further notice. Just as I have not attempted to present a detailed exposition of such views, however, it is also not my intention here to develop a lengthy case against them. Indeed, it would seem very doubtful whether any firm acceptance or rejection could ever be established in the abstract, and without reference to relevant empirical data. And if this is so, then it is one very strong reason for avoiding the passing definitive sounding judgements either way at this early stage in the history of ethnomethodology and conversational analysis.

None of this, it should be stressed, is designed to be critical or dismissive of the achievements of conversational analysis thus far, nor even of the wisdom of advising caution in any attempts to extend the work beyond the conversation data base on which much of the work was founded. If, however, the systematics of turn-taking for conversations as synthesized by Sacks, Schegloff and Jefferson (1974) are as powerful and rigourous in their empirical application as some of us believe, then there is every reason to expect and hope that the importance will not be confined to or stop short at the level of "mundane" conversations. To resort to a botanical analogy, it might be said that if some of the structure of organic matter had been unearthed in the course of research into flowers, it would be perfectly reasonable for some researchers to try using that knowledge (albeit cautiously) to start looking at vegetables, shrubs and trees, while others continue to dig more deeply into the structure of flowers. And if those who tread beyond the realm of flowers look carefully and cautiously enough, they will presumably discover sooner or later whether such attempts to extend the enterprise are or are not worthwhile.

DATA

1	C O :	Be upstanding in Court for her Majesty's Coroner.
2		Take the book in your right hand and read from the
3		card. That's it.
4	W :	I swear by Almighty God that the evidence I shall give
5		shall be the truth, the whole truth and nothing but
6		the truth.
7	C O	Thank you. Could you just keep your voice up please.
8	C :	Now your name is Alfred James Smith?
9	W :	Yes
10	C O :	Press Operator in sheet metal works.
11	W :	Yes.
12	C :	And live at 33, Rose Hill Drive, Seatown.
13	W :	Yes.
14	C :	On (date) you came to Localtown General Hospital
15		and identified the body lying there as that of your
16		mother.
17	W :	Yes.
18	C :	Full name Amy Smith, formerly Amy Jones, and she was
19		a widow aged 48, born (date) at Docktown.
20	W :	Yes.
21	C :	And she formerly resided with you at 33, Rose Hill
22		Drive, Seatown.
23	W :	Yes.
24	C :	From which she became a patient at the (name of
25		mental hospital) here. She enjoyed good health
26		apart from minor ailments until 1968.
27	W :	Yes.

28	C :	Then what happened?

29	W :	She had an upset with my dad and she took some pills.

Version II

1	CO:	Be upstanding in Court for Her Majesty's Coroner.
2		(30 second pause) (inaudible utterance) (5 second pause)
3		Take the book in your right hand and read from the
4		card.

5	W:	I swear by Almighty God that the evidence I shall give
6		shall be the truth, the whole truth and nothing but
7		the truth.

| 8 | CO: | Thank you. Could you just keep your voice up please. |
| 9 | | (12 second pause) |

| 10 | C: | Now your name is Alfred James Smith. |

| 11 | W: | Yes. |
| | | . . . .(continues as from 10 in Transcript A1) |

Version III

| 1 | | (Some people standing, some walking about, some |
| 2 | | sitting; several conversations going on) |

| 3 | CO: | Be upstanding in court for Her Majesty's Coroner. |

30 secs
4		(The sitters stand, the walkers and some standers walk
5		a few paces before standing still, CO stands still;
6		everyone stops talking)
7		(Coroner enters and sits down)
8		(Everyone else except CO sits down)
9		(CO walks to where W is sitting)

| 10 | CO: | (Inaudible utterance) |

5 secs
| 11 | | (W stands up and walks with CO to witness box, which he |
| 12 | | enters and stands still) |

13	CO:	Take the book in the right hand and read ⌈from the card.
14		That's it. ⌊W takes book
15		

16	W:	I swear by Almighty God that the evidence I shall give
17		shall be the truth, the whole truth and nothing but
18		the truth.

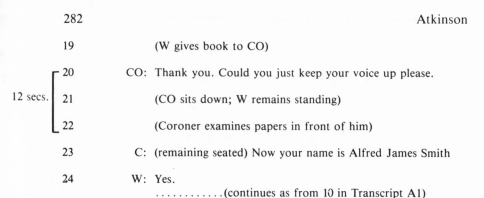

19   (W gives book to CO)

20   CO: Thank you. Could you just keep your voice up please.

12 secs. 21   (CO sits down; W remains standing)

22   (Coroner examines papers in front of him)

23   C: (remaining seated) Now your name is Alfred James Smith

24   W: Yes.
                . . . .(continues as from 10 in Transcript A1)

*Pause lengths are indicated on the left hand side. Square brackets indicate ap-
proximate start and completion points of an oriented-to activity which overlaps
with an utterance.

NOTES

1. This paper was presented at the International Institute in Ethnomethodology and
Conversational Analysis, Boston University, Department of Sociology (8-12 June 1977).
It is a modified and somewhat extended version of the later analytic sections of a much
longer paper which dealt more generally with problems of studying courtroom interaction (Atkinson 1976), and which was presented at a Conference organized by the
Sociology of Law Research Committee of the International Sociological Association at
Balatonszeplak, Hungary (20-25 September 1976). An earlier and more preliminary draft of
that paper was also given at a Seminar on the Sociology of Law and Legal Procedures held
at the Centre for Socio-Legal Studies, Wolfson College, Oxford (28-29 May 1976). Various
parts of the work have also been presented at seminars in the Universities of Stockholm,
Umeå, Bristol, and Oxford. The research was made possible by the (British) Social-Science
Research Council through its funding of the Centre for Socio-Legal Studies, and is a small
part of a much more extensive programme of multidisciplinary research in Law and Social
Science currently being done there. I am particularly grateful to Donald Harris, the
Director of the Centre, and other colleagues there and elsewhere for the helpful and
tolerant encouragement I have received in developing this work. I also have a more long-
standing debt of gratitude to Rod Watson, John Heritage, Paul Drew, and Christian Heath
for their patience in listening to my various analytic obsessions these past few years.
2. A notable exception to this is the work of Paul Drew, who has been engaged in
analyses of transcripts of a Tribunal of Enquiry for several years. See, for example, Drew
1977 and 1978 (forthcoming), and Benson and Drew 1976.
3. This approach is one of several involved in the program of research into the Social
Organisation of Judicial Procedures, which is one of the several collaborative projects currently being carried out at the Centre for Socio-Legal Studies.
4. Throughout this paper, the term *conversational analysis* is used to refer to the pio-
neering studies of the late Harvey Sacks and his co-workers, and the resulting corpus of
work which has been accumulated during the past 10-15 years. Given that the present study

has derived so much inspiration from that corpus, it would have been extremely difficult to have provided precise bibliographical citations whenever they became due and would, among other things, have meant cluttering up the text excessively with references. Hopefully, then, my debts even to the studies which are not mentioned will be evident in the course of the discussion.

5.   This and a number of other points about the organization of turn-taking in court hearings were elaborated in more detail in the earlier paper from which this one is derived (Atkinson 1976). Given that this present paper focuses increasingly on a specific problem in the organization of turn-taking, it may be as well to note in passing that the official rules of evidence and procedure relate to a great deal more than turn pre-allocation and the sequencing of court proceedings. There are, for example, large numbers of (mostly exclusionary) rules of evidence which are designed to control topic coherence or relevance. Thus, one problem with which lawyers are confronted and have to resolve is what they refer to as the "multiplicity of issues," which appears to be almost synonymous with what is referred to in ethnomethodological writings on description as the "etcetera problem" (see Sacks 1963, Garfinkel 1967, Garfinkel and Sacks 1970). In short, the potentially indefinite extendability of talk is but one of the many pressing practical problems which courts have to resolve.

6.   It will be noted that the term *unspoken activities* is used throughout this paper in preference to other more usual descriptors, such as "nonverbal activities." One reason for this is that the latter term tends to be associated with such phenomena as glances, winks, etc. and, as these do not provide the topic here, it seemed as well to make some sort of explicit distinction. It is also the case that to differentiate between "utterances" on the one hand and "nonverbal activities" on the other is to risk implying that utterances are not (or are something other than) activities, which seemed to be a suggestion worth avoiding.

7.   There appear to be a variety of ways in which unspoken activities may be tied in with the sequential ordering of talk. In the data examined in this paper, they seem to feature as turns in the opening sequences of the hearing. Later on in a court's proceedings, however, standing up and sitting down appear to serve as visible markers of utterance turn beginnings and endings, respectively. Observations of other settings (e.g., videotapes of doctor-patient consultations) made jointly with Christian Heath of the University of Manchester suggest that spoken and unspoken activities are coordinated in a range of other ways, too. As yet, however, it is too early even to begin any attempt to be more specific about them.

8.   A further possible combination which occurs in the data considered here, but which is not analyzed in any detail, is an utterance which projects *two* second parts, one spoken and one unspoken. Thus, the "That's it" at line 15 in Version III presumably acknowledges the proper completion of the unspoken activity (taking the book) projected earlier in the same turn as that which also projects the next utterance ("I swear by . . ."). In other words, the utterance at line 13 (Version III) projects *both* sorts of activities as sequentially relevant next turns. Interestingly, the two activities done together (i.e., holding the book and reading from the card) are constitutive of another *single* (describable) activity, namely "swearing the oath."

9.   The collection of the data examined here was made possible by the award of (British) Social Science Research Council Grant HR 1496/1 ("Community Reactions to Deviance"). With reference to Coroners' Courts, it should perhaps be noted that they are the final stage of the procedures for deciding the causes of sudden deaths in England and Wales. Not all such deaths get that far in the process, but the categorizations of accidents, suicides, and one or two more obscure types of death can only be done at a Coroner's Inquest. The official procedures operative at these hearings are markedly different from those more usually associated with English courts in that, for example, the normal rules of evidence do not apply, and the "adversarial" format is noticeably absent.

10.   This abbreviated form is used throughout to refer to the whole of the first utterance, i.e., "Be upstanding in Court for Her Majesty's Coroner."

11.   By this is meant that, ecologically speaking, the Coroner's Officer was the only person then on the raised platform, and was separated by the largest distance of anyone in the courtroom from the various other clusters of people there. Without wishing to become stipulative about some minimal number of yards within which parties to talk must be standing for their verbal exchanges to be regarded as "a conversation," it may also be noted that he was far enough away from everyone else for it to have been very equivocal as to whether his utterance could be recognizably describable by observers as part of "a conversation."

12.   This observation (and others not reported here) was made possible by the award of a Council of Europe Criminological Fellowship which facilitated a three-week stay at Stockholm University in November 1976. I am particularly grateful to Professor Knut Sveri and Ingemar Rexel of the Institute of Criminology for having helped me to find my way around some of the courts in Stockholm.

13.   I am grateful to a member of the audience which heard this paper being given in Boston for having drawn my attention to this example.

14.   The close ordering implications that commands (as compared with requests) seem to have when they occur as first parts in U-A adjacency pairs may well have something to do with the accomplishment and recognizability of degrees of politeness. Consider, for example the following sequences:

Example (A)	1	Child: Pass the cornflakes
	2	Parent: What's the little word?
	3	(Pause)
	4	Child: Please
	5	(Parent passes cornflakes)

Example (B)	1	A: Could you pass the salt?
	2	(B passes salt)
	3	A: And the pepper.
	4	(B passes pepper)
	5	A: And the mustard.
	6	B: Who do you think I am, your bloody slave?

In both these examples, the business of completing U-A sequences seems to be a highly delicate matter. Once they cease to be babies, children find that the summons parts of summons-answer pairs require more careful design than was the case with their cries and screams of the past, if they are to get others to do unspoken activities for them. For, as can be seen from Example (B), recipients of first parts may find, as the sequence unfolds, grounds for making a complaint. Yet this could easily have been avoided by A had he, for example, prefaced the second or third of his utterances with an apology. In short, the sequential ordering of spoken and unspoken activities would seem to have a good deal to do with the recognizability of politeness and impoliteness.

15.   See, for example, the discussion of how to repudiate the authority of courts by Bankowski and Mungham (1976, pp. 110-139), and the way such methods are recommended as ways of achieving such a goal.

16.   Such situations would also seem to involve a good deal of close coordination of spoken and unspoken activities, and would again seem to point to another relevant data source for the kinds of issues being discussed here.

17.   A more general point being hinted at here is that in settings where unspoken activities requiring close monitoring are taking place there may be a preference for silence. Thus, just as it is extremely difficult to monitor talk while talking (e.g., even professional simultaneous interpreters can only work in bursts of a few minutes at a time), so also may talk interfere with the monitoring of certain sequences of unspoken activities. Conversely, to

talk during an unspoken activity being done by another party may be to fail to exhibit an understanding that the activity in question requires the full concentration of the party who is doing it. People may therefore complain at being "interrupted" while doing some unspoken activity, or the "interruptors" may preface utterances made at such points with apologies, where the apology can be heard to be orienting to the fact that this is a delicate moment in time to be talking at all.

18. In saying that this point is "programmatic" and "controversial," I do *not* mean that it has to do with some general case for or against doing ethnomethodology, but that it is a matter for discussion *between* researchers actively engaged in such work. These remarks and the summary of some of the lines of argument which follow are derived mainly from casual conversations with others who participated in the International Institute in Ethnomethodology and Conversational Analysis at Boston University (June 1977).

REFERENCES

Atkinson, J.M. (1968). On the sociology of suicide. *Sociological Review* 16:83-92.

_____ (1971). Societal reactions to suicide: the role of coroners' definitions. In *Images of Deviance,* ed. S. Cohen, pp. 165-191. Harmondsworth, Middlesex: Penguin.

_____ (1976). Order in court: some preliminary issues and analyses. Paper presented at the Annual Conference of the International Sociological Association Research Group on the Sociology of Law, Balatonszeplak, Hungary, September, 1976.

_____ (1977). *Discovering Suicide: Studies in the Social Organisation of Sudden Death* (London: Macmillan).

Bankowski, Z., and Mungham, G. (1976). *Images of Law.* London: Routledge and Kegan Paul.

Benson, D., and Drew, P. (1976). "Was there firing in Sandy Row that night?": the social accomplishment of historical fact. Paper presented at the Seminar on the Sociology of Law and Legal Procedures, Wolfson College, Oxford, 28-29 May 1976 (forthcoming in *Sociological Inquiry*).

Carlen, P. (1974). Remedial routines for the maintenance of control in magistrates' courts. *British Journal of Law and Society* 1:101-117.

_____ (1975). Magistrates' courts: a game theoretic analysis. *Sociological Review* 23:347-379.

_____ (1976a). *Magistrates' Justice.* London: Martin Robertson.

_____ (1976b). The staging of magistrates' justice. *British Journal of Criminology* 16:48-55.

Drew, P. (1976). Accusations: the occasioned use of religious geography in describing events. University of York (England), Department of Sociology, mimeo (forthcoming in *Sociology,* January 1978).

_____ (1977). The production of excuses and justifications in cross-examination. University of York (England), Department of Sociology, mimeo.

Emerson, R.M. (1969). *Judging Delinquents.* Chicago: Aldine.

Garfinkel, H. (1967). *Studies in Ethnomethodology.* Englewood Cliffs, New Jersey: Prentice Hall.

Garfinkel, H. and Sacks, H. (1970). On formal structures of practical actions. In *Theoretical Sociology: Perspectives and Developments,* ed. J.C. McKinney and E.A. Tiryakian, pp. 338-366. New York: Appleton-Century-Crofts.

Sacks, H. (1963). Sociological description. *Berkeley Journal of Sociology* 8:1-16.

_____ (1972a). On the analyzability of stories by Children. In *Directions in Sociolinguistics: The Ethnography of Communication,* ed. J.J. Gumpertz and D. Humes, pp. 329-345. New York: Holt, Rinehart and Winston.

——— (1972b). An initial investigation of the usability of conversational data for doing sociology. In *Studies in Social Interaction,* ed. D. Sudnow, pp. 31-74. New York: The Free Press.

Sacks, H., Schegloff, E.A., and Jefferson, G. (1974). A simplest systematics for the organization of turn-taking in conversations. *Language* 50:696-735.

Schegloff, E.A. (1968). Sequencing in Conversational Openings. *American Anthropologist* 70:1075-1095.

Schegloff, E.A., and Sacks, H. (1973). Opening up closings. *Semiotica* 8:289-327.

Turner, R. (1972). Some formal properties of therapy talk. In *Studies in Social Interaction,* ed. D. Sudnow, pp. 367-393. New York: The Free Press.

Appendix I

The Transcript Symbols

Devised by Gail Jefferson; adapted here from H. Sacks, E. Schegloff and G. Jefferson, A Simplest Systematics for the Organization of Turn-Taking in Conversation, *Language,* 50 (1974): 731–734.

/ / V: Th'guy says tuh me- 'hh my son / / didid.

M: Wuhjeh do:.

The double obliques indicate the point at which a current speaker's talk is overlapped by the talk of another.

V: I / / left my garbage pail in iz / / hallway.

C: Vi:c,

C: Victuh,

A multiple-overlapped utterance is followed. in serial order. by the talk which overlaps it. Thus, C's "Vi:c," occurs simultaneously with V's "left," and C's "Victuh" with his "hallway."

((M: ((I mean no no n'no.
V: P't it back up,

Double brackets placed in front of two serially transcribed utterances indicate that they start simultaneously.

* M: I mean no-no n'no.*
V: P't it back up,*

M: Jim / / wasn' home* uh what.
V: Y'kno:w?*

An asterisk indicates the point at which two overlapping or simultaneously-started utterances end, if they end simultaneously, or the point at which one of them ends in the course of another, or the point at which one utterance-component ends vis-a-vis another.

= R: Wuhjeh do:. =
V: = I said did, he, get, hurt.

V: My wife / / caught d'ki:d, =
R: Yeh:
V: = lightin a fiyuh in Perry's celluh.

V: Well my son didit = I'm gladjer son didn' get hu:rt, 'hhh I said but . . .

In general, the equal signs indicate "latching"; i.e., no interval between the end of a prior and start of a next piece of talk. It is used for the relationship of a next speaker's talk to a prior speaker's; for the relationship of two parts of a same speaker's talk, and as a transcript convenience for managing long utterances which are overlapped at various points, in which case a through-produced utterance may be more or less arbitrarily broken up.

(0.0)	V:	. . . dih soopuh ul clean it up, (0.3)	Numbers in parentheses indicate elapsed time in tenths of seconds.
	( ):	hhehh	The device is used between utter- ances of adjacent speakers, be-
	V:	No kidding.	tween two separable parts of a
	M:	Yeh there's nothin the:re? (0.5)	single speaker's talk, and between parts of a single speaker's inter-
	M:	Quit hassling.	nally organized utterance.
	V:	She's with somebódy y'know ˙hh ennuh, (0.7) she says Wo:w . . .	
? ? ! , .	V:	Becuss the soopuh dint pudda bu:lb on dih sekkin flaw en its burnt ou:t?	Punctuation markers are not used as grammatical symbols, but for intonation. Thus, a question may be constructed with "comma" or
	V:	A do:g? enna cat is diffrent.	"period" intonation, and "ques-
	R:	Wuhjeh do:.	tion-intonation" may occur in as- sociation with objects which are not questions.
: :	V:	So dih gu:y sez ˙hh	Colon(s) indicate that the prior syllable is prolonged. Multiple
	M:	Yeh it's all in the chair all th/ /at junk is in the chair.) =	colons indicate a more prolonged syllable, as in the second instance,
	V:	Wo : : : : : : : : w) =	in which V's "Wow" covers five
	V:	= I didn' know tha:t?	syllables in M's overlapped utter- ance.
—	V:	I sez y'know why, becawss look.	Underscoring indicates various forms of stressing, and may in- volve pitch and/or volume.
	V:	'M not saying he works ha:rd.	The relationship between stress and prolongation markers indicate
__:	V:	I I don' work ha:rd.	pitch change (or nonchange) in the course of a word. In the first in-
:__	H:	Does he work ha:rd?	stance, with stress only marked under the first letter, pitch does not change. In the second instance, pitch drops at the end of "ha:rd", and in the third instance, pitch rises at the end of "ha:rd?"
	V:	He said- yihknow, I get- I get sick behind it.	The dash indicates a "cut-off" of the prior word or sound.
(hh)	M:	I'd a' cracked up 'f duh friggin (gla- i(h)f y'kno(h)w it) sm(h)a(h) heh heh	The [(h)], within parentheses and within a word or sound indicates explosive aspiration, e.g., laugh- ter, breathlessness, etc.

`hh	V:	So I sez, `hh wa:l whuḍḍiyou goin do	The (h) indicates audible breathing. A dot placed before it indicates an in-breath; no dot indicates out-breath.
UC	V:	En it d̲int fall OUT!	Upper case indicates increased volume.
( )	M:	I'd a' cracked u̲p̲ 'f duh friggin (gla-i(h)f y'kno(h)w it) sm(h)a(h) heh heh	Single parentheses indicate transcribers are not sure about the words contained therein. Pairs of parentheses, as in the third instance, offer not merely two possible hearings, but address the equivocality of each. Empty parentheses indicate that no "hearing" was achieved. On occasion, nonsense syllables are provided, in an attempt to capture something of the produced sounds.
	M:	Jim wasn' home, / / °(when y'wen over there)	
	V:	I'll be (right witchu.) (back inna minnit.)	
	( ):	Tch! ( )	
	R:	(Y'cattuh moo?)	The speaker designation column is treated similarly; single parentheses indicating doubt about speaker, pairs indicating equivocal possibilities, and empties indicating no achieved identification of speaker.
(( ))	M:	((whispered)) (Now they're gonna, h̲ack it.)	Materials in double parentheses or double brackets indicate features of the audio materials other than actual verbalization, or verbalizations which are not transcribed. Occasionally an attempt is made to transcribe a cough (which might appear as "eh-khookh!'') or a razzberry (which might appear as "pthrrrp!'').
	M:	((RAZZBERRY))	
	M:	((cough))	
	V:	((dumb slob voice)) Well we u̲setuh do dis, en we use-	
	J:	They̲'re̲ fulla sh : : it.	

Appendix II

Transcription System

The following is a simplified version of the system for transcribing utterances developed by Gail Jefferson edited and expanded by Charles Goodwin. To her system Goodwin has added some symbols for coding the gaze direction of the participants.

I. Sequencing

Item		Instance	Explanation
=	J: D:	I gave, I gave up smoking cigarettes::. = = Yea:h,	Equal signs indicate no interval between the end of a prior and the start of a next piece of talk. It is used for the relationship of a next speaker's talk to a prior speaker's and for the relationship of two parts of a same speaker's talk.
	P:	Well I think what's funny is when he was in gra:de school. = wa'n it?	
(0.0)	E:	See first we were gonna have Teema, Carrie, and Clara, (0.2) a::nd myself.	Numbers in parentheses indicate elapsed time in tenths of seconds. The device is used between single speaker's internally organized utterance and between utterances of adjacent speakers.
	J: D: 	I gave, I gave up smoking cigarettes::. = = Yea:h, (0.4)	
	J:	l-uh: one- one week ago t'da:y. acshilly,	

II. Sound Production

? ,	F:	Yih ever take 'er out again?	Punctuation markers are not used as grammatical symbols, but for intonation. Thus a question may be constructed with "comma" or "period" intonation, and "question-intonation" may occur in association with objects which are not questions.
	P:	Now if ya have thirteen points:, (1.0) counting: voi:ds?	
	J:	An' how are you feeling? (0.4) °these days,	
: :	R:	Somebuddy said looking at my:,	Colon(s) indicate that the prior syllable is prolonged.
	E:	See first we were gonna have Teema, Carrie, and Clara, (0.2) a::nd myself.	
—	J: D: 	I gave, I gave up smoking cigarettes::. = = Yea:h, (0.4)	Underscoring indicates various forms of stressing, and may involve pitch and/or volume.
	J:	l-uh: one-one week ago t'da:y. acshilly,	

_ :	J:	l-uh: one-<u>one</u> week ago t'<u>da</u>:y. acshilly,	The relationship between stress and prolongation markers indicate pitch change (or nonchange) in the course of a word. In the first instance, pitch drops at the end of "t'da:y."
	C:	N<u>o</u>:?	In the second instance the pitch rises at the end of "No:?"
	E:	The <u>f</u>our of us.	In the third instance, with stress only marked under the first letter, pitch does not change.

-	C:	(Th') U:sac- uh:, sprint car dr- dirt track championship.	The dash indicates a "cut-off" of the prior word or sound.
°	J:	An' how are you feeling? (0.4) °these days,	The degree sign indicates that the talk it precedes is low in volume.

VI. Gaze Direction

Speaker:	————	E:.		A staff is used to mark some relevant features of the participants' gaze. The gaze of the speaker is marked above the utterance; that of his recipient below the utterance.
	Utterance		The four of u s.	
Recipient:	———	B:	. . . . . ————	Thus in this example E is the speaker and B is her recipient.

[		E: .		The precise point where a party's gaze reaches another party is marked with a bracket.
			The <u>f</u>our of u⌐s.	
		B:	⌐X	

. . .		E: .		A series of dots indicates that the party marked is moving his gaze toward his co-participant. The first dot marks precisely where this movement begins.
			The <u>f</u>our of u⌐s.	In this example B begins to bring her gaze toward E at "four," finishing this movement at the point marked by a bracket.
		B:	. . . . . ⌐X	

————		E:	—————————	A line indicates that the party being marked is gazing at his co-participant.
			The <u>f</u>our of u s.	In this example the speaker gazes at her recipient during her entire utterance, and the recipient gazes at the speaker during the "s" of "us."
		B:	. . . . . ___	

, , ,   R: Somebuddy said look at my:,
        C: _____ , ,

A series of commas indicates that the party marked is moving his gaze away from his co-participant. In this example the recipient, C, moves his gaze away from the speaker at the beginning of "at." The first comma marks the precise point where the act of looking away begins.

(Name) J: (Beth_____, . . (Ann)_____
             one- one week ag o t'<u>da</u>: y.
        B:
        A: . . (Beth)

Who specifically is being gazed at can be marked by placing a name above the line.

In this example the speaker moves his gaze from Beth to Ann just at the end of the word "t'da:y." Further, one of the recipients of this utterance, Ann, is not gazing at the speaker but at another recipient, Beth.

The absence of a line in Beth's "staff" indicates that she is gazing elsewhere than at either John or Ann. (Note that when a speaker moves his gaze from one recipient to another the notation of dots and commas becomes ambiguous since the speaker is simultaneously moving away from one party and toward another.)

Index

Index

(Page numbers in **bold** type refer to complete chapters in the book)